Inland Empire Electric Line

Spokane to Coeur d'Alene and the Palouse

By Clive Carter

The Museum of North Idaho, Coeur d'Alene, Idaho

Published by
Museum of North Idaho
P.O. Box 812
Coeur d'Alene, Idaho 83816-0812
(208) 664-3448
All rights reserved.
ISBN: 978-09723356-8-3

Book editing, design, production and computerized image enhancement by
Moore Graphics Studio
smoore101@verizon.net

Printed on 70lb Ultra Litho Gloss
Typeset in Caslon 540

To my wife Ann

Who provided much research

assistance and unfailing support.

PREFACE

The interurban electric railway industry was a phenomenon that started in the late 1890s and within twenty years had built hundreds of railway lines, most of which have been described in a variety of publications. The lines to the east and south out of Spokane, known as the Inland Empire System, have been an exception until now. Here, then, is the story of this industry as it came into existence, served the Spokane area for many years, and then disappeared from the scene.

The author chronicles the trials that occurred during the planning, the struggles for financing, and the various political jostling, and all are explored in detail. Rapid changes occurred in leadership and with each turnover in management the new personnel were situated further away from Spokane. Eventually ownership resided with the Great Northern Railway.

The two lines that comprised the railway were constructed with incompatible power supply and distribution systems to the railway cars: both represented the current technology at the time of construction even though they were built less than a decade apart.

The alternating current lines to the Palouse were the leading-edge technology of the day. This aspect of the system is covered along with the rolling stock used on both lines. The equipment used for the Palouse line was conceived as being usable on both the high voltage AC lines and the low voltage line to Coeur d'Alene, but proved impractical and necessitated a set of dedicated equipment for each power system.

The line to the south also proved to be a financial albatross to the profitable Coeur d'Alene line due to the huge capital costs involved in the construction of the line. This resulted in some financial separations and recombination of the two lines. The system, however, developed into a very significant freight feeder to the Great Northern Railway and that company felt that it could not afford to lose the traffic that it generated. As a result the company bought out the stock and bond-holders. This resulted in all this trolley equipment being proudly labeled for the parent company with small letters identifying the operating company.

Despite its turbulent career and financial precariousness, the Inland Empire System served the area well for many years and outlasted all the other electric interurban lines in the State of Washington.

Robert R. Lowry
November 2005

ACKNOWLEDGMENTS

The author is grateful to the following who supplied photographs and/or information: Walt Ainsworth, Phil Beach, Tom Burg, Daniel Cozine, Jim Davis, Michael J. Denuty, Ted Holloway, Warren Wing and Richard Yaremko. The help of Sheldon Perry, who went out of his way to find illustrations, is gratefully acknowledged. James C. Mattson generously supplied information on the railroad's infrastructure.

Ted Holloway, Robert R. Lowry, Charles V. Mutschler, Kenneth R. Middleton, Sheldon Perry and John V. Wood kindly reviewed the manuscript. They made helpful suggestions and corrected errors. However, the final responsibility for the content belongs to the author.

TABLE OF CONTENTS

ACRONYMS USED

AC	Alternating Current
AC&F	American Car & Foundry
B-B	2 axle truck-2 axle truck
Cd'A&S	Coeur d'Alene & Spokane Railway
CM&St.P	Chicago, Milwaukee & St. Paul Railroad
CMSt.P&P	Chicago, Milwaukee, St.Paul & Pacific Railroad
DC	Direct Current
EMD	Electromotive Division of General Motors
GN	Great Northern Railway
I&WN	Idaho & Washington Northern Railroad
IE	Inland Empire Railroad
l.c.l.	Less than car load lot
MB	Motor Baggage car
MBE	Motor Baggage and Express
MBP	Motor Baggage and Passenger car.
MP	Motor Passenger car
NP	Northern Pacific Railway
OR&N	Oregon Railroad & Navigation Company
OWR&N	Oregon-Washington Railroad & Navigation Company
RPO	Railway Post Office
S&E	Spokane & Eastern Railway and Power Company
S&I	Spokane & Inland Railway
S&IE	Spokane & Inland Empire Railroad
SC&P	Spokane, Coeur d'Alene & Palouse Railway
SIR	Spokane International Railway (Railroad from 1941)
SP&S	Spokane, Portland & Seattle Railway
ST	Spokane Traction Company
TL	Trailer Parlor car
TP	Trailer Passenger car
WI&M	Washington, Idaho & Montana

LIST OF FIGURES

Diagrams are show in italics.

Chapter 1

INTRODUCTION

Great Northern Railway's (GNR) electrified main line that ran through the Cascade Mountains between Skykomish and Wenatchee in Washington State is well known. What is perhaps less recognized is that the Great Northern operated an electrified interurban system 175 miles east of Wenatchee. Indeed, the 176 miles of electrified road extending out from Spokane, Washington was over twice as large as its illustrious sister. This book presents a history of the system from inception in 1902 to the few remnants that remain a hundred years later.

Previous authors have addressed particular aspects of the interurban system in their treatment of broader topics. John Fahey truncated his review at 1911, while Grande's coverage was essentially pre-1920. Mutschler et al. concentrated on the history and operation of the system's Spokane streetcar lines. In view of the latter contribution, treatment of the streetcar business is omitted within these pages.

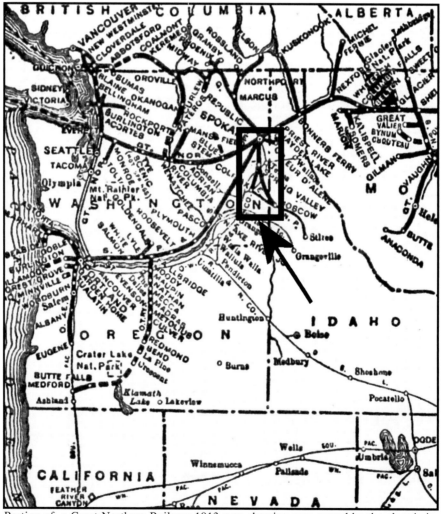

Portion of a Great Northern Railway 1913 map showing area served by the electric interurban system.

1

The interurban was unique in that a dozen different companies owned either the whole system or parts thereof during its life. Among the reasons were sale, merger and foreclosure. The longest period of solidarity, prior to GNR ownership, was 1908-1919 when the Spokane & Inland Empire Railroad Company (S&IE) owned the complete system. The S&IE had merged four companies, each having a specific function: two railroads, a streetcar business, and a Spokane terminal operation. Financial problems caused the downfall of the Spokane & Inland Empire Railroad. Two newly incorporated companies took over at the beginning of 1920.

Great Northern Railway purchased the interurban system in 1927, establishing a subsidiary as the beneficiary - the Spokane Coeur d'Alene & Palouse Railway Company (SC&P). To do this, the GNR reorganized and renamed a dormant "paper" company that it had owned for 30 years.

Great Northern's relationship with the interurban system actually dated back two decades before purchase. The GNR transcontinental main line and its branches did not penetrate areas served by the S&IE. Hence, the electric lines acted as a feeder of otherwise inaccessible traffic. To solidify interchange arrangements, the two companies signed a traffic agreement in 1907.

Even more significant in the budding relationship was the purchase of S&IE shares by GNR President James J. Hill. He acquired a controlling interest in 1909, dividing the stock equally between the Great Northern and Northern Pacific Railway companies. Their subsidiary, the Spokane, Portland & Seattle Railway, was subsequently given overall management responsibility. While this gave the GNR some control of the S&IE, loans had to be made to cover the company's debts. The S&IE went into receivership in 1919 with the GNR (and NP) losing the money invested and loaned.

For the next several years the company had no financial ties to the interurban system. However, Ralph Budd was appointed president of the Great Northern Railway in 1919. Earlier, he was chief engineer for the Spokane & Inland Empire Railroad and thus quite familiar with system's strengths and weaknesses. When the opportunity arose to purchase the system in 1927, the GNR directors, on Budd's advice, agreed to buy it for a reasonable price.

At the time of acquisition, the two primary railroad routes were (1) a DC electrified line extending east from Spokane to Coeur d'Alene, Idaho with branches to Liberty Lake, Washington and Hayden Lake, Idaho; and (2) an AC electrified line running south from Spokane, splitting into branches for Colfax, Washington and Moscow, Idaho (Table 1.1). The streetcar business had been sold in 1922

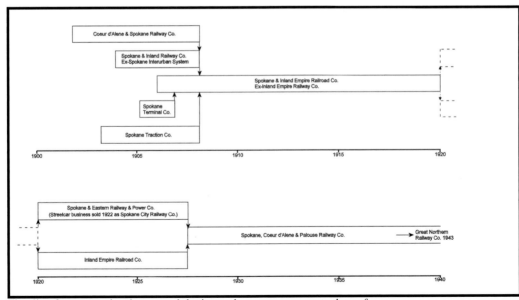

Timeline for companies that owned the interurban system or parts thereof.

Table 1.1. Mileage of Lines Owned and Operated by Spokane & Inland Empire Railroad Company in 1916.

	Main Track	Second Track	Yard Tracks and Sidings
TERMINAL DIVISION	1.110	0.791	5.234
COEUR D'ALENE DIVISION			
Terminal Junction to Coeur d'Alene	30.738	17.475	10.271
Coeur d'Alene to Hayden Lake	8.200		3.185
Liberty Lake Branch	2.198		0.593
INLAND DIVISION			
Terminal Junction to Spring Valley	38.371		7.928
Spring Valley to Colfax	36.817		6.777
Spring Valley to Moscow	50.783		8.668
TRACTION DIVISION			
City Lines	35.478	12.011	5.956
Opportunity Line: Spokane city limits to Flora Junction	8.527		1.248
Total Mileage	**212.222**	**30.277**	**49.860**
Total Mileage Excluding City Lines	**176.744**	**18.266**	**43.904**

after being incorporated as the Spokane City Railways Company. Passenger trains remained in operation, but freight serving agricultural and lumber industries was becoming the dominant revenue source.

New management, made up of GNR officers, set about reducing the cost of SC&P operations and increasing interchange business with the GNR. Passenger train services were condensed immediately and abandoned in 1940. Electric operation ceased the following year. Great Northern formally acquired the Spokane, Coeur d'Alene & Palouse Railway Company in 1943 and absorbed the railroad into the Spokane Division.

Creation of Burlington Northern in 1970 signaled the end of the lines. Northern Pacific Railway lines served the same territory and were retained by BN. Essentially all of the interurban tracks were lifted by the end of the 1980s.

The convoluted corporate and financial history of the interurban system is presented in Chapter 2. Construction of the lines is described in Chapter 3. Chapters 4 and 5 deal further with infrastructure while rolling stock is covered in Chapter 6. Passenger and freight train services are outlined in Chapter 7. Interchange and relations with neighboring railroads are summarized in Chapter 8 and Chapter 9 reviews the traffic carried. Collisions were fortunately rare with Chapter 10 covering those that did occur. An illustrated tour over the system is offered in Chapter 11. Piecemeal abandonment of the system is treated in Chapter 12.

Primary sources used in preparation included the Interstate Commerce Commission valuation records preserved at the National Archives in College Park, Maryland; the Great Northern Railway and Northern Pacific Railway records held by the Minnesota Historical Society in St. Paul, Minnesota; annual reports filed in the State Archives in Olympia, Washington; the photograph collection at the Museum of North Idaho in Coeur d'Alene, Idaho; and materials collected by the Northwest Museum of Arts and Culture in Spokane, Washington. Technical publications were referred to at the Colorado Railroad Museum in Golden, Colorado. Regional newspapers provided information with respect to construction progress and local railroad activities.

Sources

Fahey, John; Shaping Spokane: Jay P. Graves and His Times, University of Washington Press, 1994.

Grande, Walter R.; The Northwest's Own Railway, Spokane Portland & Seattle Railway and its Subsidiaries - Vol. II, Grande Press, Oregon, 1997.

Mutschler, Charles V., Clyde L. Parent and Wilmer H. Siegert; Spokane's Street Railways: An Illustrated History. Spokane, Inland Empire Railway Historical Society, 1987.

Peabody, Houghteling & Co.
First National Bank Building
CHICAGO

(Established 1865)

Cable Address "Hought, Chicago,"
Codes used: Lieber and A. B. C. 5th Ed.

$500,000

First Mortgage 5% Gold Bonds

OF THE

Coeur d'Alene & Spokane Railway Company, Ltd.

Dated November 1, 1903. Due January 1, 1929. Redeemable on or after January 1, 1914, at 105 and Interest. Interest Dates, January 1st and July 1st. Coupon Bonds of $500 and $1,000 each, with Privilege of Registration as to Principal. Principal and Semi-Annual Interest Payable at the Office of the TITLE GUARANTEE & TRUST COMPANY of New York, TRUSTEE.

A sinking fund, being 5% of the net earnings of the Company each year, beginning with the fiscal year 1904, is reserved to retire the bonds at 105

These bonds are secured by a *closed* first mortgage on all the property now owned, or hereafter to be acquired, by the Coeur d'Alene & Spokane Railway Co., Ltd. *While the actual cost of the property is at the rate of $27,000 per mile of main track, these bonds are issued at the very conservative rate of $14,700 per mile.*

Capitalization

CAPITAL STOCK		
Issued and paid in at par	$388,400.00	
In Treasury	111,600.00	
Total Authorized		$500,000.00
BONDS		
Issued	$300,000.00	
Now being issued (at the rate of 90% of the cost of improvements),	200,000.00	
Total Authorized		$500,000.00

Investment in the Property

The following statement from the attached letter, signed by the President of the Company, shows the investment in this property when the bonds are issued:

Investment of Stockholders	$418,339.94
Investment of Bondholders	500,000.00
Total investment in property	$918,339.94

This large cash investment behind the bonds is the best possible assurance to the bondholders of the value of the property and of its safe and capable management.

Earnings

As certified by The Investors Audit Company for a period of *eleven months* from the commencement of operation to November 30, 1904:

Gross Earnings	$105,845.53
Operating Expenses	69,563.95
Net Earnings	$36,281.58
Bond Interest	6,341.64
Surplus	$29,939.94

From the above statement, it is evident that the net earnings of the Company during the first eleven months of operation were nearly six times the interest charge on its bonds outstanding for the same period, and about 50% more than the maximum annual interest requirements on its entire authorized bonded debt. Extensions, and additions to equipment, which will be provided from the proceeds of the $200,000 bonds now being issued, will enable the Company to handle its rapidly increasing traffic in the most economic manner. The net earnings for the year 1905 will be approximately $65,000, and, with the inevitable development of the territory served, should continue to increase for many years to come.

Notice of Coeur d'Alene & Spokane Railway Company mortgage bond sale. All were sold by May 1905. Holders were unaffected by the S&IE foreclosure in 1919 and the bonds were redeemed at face value in January 1929.

Chapter 2

COMPANY GROWTH AND FINANCES

An electric railway between Spokane and Coeur d'Alene was first proposed in April 1892. Intentions became clear on July 6, 1892 when A.A. Newberry, D.M. Drumheller and W.S. Norman incorporated the Spokane & Coeur d'Alene Railway & Navigation Company in the state of Idaho. Allegedly, a survey was made and arrangements for bond flotation completed. The plan foundered in the economic collapse of 1893.

Ten years later, two companies were incorporated that would lead to the building of an electric railway. A local investor, Jay P. Graves, who had made his money in the mining industry, bought the moribund Spokane and Montrose Motor Railroad Company in November 1902. He planned to use its tracks as a nucleus for a streetcar system to compete with the Washington Water Power Company, which held a monopoly in Spokane. Reorganized as the Spokane Traction Company (ST), the company filed its articles of incorporation on March 11, 1903. Capitalized for $500,000, the capital stock was increased to $1 million in July 1905. Incorporators were Jay P. Graves, Clyde Graves, Fred B. Grinnell, Charles G. Reeder and A.L. White. Mutschler, et al. have reviewed the history of Spokane Traction.

The second company was the Coeur d'Alene & Spokane Railway (Cd'A&S). The driving force behind its organization and construction was Frederick A. Blackwell and Ambrose Bettes. Blackwell came from the logging industry, where he had been manager and then a director of the North Bend & Kettle Creek Railroad in Pennsylvania. Owned by a lumber company, this logging railroad also operated a passenger service. Bettes had served as a general manager with the Detroit, Rochester, Rome & Lake Ontario Electric Railway.

They recognized the potential for a direct line from Coeur d'Alene to Spokane to support the growing lumber industry and to compete with the inadequate train service offered by the Northern Pacific Railway. The Coeur d'Alene & Spokane Railway was incorporated October 20, 1902, under the laws of Idaho, to construct the railway. Incorporators were F.A. Blackwell, F.S. Robbins and C.P. Lindsley. Officers included F.A. Blackwell as president, A. Bettes as general manager, and local bank president W. Dollar as treasurer. Five thousand shares at $100 each were authorized. Stockholders approved a $500,000 issue of first mortgage bonds on November 11, 1903.

Jay Graves joined forces with Blackwell. A traffic agreement was signed between their two companies in April 1903. Spokane Traction Company was subsequently awarded franchises to build streetcar lines within Spokane city limits with the council approving their operation over ST tracks. This gave Blackwell a way for his trains to enter the city. Graves became a director of the Cd'A&S in October 1904. Familiarity with Spokane politics and country-wide financial markets were other benefits that he brought to the company.

The Cd'A&S got off to a good start. Revenue more than doubled between 1904 and 1906:

	1904	**1905**	**1906**
Gross Revenue	$127,125	$193,129	$287,093
Net Revenue*	$48,563	$57,568	$122,348

* After deducting operating expenses, taxes and dividends.

Three 3% dividends were paid on the stock during 1905. At the end of that year the company reported to the Interstate Commerce Commission that the road had cost $691,578 (equivalent to an economical $20,000 per mile) and equipment $175,969. A surplus of $118,904 was declared in December 1906.

With the Cd'A&S established, Graves and Blackwell turned their attention to building an interurban line south from Spokane, across the Moran Prairie and through the Palouse country to Moscow, Idaho and eventually to Lewiston, Idaho. Cost of the line was estimated at $3-4 million. Funding sources were explored and a consulting engineer assessed the plans for eastern bankers. When Graves and Blackwell returned from a trip to the east in October 1904 they reported funds were practically assured. With this backing, the Spokane Interurban System was incorporated in the State of Washington on December 17, 1904 to construct and operate railways from Spokane to towns in Washington and Idaho and to develop electric power. Incorporators were A. Coolidge, the president of two local banks; J. Twohy, a railroad contractor; F. Lewis Clark, one of the largest property owners and richest men in Spokane; and W.G. Graves, together with Jay Graves and Blackwell. Electric operation of passenger and express services and steam movement of freight at night were proposed. Capitalized for $3.5 million, the articles were amended on January 12, 1905 to change the name to Spokane & Inland Railway Company (S&I). The incorporators invested $200,000, receiving $1 million worth of stock.

An immediate difficulty faced by the S&I was that the Spokane Southern Traction Company had organized in 1903 to run a line south to Waverly and possibly extend to Colfax and east to Lake Coeur d'Alene. Washington Water Power offered its lines for entry into Spokane. After a series of clashes, the two competitors finally reached agreement on April 1, 1905, leaving the way open for the S&I to proceed. A provision of the agreement stipulated that S&I's power be purchased from WWP.

Immediately after organizing the S&I, Graves and/or his co-incorporators arranged a series of town meetings in the Palouse country. The purpose was to inform citizens about the planned railway and, more importantly, to promote the sale of stock and donation of right-of-way. Failure to support the venture could result in the line bypassing the town was the not-so-subtle message. Doubling of the value of Cd'A&S shares was claimed as an example of potential return - the new line was said to be an even better investment. Each town organized action groups to respond to the appeal. Most promised free right-of-way, as did farmers and landowners in country areas. By March 1905, they had subscribed for $150,000 of stock. With $200,000 from Spokane investors and a similar sum from the incorporators, the combined investment reached $550,000. The directors declared that this was sufficient for construction work to begin.

A third company was formed to build passenger and freight terminals, car barns and other business accommodations in Spokane, with appropriate tracks to serve the existing and planned lines. The Spokane Terminal Company filed articles of incorporation on March 4, 1905. Capitalized for $300,000, the stock was equally divided between the three transportation companies. Issue of bonds up to $.5 million was authorized and guaranteed by the stockholders. The company was to receive 3½ cents for every passenger carried in or out of Spokane.

Graves and his associates decided that a larger business unit would be more attractive to investors. To do this, they formed the Inland Empire Railway Company to consolidate the four companies. Articles of incorporation were filed in the State of Washington on January 19, 1906, authorizing it to build and operate steam and electric railroads to connect Spokane with stations in Washington, Idaho, Oregon and British Columbia and to buy or develop electric generating plants in these places. At a special meeting of stockholders on October 25, 1906 the name of the company was amended to Spokane and Inland Empire Railroad Company (S&IE). It was destined to last for fourteen years. At the time of incorporation (November 7, 1906), mortgage bonds had been issued by three of the merger companies, Graves and Blackwell having persuaded bond companies to place them on the market. Authorized securities (in millions $) amounted to:

	Stock	Bonds
S&I	3.5	0.0
Cd'A&S	0.5	0.5
Spokane Traction	1.0	0.366
Spokane Terminal	0.3	0.35
Total	**$ 5.3**	**1.216**

Inland Empire Railway Company was capitalized for $10 million. The 100,000 ordinary shares at $100 par were subscribed by the incorporators of the merger companies. Jay Graves took 45,000 shares, Blackwell and Clark 25,000 each, and Aaron Kuhn 1,500; W. Paine, W.C. Davidson and W.G. Graves collected 500 each. They did not invest money; instead, they traded stock from their existing holdings for new stock and donated their service as officers. An issue of $10 million preferred rights "stock" paying 5-7% was authorized concurrently; this did not confer the voting power inherent in ordinary stock. Blackwell was elected chairman, Jay Graves president and Lewis Clark vice-president. Soon afterwards, arrangements to purchase the stock of the Cd'A&S and Spokane Traction Company were announced.

Rights and properties of Spokane Terminal Company were conveyed to the S&IE on November 27, 1906. Conveyance of the other three companies was not finalized until February 13, 1908, when the trustees resolved that the S&IE acquire all property of the S&I, Cd'A&S and Spokane Traction companies and assume their indebtedness. Spokane & Inland Company was disincorporated on June 21 1909, having discharged its debts; the others could not follow suit because they had bonds outstanding.

One reason for the delay in conveyance was a problem with a fledgling competitor, the Spokane-Pend d'Oreille Rapid Transit Company. This company had incorporated in early 1906 to build a line northeast from Spokane to Squaw Bay on the southwest arm of Lake Pend d'Oreille in Idaho. At the same time, the Inland Empire Railway Company planned to extend a branch to a nearby area from its Hayden Lake line. To provide right-of-way, F.A. Blackwell purchased land near Squaw Bay, even though the Rapid Transit had already acquired an option on the property. In reprisal, Rapid Transit promoters holding stock in the Spokane & Inland Company aimed to block the merger by refusing to sell their stock (less than 200 shares) to the S&IE. Under the laws of Washington a company could not be disincorporated without the unanimous consent of the stockholders. Purchase of the final 58 shares, held by two dissenters, was announced at an S&IE trustees meeting in June 1907.

In April 1906, the trustees of the Inland Empire Railway Company had authorized $10 million of 5% mortgage bonds. Arrangements with a Chicago banking and finance company provided for the sale of $4,036,000 in bonds. Together with the outstanding bonds previously issued by the merger companies, the interest incurred was $0.25 million per year.

Sale of preferred rights in 1907. No dividend was paid after that year and the stock became worthless twelve years later. Caveat Emptor!

Construction costs of the Inland lines and a new power station began to rapidly inflate, and despite an influx of cash from the bonds and the sale of over 61,000 preferred rights shares, the S&IE ran short of money in 1907. Preferred stock had sold below par, as low as $52 per share. To promote sales, a proportion of ordinary stock was offered as an inducement. Downturn in the market at that time did not help raising money on Wall Street. A series of short-term loans were arranged with local and New York banks and undisclosed sources during the next 18 months.

One stock buyer was James J. Hill, who directed the affairs of the Northern Pacific and Great Northern Railways, both of which had connecting lines to the S&IE. Graves and Hill were well acquainted, being major stockholders in the Granby Consolidated Mining, Smelting & Power Company. Hill owned a large block of S&IE stock by February 1907. Two years later, his holdings

E. H. ROLLINS & SONS
BOSTON CHICAGO DENVER
SAN FRANCISCO

$2,743,000

SPOKANE & INLAND EMPIRE RAILROAD COMPANY

FIRST AND REFUNDING MORTGAGE FIVE PER CENT GOLD BONDS

Dated May 1, 1906. Due May 1, 1926. Optional at 107½ and interest on any interest payment day from May 1, 1911, to November 1, 1915, and at 105 and interest on any interest payment day from and after May 1, 1916.

Interest payable May 1 and November 1 at the First Trust and Savings Bank, Chicago, or the First National Bank of New York City.

Coupon Bonds of $1,000 denomination. Principal may be registered.

The Trust Deed provides for a sinking fund to be paid to the trustee to retire bonds of this issue as follows; one per cent of the outstanding bonds in each of the years 1911 to 1915, one and one-half per cent in each of the years 1916 to 1920, and two per cent in each of the years 1921 to 1925.

TRUSTEE: FIRST TRUST AND SAVINGS BANK, CHICAGO.

CAPITAL

	Authorized	Issued.
Common Stock	$10,000,000	$10,000,000
Preferred Certificates	10,000,000	2,738,500
First and Refunding Mortgage 5% Bonds	15,000,000	2,743,000
Prior Liens outstanding		1,216,000

$1,277,000 of the authorized issue are held in escrow by the Trustee to retire the $1,216,000 Prior Liens at or before maturity; $980,000 are in escrow to be issued for not to exceed 80% of the cash cost of the 9,000 H. P. hydro-electric plant on the Spokane River and for permanent extensions and additions. The balance of the bonds may be issued for not to exceed 75 per cent of the cash cost of permanent extensions and additions, but only when the net earnings for the preceding year have been at least twice the annual interest charge on the bonds outstanding and to be issued.

In our opinion the bonds of the SPOKANE & INLAND EMPIRE RAILROAD COMPANY are an investment of unusual merit, because:

1 The cash cost of the properties, as reported by the Illinois Audit Company, is twice the amount of the outstanding bonds.

2 The physical condition of the property is excellent.

3 The net earnings from the operation of fifty-eight miles of railroad are sufficient to pay the interest on all the bonds issued, and the annual net earnings from the operation of 180 miles of railroad are conservatively estimated to be in excess of twice the total annual interest charge.

4 The territory served is unusually productive and is developing rapidly, and the position of this road in that territory is sufficiently advantageous to insure it a considerable portion of the business available.

5 The management is one in which we have confidence. It has demonstrated its ability in this and other important business enterprises.

Price par and interest paying 5 per cent

The property has been examined in our behalf by various experts, and the books have been examined by the Audit Company of Illinois.

Prior to the delivery of the bonds the legality of the issue will be approved by L. C. Krauthoff, Esquire, New York City.

Bonds will be delivered at any bank desired, express prepaid, payable with exchange.

Telegrams may be sent at our expense.

For information concerning the Company and its field of operation, reference is made to the following letter from Jay P. Graves, President of the Spokane & Inland Empire Railroad Company:

Notice of Spokane & Inland Empire Railroad Company mortgage bond sale. The referenced Graves letter extolled the value of the bonds as an investment and noted that all the properties were expected to be in operation by January 1, 1907. Bond purchasers ended up as owners of the S&IE at a foreclosure sale in November 1919.

were $1,083,850 of preferred stock and $2,157,350 in common stock according to the Washington Railroad Commission. Hill also lent money to the S&IE to help pay off short-term loans; the debt to him exceeded $1 million by April 1909.

Hill gained control of the S&IE in October 1909 by purchasing more common stock. Graves had bought shares from acquaintances for this purpose, selling them to Hill along with his own holdings. The Spokane *Spokesman-Review* newspaper reckoned that Hill paid $2,535,000, but this was based on speculative data. He now held 69,305 ordinary shares and 21,667 preferred rights; NP records reveal their total cost was $5.8 million. The stock was divided equally between the Great Northern and Northern Pacific railway companies, the latter's being held by a subsidiary, the Northwestern Improvement Company. Popular opinion held that Hill made the move to prevent the expanding Chicago, Milwaukee & St. Paul Railroad from buying the company. An equally plausible reason was that Hill feared claims arising from the accident at Gibbs (see Chapter 10) two months earlier could bankrupt the S&IE and acted to save it.

Graves remained as president after Hill gained control along with his management team, but he himself fell from favor. Reputedly, Graves's resignation was requested due to his extravagant spending and grand plans. He firmly believed that adding miles of railroad was the way to increase revenue and reduce operating costs. Spokane, Portland & Seattle Railway (SP&S), jointly owned by the NP and GN, was given executive management responsibility for the S&IE in June 1911. Carl Gray, recently appointed as president of the SP&S, replaced Graves. Estimates of the book cost of S&IE property at that time included $8,469,077 for the Inland Division; $1,733,942 for the Cd'A&S Division; $1,586,453 for the Traction Division; $920,441 for the Terminal Division and $418,316 for equipment.

When Hill gained control, the financial outlook for the S&IE was beginning to show signs of weakness. Although gross revenue (including the streetcar Traction Division) had increased from 1907 to 1910, the net operating income (after deducting operating expenses and taxes) was sufficient to cover bond interest payments but little else. Dividends had not been paid on preferred rights "stock" since 1907, when three were declared, and none were returned on ordinary stock since the company was organized. The Gibbs accident, while not a fatal blow, eventually resulted in settlements by the company approaching $350,000.

Competition from road transport and rival railroads (NP and Oregon Washington Railroad & Navigation) became fierce. Gross revenue and net income declined. The company went into deficit in 1911 and year by year the annual loss grew steadily worse. To fill this gap, money was borrowed sporadically from the parent companies to pay bond interest and capital expenses; the

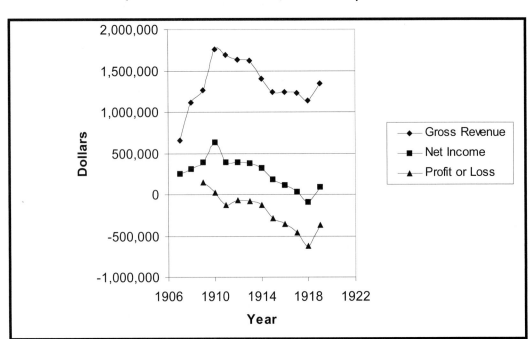

Spokane & Inland Empire Railroad financial results 1907-1919. Net income: after operating expenses and taxes deducted from gross revenue. Profit or loss: after interest deducted from net income. Source: Annual Reports to Stockholders and to Washington State.

GN and NP contributed equivalent amounts (Table 2.1). The S&IE had to pay interest on these loans. By 1918, the amount owed to the GN and Northwestern Improvement Company (an NP ancillary) had reached $6,211,242; the annual interest now exceeded that on the bonds. Adding this debt to the $4,414,500 of bonds outstanding produced a total debt of $10,625,742.

Furthermore, gross revenue by this time was insufficient to cover the operating expenses. An op-

**Table 2.1. Advances Made to the S&IE by Great Northern Railway
and Northwest Improvement Company.**

Period $	Advance	Applied to
6/1908-4/1910	2,500,015	Banks and suppliers.
5/1910-12/1910	690,560	Suppliers and construction.
1911	712,658	Suppliers and bond and debt interest.
1912	94,852	Debt interest.
1913	255,470	Bond and debt interest.
1914	214,311	Debt interest.
1915	300,256	Bond interest and taxes.
1916	75,000	Bond interest.
1917	135,844	Suppliers and bond interest.

erating deficit of $110,701, combined with annual interest, resulted in an overall loss of $624,652 for 1918. Exasperated by the whole dismal situation, the Northern Pacific president reckoned that "the NP has its own lines into the very best of this territory and should not have become a partner in this unloading by Graves and his associates."

The question of how to eliminate the need for recurrent loans had been addressed sporadically by the GN, NP and SP&S chiefs. Among the options considered were (1) to buy the bonds to acquire the company, (2) force its sale by bringing suit on the loan indebtedness, and (3) precipitate foreclosure of the mortgage. Appraisal of the salvage value of the S&IE (in the event of a forced sale) gave a figure of $5.91 million: $4 million for the railway system, $0.56 million for the traction business and $1.35 million for the power plant.

Because of the deteriorating financial position, the management trio decided to bring matters to a head and exercise option (3), withdrawing their monetary support on November 1, 1918. No advance was made for the interest payment of $92,200 due that day on mortgage bonds. As a result, the company defaulted. Terms of the bond issue were such that the principal became due two months later and, of course, the S&IE could not pay.

Upon petition by the First Trust & Savings Bank of Chicago, acting as trustee for the bondholders, a federal judge placed a receiver in charge of the property on January 10, 1919. Frank E. Connors, previously an assistant vice president with the Atchison, Topeka & Santa Fe railroad, was appointed as receiver. Claims amounting to approximately $7 million were brought against the S&IE in federal district court in April 1919, the largest (over $6 million) coming from the GN and NP followed by railroad employees for back payment of wage increases.

A receiver's sale was held in Spokane on November 1, 1919. Great Northern Railway's representative bid at the sale, but dropped out at $3.5 million. George W. Taylor from the trustee bank, acting for over 1000 bondholders located throughout the USA and Europe, purchased the property of the S&IE for $3.6 million using the mortgage bonds as payment. Excluded were bonds totaling $699,000 that remained outstanding; responsibility for them was assumed by the purchaser.

Mortgage bonds outstanding consisted of $442,000 (Cd'A&S), $176,000 (Terminal) and $81,000 (Traction). The federal court approved the sale.

In retrospect, holders of ordinary stock never received a cent from the S&IE and no dividend was paid on preferred rights after October 1907. Only Jay Graves and associates made a handsome profit, by selling their stock to J.J. Hill. Stock became worthless as a result of the receiver's sale. Adding the $5.8 million that Hill paid for his stock to the $6.2 million loans made by the GN and NP equated to a total loss of $12 million. In other words, the GN and NP lost $6 million each.

The new owners split the business into two companies. Spokane & Eastern Railway & Power Company (S&E) took over the Coeur d'Alene line, the streetcar system and the power plant, while the Inland Empire Railroad Company (IE) acquired the Palouse lines. Both companies were incorporated under the laws of Washington State January 3, 1920. The S&E was capitalized for $3 million and the IE for $1 million: each share was for $100 par value. George Taylor was appointed president, and the receiver, F.E. Connors, became vice president and general manager of both companies. Taylor held all the stock on behalf of the bondholders' protection committee, except for one share held by each director (the nine directors acted for both companies). An early action by the new organization granted wage increases to certain employee grades, the S&IE having suffered a strike because of nonpayment.

Annual net income generated by the S&E and IE is shown in Table 2.2. Combined results were somewhat better than during the final years of S&IE ownership. Nevertheless, they were insufficient to pay the $.25 million annual interest on the bonds that remained outstanding and the borrowed money. Notably, the Inland Empire Company fell short of covering operating costs throughout its life. Spokane & Eastern's net income, which easily covered the IE shortfall, actually stemmed from its ownership of Nine Mile Power Station, the plant being quite profitable. Without it, the combined total each year would have been in deficit as revealed by the 1926 results, after sale of the power station.

George Taylor's ultimate goal was to sell off major elements and distribute the proceeds among the bondholders who now owned the two companies. Leisure properties were quickly sold or leased. In February 1921, Taylor wrote to GN president Ralph Budd, to say that it was the company's intention to sell the S&E and IE during the year and asked if the GN was interested in any one or more of the divisions of either company. Budd replied that he would not consider purchase of either of the properties; he was quite familiar with them having been chief engineer for the S&IE (and SP&S) in 1910-12.

Table 2.2. Net Income Generated by Spokane & Eastern Railway & Power Company and Inland Empire Railroad Company.

Year	S&E	IE	Total
1920	$ 113,294	$ -2,108	$ 111,186
1921	126,279	-42,655	83,624
1922	275,829	-108,699	167,130
1923	199,045	-149,041	50,004
1924	202,671	-86,207	116,464
1925	116,882	-87,783	29,099
1926	*	-115,524	-115,524

Net income shown after taxes; *S&E leased to IE; minus sign indicates a loss.

Sale of the Traction Division was finalized by the S&E in 1922; previous attempts by the S&IE had failed. Articles of Incorporation for Spokane City Railways Company were signed on January 9, 1922, to acquire the streetcar business (on March 22, 1922), the $1,125,000 capital stock being owned by the S&E. On July 22, 1922, this company and the streetcar interests of the Washington Water Power Company were consolidated as the Spokane United Railways Company. In exchange, the S&E was given securities in the new streetcar company.

On July 1, 1925, the railway's Nine Mile Power Station and Spokane substation, together with the Spokane United securities held by the S&E, were sold to Washington Water Power for $2.35 million. Following this sale, Budd was prompted by a Wall Street banker associate to take another look at the railway system. The trustees had advised that they would like to clean up the whole situation. Budd replied that he had always been interested in the Coeur d'Alene line and that if the directors agreed with him, he would be willing to negotiate for it on reasonable terms. His director of traffic concurred, but advised strongly against buying the Inland Empire Railroad Company because of its modest earning potential. This option vanished on December 31, 1925, when the IE formally leased the S&E, probably to forestall such an offer.

Great Northern ended up buying both properties. Under the terms of an agreement dated November 26, 1926, the S&E and IE agreed to sell to the Great Northern, or its nominee, for $1.25 million; the buyer assumed the obligation and liability for $442,000 in mortgage bonds. Sale was contingent on Interstate Commerce Commission approval so the owners continued to operate the railroad. On April 21, 1927, the ICC authorized the Spokane, Coeur d'Alene & Palouse Railway Company, a GN subsidiary, to acquire and operate the lines of the S&E and IE. Why the GN opted to go this way rather than directly acquire the property is unclear. Presumably there was a financial, or legal, benefit.

This subsidiary had been incorporated in Washington on September 15, 1909, as the Idaho Central Railway, organized for and on behalf of the GN to acquire surveyed properties of the Panhandle Electric Railway & Power Company. The latter business was incorporated on May 15, 1907, with capital stock of $100,000; the company had at least two GN employees as stockholders. The proposed railroad between Priest River (a GN station) and Priest Lake in Idaho was never built. The proposal was formally abandoned in 1929. Great Northern purchased the Panhandle Electric Railway & Power Company on October 18, 1909. A special meeting of the board of trustees held on December 7, 1926, amended the Idaho Central Railway articles of incorporation: corporate powers were expanded and the name was changed to Spokane, Coeur d'Alene & Palouse Railway Company (SC&P) effective December 11, 1926. Idaho businessmen unsuccessfully proposed the alternative name of Spokane & Idaho Northern Railway.

On May 28, 1927, SC&P issued employee timetable No.1. The deed of conveyance was transferred June 13, 1927, SC&P securing a loan from the Great Northern to buy the property. The directors, made up of GN officers, retired the outstanding bonds, which matured in January 1929, by means of an additional loan. They instituted economies to reduce expenses, but the operation remained in deficit. Annual loss in operating income reached a nadir in 1941, at $284,367. Total debt by this time exceeded $2.3 million, money having been borrowed periodically from the GN. Offsetting the loss was the revenue the GN gained from traffic interchanged with SC&P. There was a remarkable turnaround in 1942 with a net profit of $12,229 being recorded, a situation produced by the elimination of passenger trains, replacement of electric traction by diesel-electric locomotives and increased traffic due to the onset of WWII.

During that year, the GN offered to purchase all physical properties, investments, materials and supplies of the company and the offer was accepted by the board. Transfer of SC&P property and operation to the Great Northern became effective July 1, 1943. The GN annual report to stockholders noted that this was part of a "continuing policy of simplifying its corporate structure," the GN having a 100% controlling interest ($20,000 par value stock) in SC&P with a total book value of $1,496,676. The company was formally wound up and dissolved on February 3, 1959. The Spokane Division operated the lines until February 1, 1956, when responsibility passed to the Kalispell Division. Following the Burlington Northern merger in 1970, the lines became part of a newly-created Spokane Division.

Even with modern technology and after pruning the lines, rail service to the Inland territory remained unprofitable. By the mid-1980s, the revenue generated by Burlington Northern and Union Pacific was $29 million, but it cost $31 million to carry the region's grain and lumber products. Both railroads eventually sold the loss-making lines to short line operators.

Management

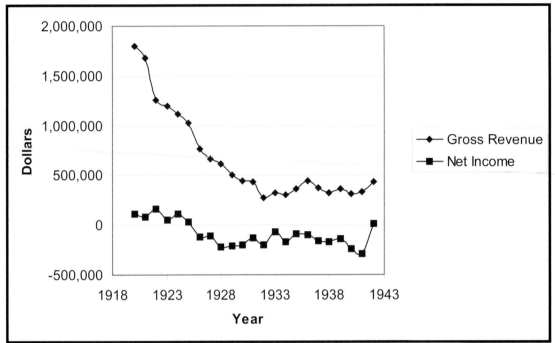

Financial results for the period 1920-1942. Spokane & Eastern Railway & Power Company and Inland Empire Railroad Company results, 1920-1926, are combined. Spokane, Coeur d'Alene & Palouse Railway Company operated 1927-1942. Source: Annual Reports to State of Washington.

When the Cd'A&S started operation, the key officers were President F.A. Blackwell, General Manager Ambrose Bettes and Traffic Manager Waldo G. Paine (as noted in Table 2.3). Bettes resigned his position in early 1904 despite being largely responsible for getting the railway into operation. He departed to promote the building of a railroad into the Big Bend country northwest of Spokane. R.F. Blackwell, son of the president, became general manager, but resigned early in 1907, leaving to pursue his lumber interests. By mid-1907 C.M. Graves was president of the railway company.

Spokane & Inland appointed their chief electrical engineer, J.B. Ingersoll, as general manager. Jay Graves held the office of president. When the S&I merged with its partner companies to form the S&IE, Ingersoll retained his engineering position. Clyde Graves became general manager of the S&IE, under his father as president. A.M. Lupfer, previously chief engineer for the S&I, assumed the same position in the consolidated company. Other S&IE officers included A.L. White, vice president, and R.C. Bowdish, superintendent. F.A. Blackwell, appointed as chairman, apparently grew bored with his new position, and went into partnership with his son to incorporate the Idaho & Washington Northern Railway in April 1907 to serve the family's expanding lumber business. He resigned from the S&IE board a few years later. As a result of the consolidation, the operating arms of the merged companies became the Coeur d'Alene & Spokane, Spokane & Inland, Traction and Terminal Divisions of the S&IE.

Table 2.3. Company Officers.

Company	Year	President	General Manager	Traffic Manager	Chief Engineer
Cd'A&S	1903	F.A. Blackwell	A. Bettes	W.G. Paine	J.C. White
Cd'A&S	1905	F.A. Blackwell	R.F. Blackwell	W.G. Paine	J.C. White
S&I	1907	J.P. Graves	J.B. Ingersoll	W.G. Paine	A.M. Lupfer
S&IE	1910	J.P. Graves	C.M. Graves	W.G. Paine	A.M. Lupfer
S&IE	1912	J.H. Young	C.A. Coolidge	W.G. Paine	R. Budd
S&IE	1916	L.C. Gilman	C.O. Jenks	W.G. Paine	A.M. Lupfer
S&E/IE	1920	G.H. Taylor	F.E. Connors	W.G. Paine	A.J. Witchell
S&E/IE	1925	M.H. MacLean	W.G. Paine	-	A.J. Witchell
SC&P	1930	R. Budd	J.H. O'Neill	M.J. Costello	J.R.W. Davis
SC&P	1936	W.P. Kenney	J.H. O'Neill	J.F. Pewters	J.R.W. Davis

Executive control of the railroad passed to the Spokane, Portland and Seattle Railway in June 1911. This action, taken at the insistence of the S&IE's majority stockholders (the GN and NP), had a devastating impact on the company's officers. Carl Grey, SP&S president, was appointed president of the S&IE by the board of trustees. A vote of thanks was accorded to his predecessor, Jay Graves, while vice president Aubrey White resigned. C.A. Coolidge, general manager of the SP&S, replaced Clyde Graves and SP&S superintendent E.E. Lillie ousted Bowdish. New appointees kept their existing positions at the SP&S. The engineering office moved to the SP&S headquarters in Portland, Oregon under SP&S chief engineer Ralph Budd. Lupfer and Ingersoll resigned their engineering positions.

Subsequent SP&S management appointments resulted in corresponding changes at the S&IE. As a result, the S&IE had four different presidents during the next several years. After Ralph Budd departed for stardom at the GN, Lupfer returned to the S&IE as chief engineer for several years.

As part of the 1920 reorganization, the chairman of the bondholders committee filled the president's role for the two new companies (S&E and IE). Frank Connors was appointed general manager and a vice president for both companies. The bondholders committee considered that he had done a good job as receiver during the previous year. Connors died in 1923, so Waldo Paine, traffic manager for the preceding two decades, assumed his du-

This assembly included Jay Graves, center on car platform in a gray greatcoat; immediately to Graves's left is F.A. Blackwell; to Blackwell's left is Clyde Graves; Spokane Traction Company director, Fred Grinnell, is center, on track. (Ted Holloway Collection)

ties. Paine died in office in 1926. Under SC&P ownership, all the officers came from the Great Northern Railway with headquarters in St. Paul, Minnesota.

Staff

By June1905 the Cd'A&S had 145 employees and grew to 208 during the next 12 months. In 1910 the S&IE reported a workforce of 865, thus making a significant contribution to local employment. Over the next twenty years, however, the number of employees decreased progressively, falling 25% by the time of receivership. Functional deployment of the 689 employees in 1916 was 45% transportation, 24% equipment maintenance, 17% track and structures, 9% power supply and 5% general administration.

Reorganization into two companies in 1920 gave the Spokane & Eastern roughly three times as many employees as the Inland Empire. More staff was needed by the S&E because it conducted rolling stock maintenance and general administration for both companies as well as operating the direct current (DC) railway, streetcars and power station. Divesting the streetcar system from the S&E in 1922 reduced its employees by one-third. The Inland Empire workforce was divided equally between the operations and maintenance organizations to run the alternating current (AC) trains.

Following the SC&P take-over, employment fell to close to 200 with the transfer of general administrative duties to the GN eliminating some 50 jobs. By 1932 there were only 122 employees, the effect of service curtailment and economies. Ten years later, when the GN acquired SC&P there were almost 200. Much of this increase had been maintenance-of-way staff hired to make necessary improvements. Distribution of manpower during the late 1930s was 40% maintenance-of-way, 30% train operation, 20% rolling stock maintenance, and 10% power supply. By that time, an average of nine pairs of motormen and conductors was sufficient to run the trains.

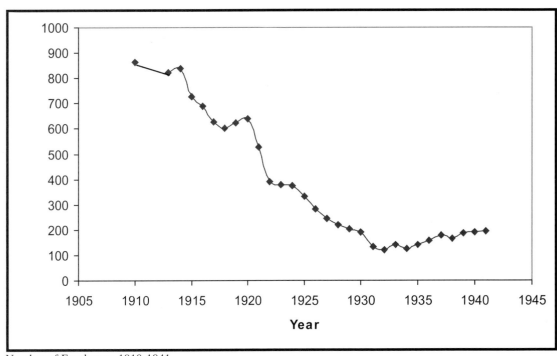

Number of Employees 1910-1941.

Sources

Interstate Commerce Commission. Acquisition of Lines by Spokane, Coeur d'Alene & Palouse Railway, Finance Docket No.6014, April 21, 1927.

Great Northern Railway Company. Branch Lines – Coeur d'Alene & Spokane Railway.

Great Northern Railway Company. Branch Lines – Spokane & Inland Empire Railroad.

Great Northern Railway Company. Branch Lines - Spokane, Coeur d'Alene & Palouse Railway.

Great Northern Railway. President's Subject File No.8759. Spokane & Inland Empire Railroad: General File.

Great Northern Railway. President's Subject File No.15831. Spokane, Coeur d'Alene & Palouse Railway.

Northern Pacific Railway. President's File No. 1340-T, No.1604, No.1604-2, No.1604-4.

Coeur d'Alene & Spokane Railway. Annual Report to the Interstate Commerce Commission, 1904 – 1906.

Spokane, Coeur d'Alene & Palouse Railway. Annual Report to Washington State, 1927 – 1942.

Spokane & Inland Empire Railroad. Annual Report to Stockholders, 1907 – 1918.

Spokane & Inland Empire Railroad. Annual Report to Washington State, 1907 – 1919.

Spokane & Eastern Railway & Power Co. Annual Report to Washington State, 1920 – 1927.

Inland Empire Railroad. Annual Report to Washington State, 1920 – 1927.

Fahey, John. Shaping Spokane: Jay P. Graves and His Times. Seattle: University of Washington Press, 1984.

Mutschler, Charles V., Clyde L. Parent and Wilmer H. Siegert. Spokane's Street Railways: An Illustrated History. Spokane, WA: Inland Empire Railway Historical Society, 1987.

Electric Railway Journal. "Spokane & Inland Empire Railroad, Spokane, Washington." December 25, 34: 1281, 1909.

Electric Railway Journal. "Inland Empire Foreclosed." November 1, 54: 840, 1919.

Electric Railway Journal. "Successor to Inland Empire Incorporates." January 24, 55:218, 1919.

Electric Railway Journal. "Spokane Sale Confirmed." March 6, 55: 493, 1919.

Electric Railway Journal. "New Name for Inland Empire Under Great Northern Control." February 17, 69: 354, 1927.

Spokane Spokesman Review.

Construction crew laying track on the Coeur d'Alene & Spokane Railway in 1903.
(Museum of North Idaho Trr-1-18)

Chapter 3

CONSTRUCTION

COEUR D'ALENE LINE & BRANCHES

Immediately after incorporation of the Coeur d'Alene & Spokane Railway Company in October 1902, the general manager was directed to secure the right-of-way. The route extended through the Spokane valley, following the course of the Spokane River. By the end of the year most of the land was secured between Spokane city limits and the state line.

Plans originally called for the line to leave Spokane along Sprague Avenue and cross the Oregon Railroad & Navigation track east of the fairgrounds. After their announcement, burgeoning land prices resulted in the route being moved further north in March 1903. This required trains to exit north along Washington Street, turn east along Sinto Avenue and over a new bridge on Boone Avenue to join the planned line. The Spokane city council granted the necessary franchises that allowed Spokane Traction Company to build these lines and operate Cd'A&S trains over them.

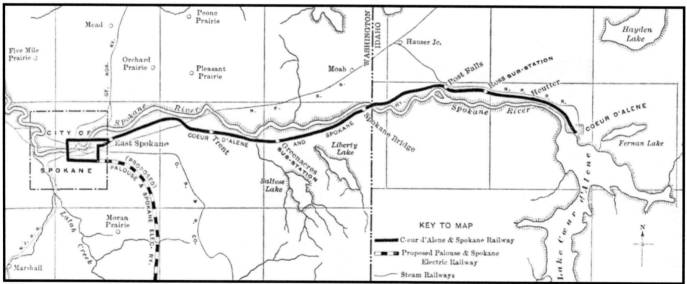

1905 map of Coeur d'Alene & Spokane Railway. The line followed the Spokane River and, east from Post Falls, paralleled the Northern Pacific branch. There were two routes over the streetcar lines into the center of Spokane by that time, as indicated by the "rectangular" path in Spokane. The original route crossed the river twice there, while the second route avoided the river and provided access to the city center for a proposed line from the south.

To enter Coeur d'Alene, the company secured a right-of-way through Fort Sherman military reservation from the U. S. Interior Department, together with 20 acres of the reserve for a lakefront park.

At a meeting in Coeur d'Alene on May 11, 1903, the directors awarded contracts for the grading of the railroad to the Spokane firms of M.D. Wright and S.A. Eslick, and for bridge construction to Porter Brothers of the same city. Contracts specified grading completion by August 1. The railway company would lay the rail, erect poles, string wires and build structures. The directors authorized the general manager to procure overhead fixtures and electrical supplies; poles and ties were already ordered. President Blackwell departed the same day for the east to purchase rolling stock and other equipment. Regular passenger service from September 1 was forecast.

Construction was underway by the end of May. The grading contractors established camps at Post Falls, Spokane Bridge, and on the outskirts of Spokane and Coeur d'Alene. By the beginning of July, three hundred men were employed. A month later, grading was 85% complete. Graders finished the job at the Coeur d'Alene terminus by mid-September. Work on the company's dock there had been completed, allowing assembly of the depot to commence (a second dock, for log movement, was completed the following year). A wooden trestle at Trent, where the electric line passed under the NP main line, and a bridge over the Spokane River at the Washington/Idaho border (Spokane Bridge) were near completion.

Ten miles of track extended east from Spokane by September 19, progressing at the rate of about two miles per day. Hewn fir ties (seven inches by eight feet) were positioned on two-foot centers and sixty-pound rail laid as it arrived. By mid-October ties were placed all the way. A hundred men were laying rail, forty more were setting poles, and wiring had started. The last rail was laid at Coeur d'Alene on October 24, the final 600 feet being witnessed by the president, general manager and half of the town population. Company officers met later that day to arrange the first train over the line.

The special train departed from Spokane OR&N depot at 8:30 a.m. on October 28, 1903, the first anniversary of the incorporation of the railway. Among the 130 guests were stockholders, lumber mill representatives, bankers, merchants and public officers. The company's steam locomotive hauled the train of three 60-foot coaches dating from around 1890, loaned by the Oregon Railroad & Navigation Company, a Union Pacific Railroad ancillary company. The train reached the new road over its connection to the OR&N; a separate franchise was granted for steam-hauled freight service over this line, along Harrison Avenue to Broadway. The connection had been used for delivery of track materials. Only the first five miles of the track were ballasted; the rest of the journey was reported as "a little uneven." Journey time was almost two hours, with several stops along the way for celebrations and photographing the entire party at Spokane Bridge.

At Coeur d'Alene when the train stopped at the new two-story depot, the front of the locomotive protruded over the company's new dock. City councilmen and the mayor welcomed the party, watched by most of the city's population. Speeches were made and a local band performed. The stockholders annual meeting was held later, followed by a return trip for the guests to Harrison on the Coeur d'Alene & St. Joe Navigation Company's new steamer "Idaho." Afterwards, the party boarded the special train for the return to Spokane.

The line was not ready for regular service at that time. Overhead wiring was incomplete, rails needed electrical bonding, electrical machinery was late and the passenger rolling stock had not arrived. Spokane Traction Company had grading and track work to do on Boone Avenue. When completed the gradual up grade from Spokane to Coeur d'Alene averaged 0.15%; the maximum was 1.2%, and the maximum curvature was eight degrees. Ballast was rock gravel, mostly taken from the right-of-way.

Regular passenger service began on December 28, 1903. A temporary terminus in Spokane was established at the junction of Riverside Avenue and Mill Street. It soon changed to the intersection of Washington Street and Sprague Avenue, with a loop laid to turn cars and a small wooden building used as the terminal. Trial trips that started four days earlier, with borrowed equipment, had demonstrated that cars could be operated over the route by electric power from Spokane without waiting for completion of the substations. In their absence, a large voltage drop was experienced at the eastern end, slowing car speed. The first freight operated the previous day with two carloads of lumber hauled to Spokane by steam locomotive.

To allow for further expansion of the railroad system, Spokane Traction petitioned the city council for two more streetcar franchises in January 1904. One extended east along Third Avenue from Sherman Street to Magnolia Street, south on Magnolia to Fifth Avenue and east on Fifth to the city limits. Third Avenue would give future interurban trains, coming in from the south side of town, access to the city center. The other route was south on Madelia Street from Olive (later Trent) Avenue to Third Avenue. Washington Water Power objected strongly at the meeting held to discuss the application, claiming invasion of their territory, but the city council granted the franchises five months later.

Cd'A&S officers announced that their railway would enter the city using both lines. Heavy grades (up to 8%) along Boone Avenue would be avoided, saving at least ten minutes on the journey time. To provide the necessary connection, the Traction Company applied for, and received, an additional franchise to extend north on Madelia Street to Broadway and east on Broadway to intersect the Cd'A&S line near the baseball park. Work started on the new streetcar lines in June, 1904. Coeur

The wiring gang takes time off for a photograph.
(Sheldon Perry Collection)

d'Alene trains began using the new route on January 27, 1905, running south down Washington Street from the Spokane terminal to gain access to Third Avenue and onward to Magnolia Street and Broadway. The 1906 Spokane map shows the route.

In early 1905 Spokane Terminal Company bought land on Ferry Avenue in Spokane for freight terminal grounds and passenger lines. The site extended east from Division Street to the river. Yard tracks were laid and a new freight depot opened in March 1906. A transfer track between the GN and NP yards crossed at the east end of the yard so a connection here gave the electric line access to both for interchange. The S&IE rerouted the transfer track in 1911 and extended the freight yard. Repair shops, to handle both streetcar and interurban rolling stock, opened in 1907 at the bend in the river.

Plans were made to build a terminal at the southeast corner of Sprague Avenue and Washington Street. After purchasing the land it became apparent that the space was insufficient for the projected traffic. Spokane Terminal Company changed the site in March 1905 to the intersection of Lincoln Street and Main Avenue, acquired the land and built a three-story terminal there.

Spokane Terminal Company obtained a franchise to lay a double track line from the terminal. The route was east along Main Avenue to Market Street, north along Market to Ferry Avenue and east to the river. The river was crossed at two points over wooden Howe truss bridges; the shops lay between them. The second bridge carried a single track that extended to a new wye (named Inland Junction) where the Cd'A&S and S&I railways joined. A one-mile extension from the baseball park to Inland Junction was necessary to make the Cd'A&S connection. Regular train service from the new terminal began on May 27, 1906.

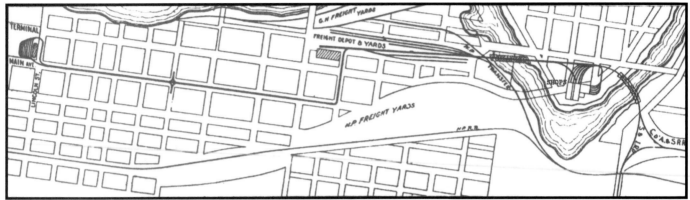

Route from the passenger terminal to Inland Junction where the Cd'A&S and S&I lines joined. The new shops were evident on this 1907 map.

The line from Spokane terminal crossed over bridge 1.5 (A) to reach Inland Junction where track 1 went to Moscow/Colfax and track 2 to Coeur d'Alene. The third leg of the wye, track 3, connected them. Track 4 belonged to the Milwaukee Road. City substation (B) was owned by the S&IE. (Ted Holloway Collection)

Thus by 1906 Cd'A&S trains had accessed Spokane city center over three different routes. Services along Boone Avenue and Third Avenue lasted only a year each. The terminal route was used until 1927 when passenger business moved to the GN depot. This change required a connecting track between the GN main line, near Division Street, to the existing electric line, close to the GN-NP transfer track crossing. Trolley wire was extended over two tracks at the GN depot.

Growth in passenger traffic indicated a need for increased line capacity, so a second track was added between Greenacres and Spokane Bridge. Double tracking of this section began in March 1907. Work was discontinued by the summer, ostensibly due to heavy traffic. By March 1908, construction had restarted, employing 200 men and equipment reassigned from the power station dam. The six miles of double track were completed a few months later. As part of the overall upgrade, track was relocated at Spokane Bridge to eliminate tight curves on either side of the river and reduce the maximum grade of 1.5% to 0.5%. Double tracking of the Greenacres-Spokane section became

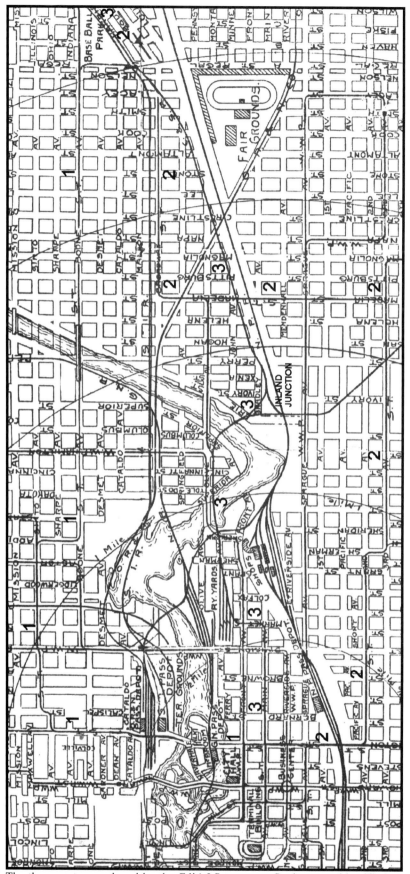

The three routes employed by the Cd'A&S to access Spokane are identified on this 1906 map as 1) via Boone Avenue and Washington Street (1903); 2) via Madelia Street, Third Avenue and Washington Street (1905); and 3) to the new terminal (1906).

necessary by 1909 because local traffic was increasing in the Spokane area. Addition of the second track got underway that year and was completed in 1910.

Hayden Lake Extension

That the Cd'A&S was considering an eight-mile extension from Coeur d'Alene to Hayden Lake, a resort area, was reported as early as February 1904. Further expansion to the wide timberlands lying to the northeast was likely. Two years later, the Cd'A&S directors approved extension to Hayden Lake at an estimated cost of $200,000. Work began early in April 1906 from Coeur d'Alene. M.D. Wright Company stored ties and electrification poles at a camp on 12th Street. Grading was completed by the beginning of June and six miles of track were laid during the next three weeks. Although the goal was to open the line for a steam train on the July 4th holiday, late delivery of rail caused a schedule slide. The line opened for electric train service on August 15, 1906, the delay having allowed wiring completion. Track work at Hayden Lake was simply a loop. The depot did not open until nine months later.

Liberty Lake Branch

Development of Liberty Lake as a resort had begun by the turn of the century. The owners asked the Cd'A&S to build a spur from the rudimentary station, named Liberty Lake, on the main line two miles distant from the lake. Railroad officials initially rebuffed the suggestion. Close proximity to Spokane made it increasingly popular and the number of passengers using the junction station grew. A survey was arranged in August 1904 and Blackwell announced that the line would be built. Two years later, the directors approved the branch and rail was laid in March 1907. Track work included a wye at the main line station, the renaming of

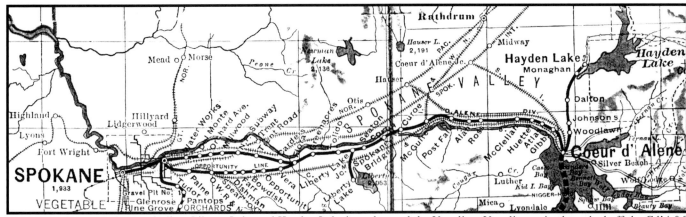

Map of the Coeur d'Alene main line, Liberty Lake and Hayden Lake branches and the Vera line. Vera line trains branched off the Cd'A&S main line at Shops Junction to run over Traction Division tracks to the Spokane city limits, passing under the main line at Madelia Street. The Vera line proper extended from the city limits to Flora.

Liberty Lake Junction, and a loop at Liberty Lake. Service began with the summer timetable introduction on June 15, 1907. Passenger facilities at both ends of the line were still under construction when the line opened.

VERA LINE

Irrigation of the Opportunity and Vera districts to the east of Spokane got underway during the first decade of the century. Jay Graves came to an agreement with the developers that the railroad would build through the area in exchange for free right-of-way and contracts to supply its electric power and light. Land was acquired by mid-November 1908 and a franchise awarded to the Traction Division to build the tracks within the city limits. In fact, the Traction Division operated the whole Vera line.

The line extended from Flora, diverging from the Coeur d'Alene main line to Vera, and then paralleled Sprague Avenue over a private right-of-way through Opportunity, Dishman, and Spear to meet the Spokane Traction line at Freya Street. From here movement was over the streetcar line to Madelia Street, via Riverside Avenue, north to Trent Avenue and west along Trent to join the terminal line at Spokane shops.

Contractors began grading west from Vera on December 7, 1908, but stopped when the cold weather set in. Work recommenced in June 1909, with a crew of 40 men and some 18 teams setting up a camp in the Vera district. Sixty-pound rail was laid to accommodate freight, as well as passenger rolling stock; fruit growing and agriculture were the local industries. Two rail laying gangs working from both ends met along Sprague Avenue on September 11, 1909. Overhead wiring was finished by the end of October. Company officials made an inspection trip on November 12 with general manager C.M. Graves as motorman. The line opened for traffic the following day, when celebrations were held under the auspices of the Opportunity Farmers Union and a barbecue was organized.

INLAND LINES

Spokane Traction stated in a 1904 franchise application that the reason for building along Third Avenue was to provide access for a railway from the Palouse country. Messrs. Graves and Blackwell had expressed interest in building such a line and surveys were conducted. Graves conducted a rudimentary market survey, requesting details of recent shipments from farmers.

In January 1905, the Spokane & Inland Railway began to plan the line south from Spokane to Moscow. A.M. Lupfer was hired as chief engineer, coming from the Great Northern Railway where he had overseen construction of the Kalispell cutoff. Three potential routes were evaluated, the preliminary favorite being through Colfax and Pullman. Cost was estimated optimistically at $3 to 4 million even though the Palouse terrain of rolling hills was much more challenging than the Cd'A&S construction.

Towns on the projected route were enthusiastic, buying shares and offering free right-of-way. By-passed towns asked for reconsideration. Rockford, four miles east of Mount Hope, requested the line be diverted to serve both it and Fairfield, but was rebuffed.

The directors gave the go-ahead in mid-March to start construction of the line. One third of the money already subscribed was allocated to start the work. A contract was immediately awarded to Porter Brothers of Spokane to grade the first 22 miles; unit cost varied according to difficulty of removal: $1 per yard for rock and 22 cents per yard for earth. The first 10.5 miles was subcontracted to other companies, most of this section requiring heavy rock work. Four months later, the next 11 miles of grading to Waverly was added to the contract. By this time, 450 men were employed on the line. Another contract was placed with Porter Brothers for the construction of seven bridges including the challenging Rock Creek, California Creek and Latah Creek sites, together with the two Howe trusses in Spokane. M.D. Wright Company, a Cd'A&S major customer, won the contract to supply ties and poles for the line.

A thousand men were grading by October 1905 when 75% of the work was complete. Fourteen camps existed along the 33 miles with subcontractors doing much of the work in one to three mile stretches. The uphill grade out of Spokane was almost finished. Most of the work was now concentrated over the Moran Prairie where heavy cuts (20 to 30 feet deep and 100 to 500 feet long) and fills (up to 70 feet deep and 800 feet long) were required. Two large steam shovels were used. The goal of having 27 miles of road ready for operation by the end of the year was not achieved. Seven miles of track had been laid by that time, with ballasting and pole installation imminent, and the construction of Hangman's Gulch bridge ready to start.

This materials storage area, which existed during the construction of the S&I lines, appears to be at Inland Junction. (Sheldon Perry collection)

Erecting poles on the S&I. (Ted Holloway Collection)

By May 1906, the 1,057 foot Rock Creek Bridge, the largest on the system, was sufficiently complete to carry work trains. This allowed track laying to progress south at the rate of 0.75 miles per day and reach Waverly by the last week of June. The first S&I train ran from Spokane to Valleyford on June 30, 1906, carrying 117 people including most of the company officials. The party left the terminal building at 1:30 p.m. in electric cars and transferred to a steam-hauled train at Inland Junction - electric power was mandatory within Spokane city limits. Equipment for the

Steam power was also used to erect the poles. (Ted Holloway Collection)

Ballasting on the S&I. (Ted Holloway Collection)

trip consisted of a contractor's steam locomotive, an NP passenger coach and a flat car fitted out with benches; new rolling stock had not arrived. Several more runs for land sales promotion were made during the next few weeks.

Overhead wiring was essentially complete to Waverly by August 1906. However, the substations were not ready when the Spokane-Waverly section opened to traffic on September 24, 1906, so a steam locomotive was attached at Inland Junction with new S&I passenger cars being used for the trains. Electric train service to Waverly was inaugurated on October 30, 1906. To celebrate this occasion, members of S&IE management and the Chamber of Commerce traveled in two sections to Waverly. Lunch was laid on in a new warehouse and a visit paid to the local sugar factory. A new schedule went into effect on November 7.

It was announced in September 1905 that the line would divide 40 miles south of Spokane at Spring Creek (subsequently renamed Springdale and finally Spring Valley) into 36 mile-long branches to Palouse and Colfax. The directors granted approval, on November 4, 1905, for immediate extension from Waverly to Rosalia (on the Colfax branch). A contract for this work and an extension to Colfax was awarded in February 1906 to a consortium of Grant Smith and Company (Chicago) and Jones, Angerud and Company (St. Paul). Both companies were already occupied with railroad

Rock Creek bridge under construction. (Sheldon Perry Collection)

Tour by railroad dignitaries during S&I line construction.
(Sheldon Perry Collection)

construction in the northwest and subcontracting was necessary. Farm workers and horses assisted when available for hire. Rail laying from Waverly to Spring Valley was complete by mid-October 1906, and the extension to Rosalia, although hampered by shortage of materials, was achieved by the end of 1906. Passenger service by electric train between Spokane and Rosalia began on February 1, 1907.

Boring a tunnel delayed the opening of the branch to Colfax; it was finished the following month. Work had been underway for a year on the tunnel, located six miles from Colfax. In the meantime

Entrance to the Manning tunnel when the Colfax line was built. (Sheldon Perry Collection)

North portal of the Manning tunnel, photographed after closure. The portal carried a date a decade later than when the tunnel was bored. (Ted Holloway Collection)

grading had been completed to Colfax and in the yards there. Once the tunnel was ready, track laying crews were immediately transferred from the Palouse area to complete the 26 miles to Colfax, five miles of track having been already laid south from Rosalia. A large crowd at Colfax watched installation of the last rail on July 6, 1907. Following surfacing and ballasting, the line opened for traffic on August 1, 1907. Steam haulage was necessary between Rosalia and Colfax until October 7, when electric power was turned on. Extensive reconstruction was required at Colfax after flooding by the South Palouse River in March of 1910.

Construction of the Palouse branch, by the Palouse Construction Company, got underway in February 1906. Work teams were assigned to Spring Valley junction, Garfield and Palouse. A 500-foot tunnel was planned to gain entry to Palouse at the north end, through an area of rock. After several weeks of boring, it was found that the rock had insufficient strength to support the tunnel and a cut, 740 feet by 50 feet by 28 feet, was made instead at a cost of $65,000. A 30 by 774 foot reinforced concrete retaining wall, parallel to Washington, Idaho and Montana Railway tracks, became necessary. The south end of the depot was adjacent to the wall.

Track was laid from Spring Valley to Geary (10.73 miles) by the end of 1906 and electric passenger service to Oakesdale began on April 15, 1907. The remaining section, Oakesdale-Garfield-Palouse, had just been laid by that time. Service to Palouse was inaugurated on June 1, 1907; steam haulage from Garfield may have been necessary for a short time. Three trains ran each way between Palouse and Spokane, non-stop north of Spring Valley. Running time was three hours until the roadbed settled.

Uncertainty as to whether the route to Moscow would encompass Colfax/Pullman or go via Palouse had persisted until June 1906 when the latter, shorter line, was selected. Public announcement of this decision was muted, being briefly mentioned in an advertisement selling S&IE bonds. Surveys were conducted the following month and most of the right-of-way purchased between Palouse and Moscow. By January 1907 work had commenced on a 52-span timber trestle at Palouse

Steam shovel at work between Palouse and Moscow. (Sheldon Perry Collection)

that extended south from the depot over the Washington, Idaho & Montana tracks and Main Street. Further south, workers were busy grading by June 1907, helped by a steam shovel, but then stopped for several months. Labor shortage was blamed, but more likely a lack of money was the cause.

Grading restarted in March 1908, when several car loads of equipment and horses arrived. Old grade had to be built up in many places where it had been washed out by the fall and spring rains and two large cuts were still needed. Crews worked in both directions to complete the grade. Ten miles of track had been laid east to Viola by the end of May; overhead wiring was only a day behind. A delay resulted from making a big cut 1½ miles west of Viola, the dirt excavated being moved to make a large fill to the east. Between 300 and 400 men made the cut, but keeping the team intact was difficult due to the attractions of other fields of work. Otherwise all grading was done. By mid-August, 6½ miles of track remained to be laid.

Construction of the trestle underway at Palouse, looking north. (Ted Holloway Collection)

The reinforced concrete wall built at Palouse is on the right-hand side of this relatively modern photograph. The wall was 774 feet long, of 30 feet maximum height and 13 feet thick at the base tapering to 1 foot wide at the top. The depot on the left belonged to the Washington, Idaho & Montana Railway, its tracks continuing west under the trestle carrying the electric line. (Sheldon Perry Collection)

The Palouse-Moscow section opened on September 15, 1908, with two electric trains running each way daily between Moscow and Spokane. Steam haulage between Viola and Moscow had been expected, but the assignment of extra men to the electrification work allowed completion in the time for the opening.

The territory traversed by the alternating current (AC) railroad necessitated numerous curves and grades. The longest tangent was a little over two miles in length and there were several 12 degree curves. The longest piece of level track was 1½ miles, but this stretch contained four reverse curves of 4 to 8 degrees. Maximum grade on the main line was 2%, the longest stretch at that grade being the seven-mile climb out of Spokane. At many stations south of Spring Valley, trains faced an adverse grade departing in either direction.

In summary, construction of the Inland lines, from start to finish, took over 3 ½ years. Full operation of the Inland lines had been anticipated by January 1, 1907. Delays incurred in opening line segments after that date were:

Waverly-Rosalia   1 month
Rosalia-Colfax   8 months
Waverly-Palouse   6 months
Palouse-Moscow   21 months

The cost was close to double the original estimate.

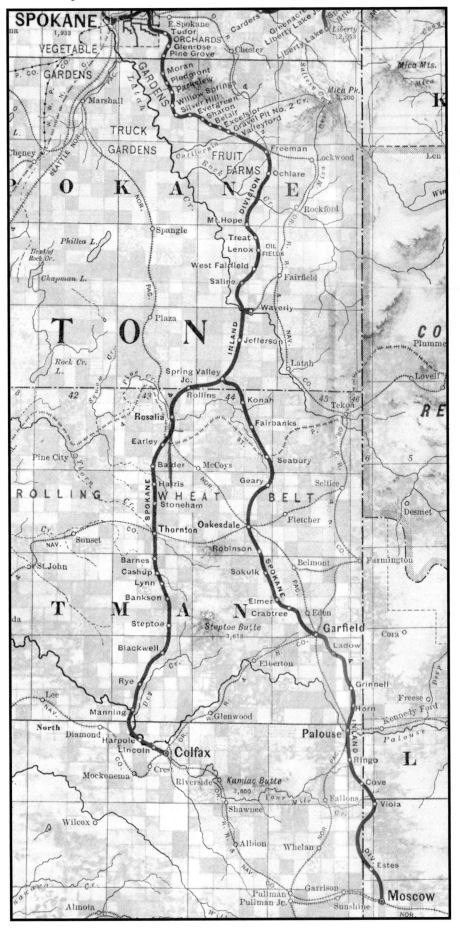

Spokane & Inland Railway lines showing station locations.

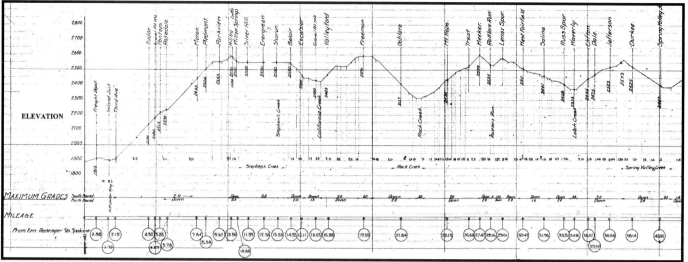

Profile of the Spokane to Spring Valley line.

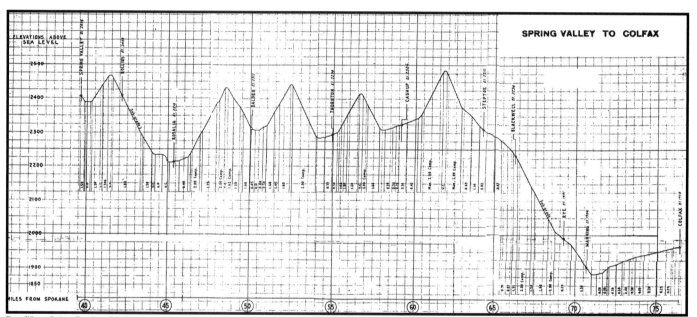

Profile of the Spring Valley to Colfax line.

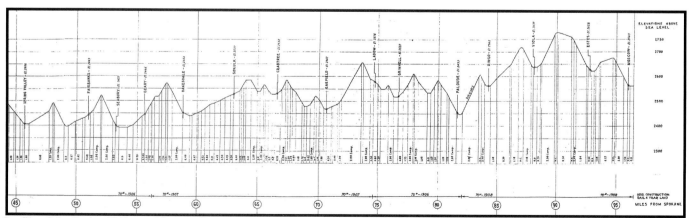

Profile of the Spring Valley to Moscow line.

PROPOSED LINES

As with many railroad companies, the promoters of the electric railway had grand ideas for growth. Probable extension around Lake Coeur d'Alene to Wallace was publicly voiced. A branch from Waverley to Lake Coeur d'Alene was fleetingly considered when the Inland line was under construction. The possibility of extending from Colfax to Walla Walla surfaced later. Several potential routes were more actively pursued, surveys conducted and right-of-way procured, only to be aborted later. They are discussed below.

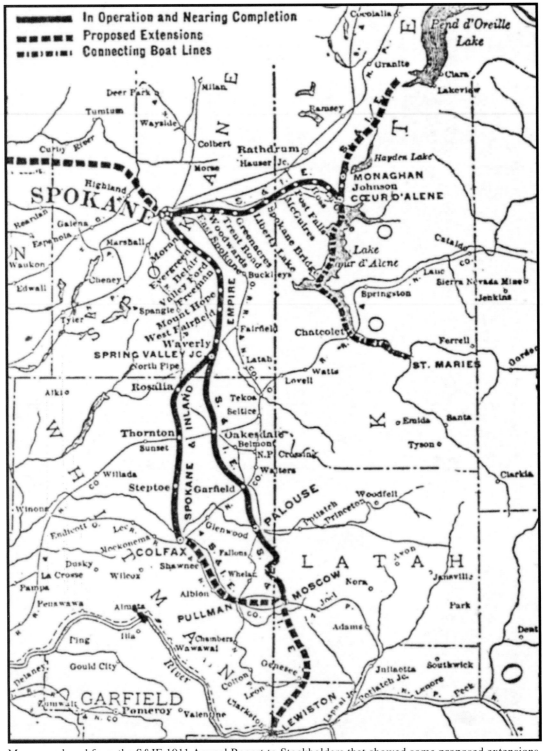

Map reproduced from the S&IE 1911 Annual Report to Stockholders that showed some proposed extensions.

Lake Pend Orielle and Athol

A line extending via Hayden Lake to the timberlands near Athol and on to Newport was under consideration by the Cd'A&S as early as 1904. In mid-1906, F.A. Blackwell said that the railway company expected, within a year, to have an electric line to Squaw Bay, on the southwest arm on Lake Pend Orielle. Estimated length was 24 miles.

Blackwell had already paid cash for 17,000 acres bordering Squaw Bay to provide right-of-way and for resort development. However, a fledgling competitor, the Spokane-Pend Orielle Rapid Transit Company had previously made arrangements to acquire the property. This company had incorporated in early 1906 to build a 51 mile line from Spokane to Squaw Bay. The new company instituted suit, delaying S&IE preparations to build the line. Legal action dragged on in the courts until November 1908 when the Idaho Supreme Court ruled in Blackwell's favor.

Meanwhile, surveyors had been busy and a modified route to Athol and Squaw Bay was proposed. Such a branch was said to have the potential to attract timber and agricultural business in the area, while the Acme Cement Company (Jay Graves, vice president) proposed to build a plant at the south end of Lake Pend Orielle. Nothing more was heard of the proposed line. A similar request four years later by the Portland Cement Company, for limestone movement, was turned down as uneconomic.

In 1923, the Ohio Match Company made an interesting proposal. The company had purchased seventy million feet of white pine from the United States Government for the manufacture of matches. The National Forest was northeast of Spokane. To move the timber, the plan was to build a railroad to the upper end of Hayden Lake, thence by water and electric line transportation to their new sawmill at Huetter. After considerable negotiation with the match company, the Spokane International Railway induced them to build an extra ten miles of railroad to connect with the SIR line to Canada.

Lewiston

When Jay Graves announced his intention to build an electric line south from Spokane, he made it clear that the eventual goal was Lewiston. He reiterated this during the next few years. Preliminary surveys began in 1906 from Palouse and Moscow. Two years later, the S&IE organized surveys to Lewiston from (1) Moscow, over alternative routes through Hatwai Canyon and Little Potlatch Canyon and (2) Pullman, via Steptoe Canyon and Clarkston.

By 1908, Graves had practically made up his mind to wait at Moscow with the existing terminal and let developments tell whether further extension should be made or not. His uncertainty was compounded by an offer for him to take over the Lewiston & Southeastern Electric Railway Company, which intended to construct 70 miles of line from Lewiston through the Camas Prairie to Grangeville, Idaho. He turned to NP's president Howard Elliot for guidance. Elliot advised that it would be safer to stop at Moscow, not because the NP was interested in that part of the country, but because it would be too heavy a load for the S&IE to undertake in a thinly populated area. Graves followed the advice.

Pullman

A strong possibility of the S&I building a line to Pullman existed for a while. Management informed Pullman businessmen in January 1905 that a favored route between Spokane and Moscow lay through Colfax and Pullman. Later that year, right-of-way through Colfax was obtained for the necessary extension. Eventual selection of the Palouse branch for the route to Moscow effectively eliminated any chance of extending south from Colfax. Failure to provide the line to Pullman by January 1, 1907, resulted in the S&I forfeiting a bonus of several thousand dollars that the city had previously collected at the railroad's request.

Jay Graves later presented Howard Elliot with an expansion plan. Elliot replied that after discussion with J.J. Hill, they had decided that "as to building between Colfax and Pullman, and then electrifying the Northern Pacific to Moscow, …such work will probably be desirable one of these days, but… it seems best to wait and not attempt to spend any money in this direction, until we know something more about the course of general business in the United States."

Big Bend Country

"Building of an electric line down the Spokane River toward Nine Mile Bridge will commence…" announced Jay Graves on August 30, 1906. Surveys were underway on both sides of the river and land purchases made. Graves refused to say how far the line would be built, leading to speculation that it was the first step in the electric railway system extending to the Big Bend country (the term Big Bend referred to a right angle bend in the Columbia river, about 30 miles northwest of Spokane). Haulage of large electrical machinery to the company's new power station was believed to be the immediate purpose.

Intentions became clearer two years later when the Spokane, Columbia and Western Railway Company (SC&W), an S&IE subsidiary, was incorporated in Washington on August 28, 1908. Trustees were W.G. Davidson, W.E. Turner, L.C. Gilman, W.G. Graves, and W.G. Paine; Gilman was president. The articles of incorporation authorized the company to construct and operate electric railroads connecting Spokane with adjacent towns in Washington, Idaho, Oregon and British Columbia. Capital stock authorized was 30,000 shares of $100 each; shares were subscribed but not issued.

The proposed route followed the S&IE high-tension power line between Spokane and the Nine Mile Dam as far as the Seven Mile Bridge. At that point it crossed the Spokane River to the south bank and extended to Mondovi and Davenport. Right-of-way to Davenport and through that town was sought. From Davenport the route ran along Hawk Creek to the Columbia River. From there the route ran almost directly north along the east bank to Miles where it crossed the Spokane River into the Spokane Indian Reservation. Right-of-way and a terminal site could only be secured on the Reservation by congressional act. A 1% grade was a goal to enable the road to handle large wheat crops; fruit traffic was expected to become another source of revenue. Connection with a boat line operating on the upper Columbia was anticipated.

On March 10, 1910, the Spokane Daily Chronicle reported that the proposed line had been abandoned. After acquiring much of the right-of-way at an estimated cost of $10,000, it had been announced that the line would not be built. Newspapers attributed this change of heart largely to the Hill interest in acquiring of control of the S&IE. This was quite likely, since Northern Pacific's Washington Central branch already served Davenport and the local wheat growing country. Great Northern also had plans for the area. In 1912 the GN graded from Bluestem, 40 miles west of Spokane on its main line, in a northerly direction much as proposed by the S&IE. Track was never laid.

Graves did not give up. He applied for a franchise to operate S&IE streetcars to the northwest of Spokane, with an eye to future extension into the Big Bend country. Hill and Elliot belatedly vetoed his action because "we feel extension of city lines is not desirable at this time."

Spokane Subway

During the week before Christmas 1907, the S&IE submitted a proposed franchise to Spokane city council to build a subway connecting the passenger and freight terminals. The tunnel was to be almost a mile in length and about 30 feet below ground. Nominal width was 23 feet and a maximum of 60 feet. Electric and steam locomotives would have access as would freight and passenger trains. From the terminal station, the double track tunnel would extend east under Front Avenue to Center Street and then diagonally (northeast) from Front Avenue, coming out at a portal in company freight grounds at a point between Division and Sheridan Streets. Most of its length lay under Front Avenue. Terminal station tracks were to be below ground, circling the depot as on the surface. Public access would be provided for in the business district with elevators carrying passengers to the trains. Recent completion of a tunnel under Seattle by the Great Northern may have stimulated this proposal.

Benefits claimed by railroad were (1) reduced time taken to get from the terminal, through city streets to Inland Junction and thus shorter passenger journey time, (2) elimination of potential dangers associated with passage of heavy trains through the city, (3) access to the city for a line from the northwest, though the western portal. Estimates put the cost close to a million dollars and construction time of two years.

The draft franchise was approved two months later by the city council with little change. One amendment required that work would commence within two years and be completed within five years. Citizens welcomed the tunnel project, although some disquiet was expressed that the franchise was too generous to the railway company. In particular, the city derived no compensation; the franchise could be sold to another railroad, the surface lines could continue to operate and steam power was authorized in the tunnel (the company said steam would only be used in the event of electric power failure).

By the end of 1908, it became clear that the subway plan had been abandoned. Railway-owned land at the western approaches to the tunnel was for sale. Not a stroke of work had been done and the time limit set by the franchise had almost expired. Plans for extension to the west through the Fort Wright grounds had been blocked by severe demands by the War Department. The proposed Big Bend line was planned to access the freight yards by a different route, not via the subway.

As a final note, it can be mentioned that in 1928 that the Great Northern took a brief look at a potential branch west from Colfax, through LaCrosse, to connect with the SP&S main line near Hooper. The aim was to shorten wheat movement mileage to Portland. Great Northern representatives reviewed tonnage and passenger activity in the area, but no surveys were made.

Sources

Northern Pacific Railway President's File No.1340.

Northern Pacific Railway President's File No.1603.

Street Railway Journal, February 11, 1905, 25: 263. "The Coeur d'Alene & Spokane Railway."

Street Railway Journal, April 27, 1907, 29: 725. "Notes on the Inland Empire System Operating from Spokane, Washington."

Street Railway Journal, June 8, 1907, 29: 1045. "Another Division of the Spokane & Inland."

Electric Railway Journal, December 31, 1910, 37: 1281. "Spokane & Inland Completes Bridge over Spokane River."

Spokane Spokesman Review.

Coeur d'Alene Independent.

Coeur d'Alene Journal.

Substation and battery house at Greenacres in 1929. The substation consisted of a two-story 45 by 52 foot brick portion attached to a 32 by 40 foot room made of concrete block. By 1919 electrical equipment was housed in the larger building and the 32 by 80 foot brick battery house was redundant. (National Archives)

Chapter 4

ELECTRIC POWER SYSTEMS

DC POWER

The Cd'A&S and Vera lines operated at 600 volts DC (direct current), the conventional choice for city streetcars and interurban railroads at the start of the twentieth century. Spokane Traction already ran at this voltage and there were the additional benefits of simple control systems and wide experience in the United States. High tension AC (alternating current) power was purchased from Washington Water Power Company (WWP) and converted to the DC voltage at railroad owned substations. Nine Mile hydroelectric power station, built and owned by the S&IE, eventually became the source.

Spokane Traction's substation and overhead system initially powered Cd'A&S cars within the city. Beyond the city, a WWP 63,000 volt transmission line, which extended from Spokane to the Coeur d'Alene mining district, fed a transformer station at Greenacres. From here, a pole line along the right-of-way carried 23,000 volt, three-phase, AC power to the substations. High voltage was essential for long-distance transmission to minimize voltage drop and transformers could handle only alternating current. A second pole line, on the opposite side of the track, carried 600 volt DC feeder wires to a single trolley wire (0000, figure eight pattern copper wire) supported 22 feet above the rails by span wire construction (5/16 inch wire). Telephone lines were carried on the poles. The power poles, 100 feet apart, were located 20 feet from the track center.

At first, Cd'A&S substations were located at Greenacres and Ross, 14 and 25 miles respectively from Spokane. Due to the late delivery of equipment, Spokane was the single source of 600 volts DC for the 30-mile-long trolley wire when the railway opened. Greenacres substation became operational in March 1904, followed by Ross two months later. Each substation had three 100 kW oil-insulated transformers and a 200 kW rotary converter, to convert the AC power to 600 volts DC. Capacity was found inadequate to handle the growing traffic, so three 150 kW transformers and a 400 kW rotary converter were ordered for each site in 1905. New buildings, 34 by 40 by 30 feet high, were erected to house the electrical equipment. Designed by architect George Williams, the Ross substation was brick, while that at Greenacres was concrete block; the original structures had been wood.

A brick substation was built at Coeur d'Alene to supply the new Hayden Lake extension, local builder J. H. Jones being given the contract in March 1906. The 23,000 volt AC pole line was extended from Ross to the new substation.

Washington Water Power commissioned Post Falls hydroelectric power station in 1907. This plant immediately became the main power source for the Cd'A&S, being halfway along the main line to Hayden Lake. Transformers were moved into the plant from their previous site to deliver 23,000 volts AC to the railway. The location of a new substation at McGuires may have been related to this change.

Coeur d'Alene substation built in 1906 and is now on the National Register of Historic Places. Batteries and equipment were accommodated in the 32 by 148 foot brick building, the batteries occupying 109 feet. (Museum of North Idaho Trr-1-44)

McGuires' 22 by 45 foot reinforced concrete substation was attached to a brick 32 by 89 foot battery room. (National Archives)

The power supply contract required the railway to purchase power from Washington Water Power Company for ten years, at a guaranteed minimum level of 3800 hp. Monthly power consumption was determined as 75% of the peak value recorded by WWP during that month. Momentary peaks, several times larger than required for normal running, were common on the railway. To stabilize the figure closer to the guaranteed minimum and hence minimize the monthly bill, the railroad adopted a system of storage batteries having sufficient capacity to handle peak loads. A typical battery had about 300 cells and 800 amp-hour capacity; cells were made of wood and were lead lined. A single story, flat roof, brick storage room, typically 32 feet wide and 80 to 100 feet long, accommodated the rows of cells. Storage batteries were provided at Spokane, Greenacres, Ross, McGuires and Coeur d'Alene substations.

Rows of lead-lined wooden cells housed in a battery room. (Ted Holloway Collection)

In 1911 the S&IE completed construction of a 60,000 volt AC transmission line from Nine Mile power station to Hayden Lake, along the railroad right-of-way from Spokane. While the intention was to expand commercial business (irrigation, lighting, etc.) prospects for the power station, the Coeur d'Alene Division could also draw power from the line to supplement that bought from WWP. A small frame substation was built at Hayden Lake to house two rotary converters along with the necessary transformers and auxiliary equipment.

After the WWP contract expired in October 1916, Nine Mile station supplied all the power over the 60,000 volt AC transmission line. Coeur d'Alene substation was remodeled to receive 60,000 volts AC, instead of 23,000 volts AC, with two sets of three 200 kW transformers and a rotary converter being installed. The 23,000 volt AC transmission line was dismantled from Coeur d'Alene to Liberty Lake Junction in 1917 and redundant transformers removed from WWP's Post Falls plant.

Other substations were modified appropriately, their DC conversion equipment in 1919 being:
- Hayden Lake: two rotary converters, 400 and 500 kW;
- McGuires: 500 kW rotary converter; and
- Greenacres: 400 kW rotary converter and a 750 kW motor-generator set.

Power storage was no longer necessary so the batteries were taken out at Greenacres in 1916; Coeur d'Alene and Spokane in 1917; and McGuires in 1921.

AC POWER

Single phase power at 6600 volts, 25 cycles, was chosen to operate the Spokane & Inland Railway to Moscow and Colfax. Estimates showed a large saving in initial investment and annual operating expenses compared to the DC system. Alternating current was claimed to be preferable for heavy traction, freight haulage being the primary mission of the railway. The decision was a particularly brave step for the Inland, since this AC system was untried technology. Concurrent selection of a similar 11,000 volt scheme by the New York, New Haven & Hartford Railroad may well have increased the S&I's confidence level. Inland's electrical superintendent, J. B. Ingersoll, was certainly in favor, having been a Westinghouse engineer and in charge of installing such a system for the Indianapolis & Cincinnati Traction Company. Jay Graves, too, had knowledge of AC applications through his mining interests. The power choice called for conversion of three-phase power to 45,000 volts single phase, transmission to trackside substations and step down to 6,600 volts. Electrical equipment was ordered from the Westinghouse Company, the promoter of this form of traction.

Power was purchased from WWP at 4000 volt, 60 cycle, three-phase. Conversion to single-phase required a new facility – a frequency-changing station. P.L. Peterson Company was given the construction contract by the S&I in 1906. Located close to the Inland right-of-way at East 1420 Celesta Avenue, Spokane, the brick and cement block building was 60 by 100 by 31 feet high with a 40 by 90-foot battery room wing. Four 1000 kW frequency changing sets converted 4000 volt, 60 cycle current to 2200 volt, 25 cycle. Each set consisted of a 1000 hp, 60 cycle, three-phase, 4000 volt induction motor, and a 1000 kW 25-cycle 2200 volt, single-phase generator, with an integral 750 kW, 550 volt DC generator/motor; all were mounted on the same shaft and a single bed-plate. Total cost of the frequency changing station was $300,000.

Frequency changing station located in southeast Spokane on Celesta Avenue. It was converted to a private residence. (Ted Holloway Collection)

Frequency changing equipment. (Ted Holloway Collection)

The motor-generator unit, incorporated into each set, operated in conjunction with a 275-cell storage battery to maintain a constant load on the power station. During periods of low demand, the unit functioned as a DC generator, charging the battery. When demand was high, the unit operated as a motor, drawing power from the battery to assist in driving the alternator. General manager Ingersoll designed this novel method of storing AC power. Two booster sets were added to supplement the battery which survived until 1923.

Switchboard in the frequency changing station. (Ted Holloway Collection)

Kiesling substation supplied 6,000 volt single phase AC to a section of the Inland Division line. Part of the adjacent depot is visible. (National Archives)

Five water-cooled, 1250 kW transformers raised the 2200 volt output from the frequency changing sets to 45,000 volts for transmission to the substations. The frequency changing station additionally functioned as a substation with three 2200-6600 volt transformers feeding the local section of the Inland AC line. A 20-panel switchboard of electrically-operated oil circuit breakers and lightning protection completed the station equipment.

The 45,000 volt, single-phase line, consisting of two wires (No.2 medium hard drawn copper wire), was carried from the frequency changing station to the transformer substations and stepped down to 6,600 volts (700 volt AC was required by some towns for safety). Substations were located approximately 12 miles apart at:
- Kiesling, Mount Hope and Waverly between Spokane and Spring Valley;
- Rosalia, Thornton and Colfax between Spring Valley and Colfax;
- Fairbanks, Oakesdale, Garfield and Palouse between Spring Valley and Moscow.

Typically 34 by 42 feet, brick-built and two stories high, each substation housed three 300 kW, oil-insulated, self-cooled transformers and ancillary electrical protection equipment. The station agent acted as the attendant, an alarm bell sounding the tripping of a circuit breaker. Moscow never had a substation; Fairbanks and Colfax closed by 1930 due to traffic conditions.

Single catenary construction was used, with a 7/16 inch messenger wire suspended from mast arms and an adjustable clipped trolley wire (000, grooved pattern copper wire). Catenary poles were spaced 100 feet apart. Trolley wire was sectionalized with circuit breakers situated near each substation, so that each section was fed from two substations. A seven-man motorcar crew maintained the overhead system and rail electrical bonds. Within Spokane city limits the council required operation at 600 volts DC.

NINE MILE HYDROELECTRIC POWER STATION

Jay Graves announced in January 1905 that he and F.A. Blackwell had secured the option and rights to build a dam and power plant on the Spokane River at Nine Mile Bridge. They planned to operate turbines generating 12,000 hp to feed the electric railway system and sell power to cities along the right-of-way in competition with Washington Water Power Company. This proposal was dropped two months later when the power supply contract with WWP was signed.

Plans were resurrected the following year. In July 1906, the S&I began construction of Nine Mile hydroelectric power station. Cost was estimated at $800,000 to $1,000,000. The site was a dozen miles northwest of Spokane where the Spokane River passed through a granite rock canyon. The

Mount Hope is believed to be the site of this AC substation. (National Archives)

plant was commissioned on July 26, 1908, and immediately began to satisfy the Inland lines power requirements. Electricity was also furnished to several towns including Rosalia. Book cost of the plant recorded in 1911 was $1,311,520.

The dam incorporated the powerhouse at the deepest part of the river, adjacent to one bank. The spillway type dam was built of concrete, faced with large blocks of granite rock. Upstream, the face was almost vertical and downstream in an S-shape. The length of the spillway was 225 feet and the height 58 feet. Reinforced concrete was used for the base (65 by 115 feet) of the 82-foot-tall brick powerhouse.

Power was generated by four turbine-generator sets although installation of two of them was delayed until 1910. Each set consisted of a 3000 kW, three-phase, 60 cycle, 2200 volt generator direct connected to a 5000 hp (nominal rating) turbine-type water wheel. There were four double-leaf headgates to each wheel chamber. The plant had a maximum capacity of 20,000 hp and a continuous capacity of 15,000 hp. Sales to customers, other than the railroads, were intended, so four 3000 kW transformers stepped up the 2200 volts to 60,000 volts AC, the prevailing standard for that area.

A power distribution center was needed to supply the railroad and commercial customers from Nine Mile so the S&IE built the "City Substation" in Spokane, a 93 by 112 foot brick building, 32 feet high with twin roofs, located immediately south of Inland Junction. Two transmission lines, erected along a private right-of-way, carried 60,000 volt, 60 cycle power from Nine Mile to the substation. Either line was capable of carrying the entire output of the plant and insured continuous service in case of damage to one. Equipment included two 1500 kW motor generators, one 2000 kW motor generator, four 2000 kW transformers and one 2500 amp booster set. Transmission to the railroad's frequency reduction station was at 4000 volts, 60 cycles, for compatibility with existing equipment

there. The city substation also supplied the power for cars operating within the city. Extension of the 60,000 volt AC transmission line from the city substation to Hayden Lake (40.38 miles) was completed in 1911.

Nine Mile dam and powerhouse around 1910. (Sheldon Perry Collection)

Closer view of Nine Mile power plant. (Library of Congress)

The S&IE-built "City Substation" was identified as C in the photo and partially hidden behind the embankment carrying the NP main line. Power generated by Nine Mile plant was distributed from here to company divisions and commercial customers. The Inland Division main line extended under the concrete bridge, along Erie Street, to Inland Junction. (Northern Pacific Railway; Walt Ainsworth collection)

Benefitting from the enlarged distribution system, the power station supplied the following customers in 1912:

Customer	Horsepower
S&IE - Inland Division	4,000-5,000
S&IE - Coeur d'Alene Division	1,200
S&IE - Traction Division	2,500-3,000
Commercial & Irrigation	4,500

Nine Mile now partially met the power requirements of the Traction and Coeur d'Alene Divisions. A contract was signed the following year to supply the Inland Empire Paper Company's new Millwood mill with practically all the secondary power generated by the power station. Secondary power was delivered during the eight months of the year when the flow of water in the river was above the minimum required for continuous output of the plant. From 1916, the approximately 10,000 hp needed by all the S&IE Divisions was furnished by Nine Mile. To meet the railway needs, some commercial contracts were dropped, including one with Inland Portland Cement Company.

After exit from receivership, the title of the newly incorporated Spokane and Eastern Railway and Power Company clearly defined where ownership of the power plant lay. Five-year results released by the company show remarkably profitable power generation:

Year	Revenue $	Net Income $
1920	135,488	78,072
1921	164,701	102,146
1922	276,878	221,828
1923	301,813	249,579
1924	284,730	223,321

Indeed, the figures significantly enhanced the overall financial results of the company.

Nevertheless, the duty of the bondholders committee was to liquidate the whole business. Sale of Nine Mile Power Station to Washington Water Power Company was agreed upon in May 1925 at a price of $1,486,839. On July 1, 1925, the power station, Spokane city substation, and the power line connecting the two were sold to WWP. The new owner entered into a long-term contract to supply the railroad. Nine Mile Power Station became another link in the chain of plants operated by the power company.

Sources
Great Northern Railway President's Subject File No.9128, S&IE History of Properties – Power Plants, Power Stations & Transmission Lines, 1919.

Northern Pacific Railway President's File No. 1340-D.

Spokane & Inland Empire Railroad. Annual Report to Stockholders. 1911-1914.

Spokane & Inland Empire Railroad. Annual Report to State of Washington. 1916-1919.

Spokane & Eastern Railway & Power Company Annual Report to State of Washington. 1920-1924.

Electrical World, August 25, 1906, 48: 473. "The Spokane & Inland Railway."

MacCalla, C.S., Electrical World, May 30, 1908, 51: 1135. "The Post Falls Development of the Washington Water Power Company-II."

Electrical World, October 10, 1908, 52: 793. "Hydro-Electric Generating Station of the Inland Empire System."

Street Railway Journal, February 11, 1905, 25, p.263. "Coeur d'Alene & Spokane Railway."

Street Railway Journal, April 27, 1907, 29: 725. "Notes on the Inland Empire System Operating from Spokane, Washington."

Street Railway Journal, September 28, 1907, 30: 726. "Storage Batteries Applied to the Single Phase System of the Spokane & Inland Railway."

Street Railway Journal, March 9, 1907, 29: 419. "New Hydro-Electric Plant of the Spokane & Inland Empire Railroad Company."

Railway & Engineering Review, February 9, 1907: 102. "The Spokane & Inland Empire System."

Electrical Railway Journal, October 10, 1908, 32: 898. "Hydro-Electric Power Plant for the Inland Empire System."

Electrical Railway Journal. November 27, 1920, 56: 1090. "Spokane's Traction Problems Are Being Solved."

Electrical Railway Journal, June 6, 1925, 65: 907. "Spokane Power Station Sold."

Spokane Spokesman Review

Coeur d'Alene Journal

The Spokane Terminal building at the corner of Main Avenue and Lincoln Street opened in 1906. Passengers were handled on the first floor, company officers housed on the second floor, and departmental offices located on the third floor. (Warren Wing Collection)

Chapter 5

BUILDINGS, BRIDGES AND ROADWAY

BUILDINGS

In 1919 the S&IE prepared an inventory of buildings. The resultant list is reproduced in Appendix A. Buildings that had an integral role in train operation are described in more detail below.

Passenger Facilities

Depots owned by the S&IE are summarized in Table 5.1. Passenger depots were built at Spokane and Coeur d'Alene, separate freight depots being provided there. Other stations had a combination passenger and freight depot or a shelter shed.

The Spokane terminal building was completed in March 1906 at a cost of $110,000 and formally opened to the public on May 27, 1906. Officers moved in before waiting rooms and other passenger facilities were finished. Design was by Albert Held, a Spokane architect responsible for many of the railway's buildings, and the contractor was P.L. Peterson. Owned by Spokane Terminal Company, the building served the Cd'A&S and S&I railways. Located in the city center, at the corner of Main Avenue and Lincoln Street, the 50 by 160-foot building was oval in shape, with rounded corners, the major axis running north and south. The exterior was buff brick with the windows, sills and coping trimmed with terra cotta.

Another view of the Spokane passenger terminal building. (Sheldon Perry Collection)

On the first floor were waiting rooms, ticket office, parcel room and newsstand, all with tile flooring. The express and baggage room was at the north end and offices at the south end. Woodwork throughout the first floor was oak, with local marble wainscoting around the wall. The main entrance, on the eastern side, was separated from the waiting room by a glass partition extending to the ceiling.

From the main vestibule, a double flight of marble stairs with iron railings led to the second floor. This floor contained the executive offices of the S&IE and its subsidiaries.

Table 5.1 Summary of Depots

Station	Built	Stories	Size	Position*	Exterior	Agent on Site				Disposition	Notes
						1912	1934	1950	1968		
CD'A&S LINE											
Spokane Terminal	1906	3	49 x 160'		Brick	X				Sold 1929	GN depot used from 1927.
Millwood	1906	1	12 x 32'	South	Drop siding	X				Removed 1948	Moved 1948 to GN Orient station for bunkhouse.
Greenacres 1st.	c 1904	1	37 x 50'	South	See notes					Replaced 1909	Temporary depot - frame construction.
Greenacres 2nd.	1909	1	16 x 54'	South	Drop siding	X	X			Razed 1944	Bay 5 x 12 feet.
Liberty Lake	c 1907	1	12 x 38'	South	Drop siding	X				Retired 1928	Bay 8 feet; 9'8" to eaves. 50 foot covered platform each side.
Spokane Bridge	1906	1	20 x 44'	South	Drop siding	X				Removed 1929	Bay 3 x 10 feet; 12 feet to eaves; 18 feet to gable.
Post Falls	1905	1	20 x 45'	South	Drop siding	X	X			Removed 1936	Bay 8 feet; 15 feet to eaves. Sold 1936; replaced by 9' x 12' shelter shed.
Coeur d'Alene 1st.	1903	2	30 x 93'	South	Drop siding	X	X	X		Retired 1964	22 feet to eaves. Remodeled 1926.
Coeur d'Alene 2nd.	1964	1	20 x 44'	East	Drop siding				X	Retired by BN	Bay.
Dalton	1907	1	12 x 36'	East	Drop siding	X				Retired 1940	Bay.
Hayden Lake	1908	1	14 x 40'	East	Drop siding	X				Retired 1931	Bay 4 x 9 feet. Covered platform each side.
VERA LINE											
Opportunity		1	16 x 70'	South	Drop siding					Removed 1935	
Dishman	by 1919	1	14 x 40'	South	Drop siding					Removed by 1936	
INLAND LINES											
Kiesling	1914	1	14 x 46'	West	Drop siding	X				Retired 1941	Bay 3 x 10 feet; 10 feet to eaves.
Valley Ford	1909	1	22 x 58'	West	Brick veneer	X	X			Removed 1939	Bay 3 x 10 feet; 10 feet to eaves.
Freeman	1909	1	16 x 52'	West	Drop siding	X	X			Retired 1938	Bay 3 x 12 feet; 10 feet to eaves.
Mount Hope	1907	1	22 x 52'	East	Brick veneer	X	X	X		Retired 1945	
Waverly	1907	1	25 x 63'	East	Brick veneer	X	X	X	X	Removed 1970	
Spring Valley	1907	2	40 x 80'	In wye	Brick veneer	X				Burned 1936	Replaced 1936 by Kiesling tool house 9 x 10 feet as shelter shed.
Fairbanks	1907	1	10 x 20'	West	Shiplap	X				Removed 1939	
Oaksdale	1907	1	22 x 90'	West	Brick veneer	X	X	X	X	Retired 1971	
Garfield	1907	1	22 x 90'	West	Brick veneer	X	X	X	X	Retired 1971	
Palouse 1st.	1907	1		East	See notes					Removed 1908	Temporary depot - frame construction.
Palouse 2nd.	1908	1	24 x 112'	East	Brick veneer	X	X	X	X	Removed 1972	
Moscow 1st.	1908	1	20 x 38'	East	Frame					Removed 1912	Temporary depot - frame construction.
Moscow 2nd.	1912	1	28 x 90'	East	Drop siding	X	X	X	X	Retired 1972	Bay 13 feet; hip roof. Survived into 1990s in private use.
Rosalia	1908	1	23 x 90'	East	Brick veneer	X	X	X	X	Retired 1971	Bay 3 x 10 feet; 12 feet to eaves.
Thornton	by 1912	1	20 x 38'	East	Shingles	X	X	X		Retired 1972	Replaced by shelter shed 6 x 12 feet and retired 1959.
Steptoe	1914	1	17 x 40'	West	Drop siding	X	X			Sold 1939	Temporary depot - frame construction.
Colfax 1st.	1908	1	25 x 34'		See notes	X				Sold 1936	
Colfax 2nd.	1912	1	24 x 100'	East	Drop siding	X	X	X		Retired 1969	Bay 24 feet. Hip roof.

X Station Agent

* Depot position relative to main track.

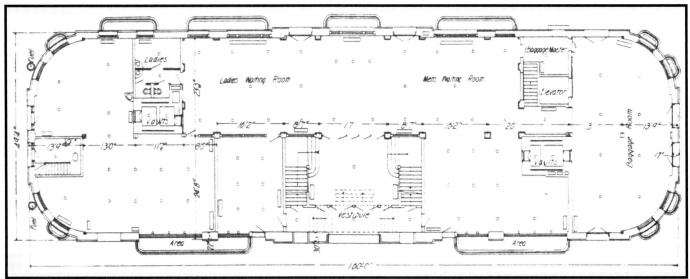

The Spokane Terminal Building's first floor plan.

Ticket office and waiting room in the terminal building. (D. Cozine Collection)

The offices, with outside windows, were on each side of a central hall, from which they were separated by a glass partition with a three-and-a half-foot-high wainscot. A telephone exchange on this floor connected the 30 offices in the building.

The double flight of stairs continued to the third floor from a common landing. On this floor were the offices of the auditing department, publicity department, chief engineer and drafting rooms. In the basement, reached by stairs descending from the waiting room, were the smoking room, trainmen's room, toilet, steam heating plant and storerooms.

Terminal grounds were 300 by 500 feet. Tracks looped around the entire building to avoid switching the cars. Several tracks were provided on the rear (west) side for train storage.

The Spokane terminal closed when acquired by the GN-owned Spokane, Coeur d'Alene & Palouse Railway. According to ICC records the last train departed on May 10, 1927. Passenger business was moved to the GN passenger depot on Havermale Island. It was sold in 1929 and demolished to make way for a Sears, Roebuck and Company store. The main branch of Spokane Public Library is now on the site.

The Coeur d'Alene two-story passenger depot was 30 by 93 feet, of frame construction with a hip roof, and cost $8,425. Passenger and baggage/express rooms were on the first floor. Offices occupied the second floor, the staff moving in at the end of December 1903 from the Exchange Bank Building. The depot lasted until 1965, when it was taken down and replaced with a 20 by 44 foot single story modern office building at 601 Northwest Boulevard, close to the railroad yard. Combination passenger and freight depots along the Cd'A&S line were single story and of frame

Coeur d'Alene's two story passenger and baggage depot was built in 1903. Offices were located on the second floor but under GN ownership the agent lived on the second floor. The building was dismantled in 1965. (Museum of North Idaho)

construction. Drop siding walls and a shake-covered gable roof were common features. Operator bays were topped by a cross gable. Kirtland Cutter, the architect responsible for the hotel at Hayden Lake, drew the plans for the adjacent depot in a compatible style; Liberty Lake got a similar one. Both of these resort depots were given covered platforms, approximately 50 feet long on each side to accommodate large crowds. All of these depots were retired by 1948.

On the Inland Division, eight depots had brick veneer exterior and were characterized by a conical turret over the semicircular office bay. The architect was Albert Held. Brackets supported the extended eaves of the hip roof that had a reduced pitch over the freight platform. There were three sizes: approximately 60 foot length (Valley Ford, Waverly and Mount Hope); 90 foot length (Oakesdale, Garfield and Rosalia); and 112 foot length (Palouse) with most of the extra space being assigned to the freight room.

Two more depots, Thornton and Spring Valley, were earmarked for this style. Spring Valley did get a brick exterior, but required two stories to accommodate the Division offices and a unique shape to fit

Coeur d'Alene depot photographed from trackside. (Ted Holloway Collection)

the site. Thornton ended up as a small frame structure. In fact, depots built after 1908, except for Valley Ford, got a wood exterior, terminus buildings at Colfax and Moscow being of this type. Examples of brick-faced depots lasted until the early 1970s while the last wooden survivor, built at Moscow in 1912, remained into the 1990s in private hands.

Many communities were too small to warrant a depot. Instead a shelter shed was provided for passengers at appropriate stations. There were close to seventy on the S&IE system; their location and size

Hayden Lake Depot. (Museum of North Idaho Trr-1-97)

The first depot built at Greenacres, shown here with train order signal, was replaced within five years. The motor baggage and express car at the station carries its original No. 152. (Ted Holloway Collection)

Depots along the Cd'A&S line were unremarkable in appearance as illustrated by the second one built at Greenacres. The second track existed between 1910 and 1920. (D. Cozine Collection)

A number of passenger and freight depots on the Inland lines had brick veneer exterior and featured a turret over the office and operator bay. Waverly, shown here, was one of them. Riders on the small vehicle were probably surveying the line for valuation by the ICC. (National Archives)

are given in Appendix A. Dimensions were typically ten by twelve feet on the DC lines, whereas six by seven feet was more common on the Inland. Usual construction had drop siding walls and a shingle roof. Many shelter sheds were retired around the time of passenger service withdrawal, but some had gone earlier: Pantops, Foch, Silver Hill, Belaire, Larkin, Rattlers Run, Horn and Konah, on the Inland lines, being retired in 1928.

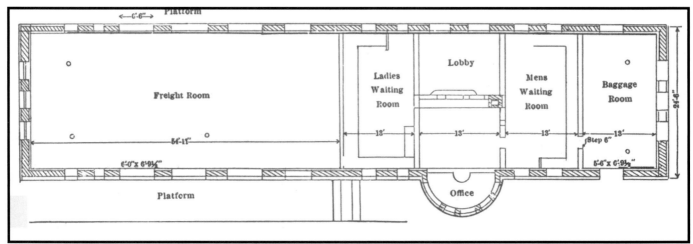

Plan of the Palouse 23 by 112-foot depot, the largest of the turret-style structures.

Moscow's first depot used secondhand materials from the original depot at Palouse. By 1911 it had deteriorated so badly that citizens and businessmen threatened to boycott the railroad and physically move the depot outside the city limits. (Ted Holloway Collection)

The Inland terminals at Colfax and Moscow were given frame depots in 1912 to replace temporary structures. The Colfax depot is shown here. (Robert A. Johnson, Warren Wing Collection)

Freight Depots

The Spokane Terminal Company opened the Spokane freight depot in March 1906. There was ready access to the site from Division Street for road carriers. This single-story brick building was 40 by 300 feet. A ten-foot roof overhang on both sides offered weather protection for the doorways. Freight moved through eight doors opening out to a rail-side, ten-foot-wide concrete platform, and thirteen doors on the opposite side faced Gray Avenue. Doors were equipped with fireproof rolling shutters. An office was located at the eastern end and three platform scales were spaced along the main floor. The basement housed a storage battery.

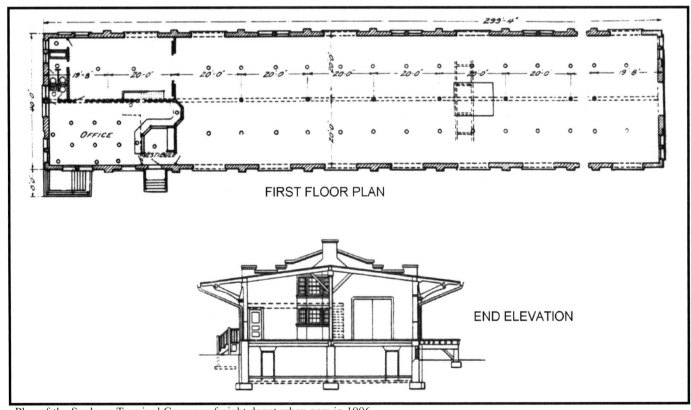

FIRST FLOOR PLAN

END ELEVATION

Plan of the Spokane Terminal Company freight depot when new in 1906.

Spokane's freight depot soon after it opened. Two Cd'A&S motor baggage and express cars were ready to depart, possibly hauling a boxcar. (D. Cozine Collection)

Road-side of the freight depot with horse-drawn vehicles present. (Sheldon Perry Collection)

The Spokane freight depot was enlarged in 1928 by SC&P for lease to a grocery company and eventually sold. The building is shown in the BN era. (Sheldon Perry Collection)

Spokane freight yard office, March 1972. (Michael J. Denuty)

The only other freight depot of significant size on the S&IE system was at Coeur d'Alene, opposite the passenger depot. The size was increased a couple of years after the photograph was taken. (Ted Holloway Collection)

The depot became redundant in 1927, following transfer of activities to the GN freight depot. To render it suitable for lease, the SC&P directors approved a $40,000 expenditure for a 60 by 260 foot addition. The C.E. Marr Grocery Company leased the enlarged building. Riverside Warehouse Company held the lease from 1937 until the GN sold the building twenty years later. It survived into the 1980s, but eventually was removed.

Coeur d'Alene's frame freight depot was on the west side of the passenger depot. The size was 20 by 126 feet, having been extended 35 feet in 1907. The depot was leased by 1929 and retired in 1961.

In 1904 the Cd'A&S built its car barns immediately north of the Coeur d'Alene passenger depot. Both were frame construction with the dual track barn on the left housing a machine shop. They remained active for some years after new shops opened in Spokane. The last building was removed in 1931.
(A. Libby, T. Holloway Collection)

Shops

The Cd'A&S shops were located at Coeur d'Alene, just north of the passenger depot. A three-track car barn (150 by 42 feet) and an adjacent two-track barn (124 by 47 feet), which incorporated a machine shop, were built in 1904-5. Both were of frame construction with drop siding walls. The larger barn was taken down in 1921-followed ten years later by the machine shop. All the motormen were initially based here.

Plans for the construction of car shops at Spokane, on the north side of the river bend, were announced by Spokane Terminal Company in

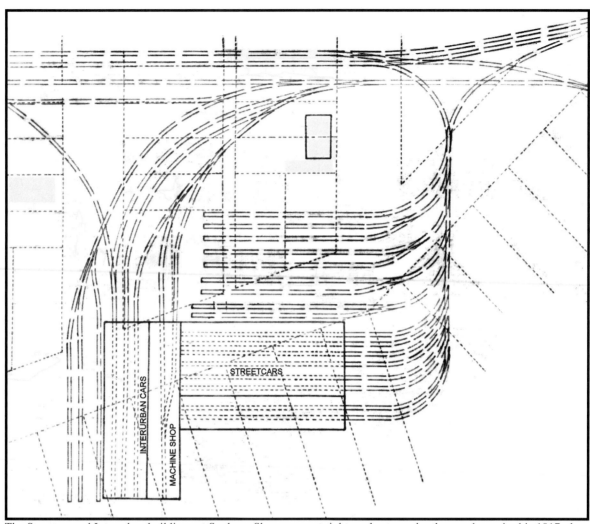

INTERURBAN CARS

MACHINE SHOP

STREETCARS

The Streetcar and Interurban buildings at Spokane Shops were at right angles to each other as shown in this 1917 plan. (Great Northern Railway)

Front of the streetcar shop. (National Archives)

late 1905. Again, the architect was Albert Held, who estimated a minimum cost of $130,000. A contract was placed with P.L. Peterson Company and foundation work got underway by February 1906. There was a rush to get the streetcar facilities finished, because a fire had destroyed the Spokane Traction car barns on Sinto Avenue. Construction of the L-shaped brick building was completed in 1907. Addition of a barn for interurban cars on the eastern side followed.

Facilities were as follows:
- Spokane Traction shop, 120 by 200 feet: car barn, five tracks; carpenter shop, two tracks; paint shop, one track.
- Machine shop, 40 by 202 feet: incorporated two half-length pit tracks for S&I repairs.
- S&I car inspection barn, 52 by 202 feet: three tracks.
- Storeroom, blacksmith shop, boiler room and armature winding facilities were appended to the main structure.
- Storage tracks for traction and interurban cars.

Four 9 foot 6 inch diameter turntables facilitated movement of trucks and materials between shops. Yard tracks provided for storage of 62 streetcars and 30 interurban cars. A 40 by 150 foot storage shed was added later because heavy materials, wheels and other materials stored in the basement beneath the machine shop required removal by crane through trapdoors.

The Machine Shop is on the left hand side of the taller building and the three-track Interurban Shop on the right. (National Archives)

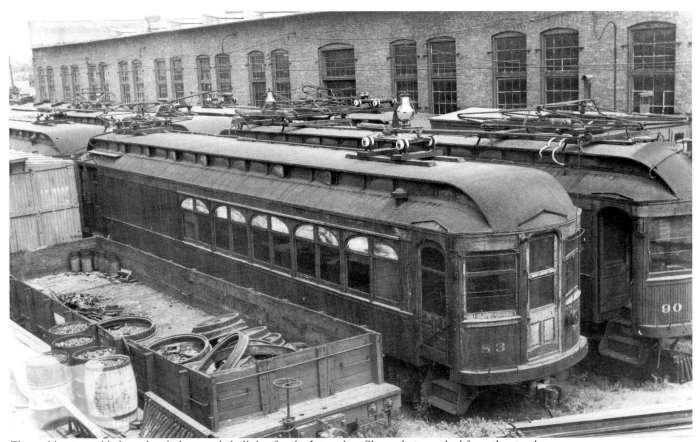

The architect provided ample windows and skylights for the Interurban Shop; photographed from the storehouse. (Harold Hill, Warren Wing Collection)

Sale of Spokane Traction eliminated streetcar maintenance and most of their outdoor storage tracks were removed. Over 40 people were employed by the shops in 1930, but ten years later there were only 21 employees. After the abandonment of electric operations, the shops took on the repair of gas-electric cars and other equipment owned by the Great Northern Railway. The shops were remodeled in 1950 to service diesel locomotives and space assigned to other GN organizations such as the signals, bridges and buildings departments. Diesel fuel and sanding facilities were removed in 1959. The structure still stands, but not for railroad purposes.

Steam Locomotive Facilities

A two-stall, frame, 34 by 75 foot engine house with 55 foot pits was built at Coeur d'Alene in 1904. A water tank, coal platform, oil/sand house and an office were nearby. The site was about 60 feet north of the substation on the same side of the main track. The engine house was there in 1919, but removed during the next decade; the company's last steam locomotive was sold in 1918. On the Inland, a water tank was originally provided at Valley Ford and Spring Valley.

Interlocking Towers

An interlocking tower, 12 by 18 feet, was needed at Colfax to control the grade crossing of the OR&N line by the S&I. The 1907-built structure had drop siding walls and a shake roof. Automatic interlocking and an electric gate machine were installed in 1928 and the tower removed.

A signal tower was installed at McGuires for the grade crossing of the Coeur d'Alene line by the Milwaukee Road following a collision there in 1915 (discussed in Chapter 10). It was retired in 1932.

Warehouses

Grain warehouses existed every few miles on the Inland lines; almost every station between Spring Valley and Moscow had one and the Colfax line was similarly endowed. There were 42 warehouses by 1914. Sizes were typically 50 feet wide and 100, 150 or 200 feet in length, the size depending upon anticipated traffic at the station.

Stockyards

A dozen stations were given stockyards when the lines were built. Spokane Bridge did not get one until 1939. Several were removed by the time the GN acquired the company. Five remained in operation by 1950 (see Table 5.2).

Milk Platforms

To facilitate shipment of milk churns, platforms were installed at stations close to milk marketers on the Inland lines. Platform size varied, ranging from three by three feet to 10 by 30 feet.

Station	Pens	Size	Notes
Coeur d'Alene	1	32' x 44'	Removed by 1950.
Colfax	2	55' x 120'	Rebuilt 1939.
Fairbanks	1	16' x 33'	Removed by 1934.
Garfield	2	50' x 92'	
Moscow	2	50' x 70'	
Oakesdale	1	50' x 50'	Removed 1938.
Palouse	1	23' x 112'	
Rosalia	2	32' x 84'	Removed 1942.
Spring Valley	1	32' x 40'	Removed 1940.
Spokane Bridge	5	40' x 200'	Built 1939; removed 1955.
Steptoe	2	48' x 108'	Removed 1937.
Thornton	2	50' x 57'	Removed by 1950.
Waverly	1	32' x 32'	12' x 32' by 1929.

Table 5.2. Stockyards.

BRIDGES

For milk movement, wood platforms were installed at numerous churn collection points. Inland train No. 9, hauled by Motor Mail & Baggage Car No. 30, makes a dairy stop about 1915 and one of the crew takes the opportunity to adjust the pantograph on the second car. (Warren Wing Collection)

Close to 150 bridges could be found on the S&IE rail system. Inland Junction to Spring Valley section and the branches to Moscow and Colfax had at least 35 bridges each. All bridges were of wood construction originally, pile trestle being the most common type. Some of the smaller bridges were eventually filled in. Individual bridges are itemized in Appendix B.

Several were notable in size. Two bridges over the Spokane River in Spokane had three Howe trusses each, the single trusses being 100 to 150 feet in length. The GN renewed both, while reducing the western bridge from dual to single track. Single track Bridge 1.5, east of the shops, was controlled by automatic block signals from 1909. Largest on the system was the 1,057.5 foot long, 135 foot high Rock Creek trestle and deck truss bridge, two miles north of Mount Hope. Other large bridges existed at Parkview (704 feet), Sharon (541 feet) and California Creek (228 feet). A bridge watchman was employed at Rock Creek and given a 14 by 26 foot dwelling there. Approaches to Palouse and Colfax depots included 52-span and 46-span timber trestles, respectively.

Great Northern replaced some of the wooden bridges with steel structures with construction projects spread over almost thirty years. Both of the river bridges at Spokane were among those changed to steel. The GN covered the Howe trusses at Harpole (near Manning) and Palouse in 1928.

Bridge 1.3 over the Spokane River at Spokane originally had three 125 foot Howe truss spans that carried double track. (Ted Holloway Collection)

Wooden Bridge 1.3 was replaced in 1944-6 by three new steel structures and changed from double to single track. The bridge was removed by explosives on August 20, 1987. (Michael J. Denuty, taken in January 1972)

Bridge 1.5 crossed the Spokane River just east of the Shops to reach Inland Junction. Three Howe trusses formed a curve. (Sheldon Perry Collection)

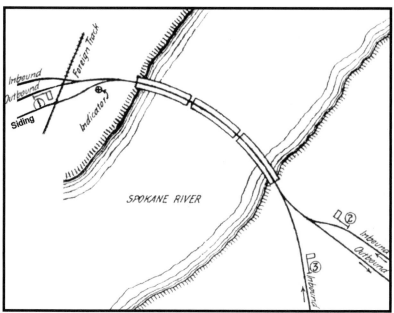

Single track Bridge 1.5 was controlled by automatic block signals. Electrically operated, normal danger, and semaphore signals were installed 400 feet from the ends of the bridge: signal 1 on the outbound track on the west side of the river and signals 2 and 3 to control inbound trains from the two tracks at Inland Junction. Track circuits and signal control were arranged so that when a train approached the bridge, the signal cleared if the single line bridge section was unoccupied. Movement of any signal to the clear position held the other two signals at stop and caused the siding indicator to display a red light.

The GN renewed Bridge 1.5 with steel members as seen here with Trent Avenue concrete road bridge behind. Burlington Northern removed the bridge in March-April 1974, two years after this photograph was taken.
(Michael J. Denuty, Photographer)

This five-span plate girder bridge was erected by the S&IE at Spokane Bridge in 1910 to replace a seven-year-old wood structure. Photograph was taken around 1928.
(National Archives)

The Rock Creek Bridge, with its 1,057 foot span, was the largest on the S&IE system. All freight trains had to stop before proceeding over the bridge and the speed of passenger trains restricted.
(Warren Wing Collection)

One of the larger bridges was the 548-foot Sharon Trestle. (Ted Holloway Collection)

Rattlers Run Bridge was still standing in 1977. (Sheldon Perry Collection)

Latah Creek Bridge, near Waverly, with three steel deck spans and trestle approaches, was erected in 1929 to replace an old trestle structure. This photograph was taken in March 1972. (Michael J. Denuty, Photographer)

A bridge was required at each end of the 655-foot tunnel between Harpole and Colfax. A postcard depicts the wooden bridge at the north end where the track curved through the bridge. (Sheldon Perry Collection)

A circa 1907 view of Palouse looking east; the S&I line is horizontal across the page. A two-car train near the substation, the bridge over the east-west WI&M tracks, and trestle to the river bridge are visible. The WI&M tracks below the S&I bridge ran west along the riverbank to interchange sidings with the NP and Inland. Tracks in the foreground were the Northern Pacific P&L line. (Ted Holloway Collection)

The GN covered two 100-foot Howe truss bridges in 1928. One was Bridge 76.3 between Manning and Colfax. This bridge is extant on private property. (Library of Congress)

ROADWAY

Inland lines passed through undulating country that necessitated numerous curves and grades. The longest tangent was a little over two miles in length and there were several twelve-degree curves. The longest section of level track was one and a half miles, but this stretch contained four reverse curves. Maximum grade of the main line was 2%, the longest haul on that grade being seven miles (out of Spokane). Coeur d'Alene grades were less severe; the route was mostly along the Spokane River valley.

The Cd'A&S line had 60-pound rail while 70-pound was used for the Inland. Ballast was generally gravel extracted from pits near Spokane on the Inland line. Wyes were provided at Coeur d'Alene, Moscow and Colfax for turning trains, the latter being one and a half miles from Colfax depot. To encourage rail shipment, the railroad laid spurs or sidings wherever warranted, governed by business prospects and potential revenue from the source. Costs were usually borne by the shipper where specifically requested, but the railroad paid for some. Passing tracks were positioned with respect to anticipated train services.

During the 1940s, the GN revamped the Inland lines to lower maintenance costs. Redundant spurs were removed and the number of passing tracks/sidings reduced. When modern grain elevators were built along the line, station tracks were modified to provide rail access. Industrial growth in east Spokane after World War II prompted the addition of several spurs along the Coeur d'Alene line.

The location and size of sidetracks along the railroad system are itemized in Appendix C. Diagrams provided in this chapter illustrate the track arrangement for the terminals at Coeur d'Alene, Moscow and Colfax. At many stations that featured a depot building, sidetracks were little more than a passing track as illustrated by Spring Valley, Fairbanks, Waverly, Garfield and Oakesdale. Additional track plans for other stations are included in Chapter 8.

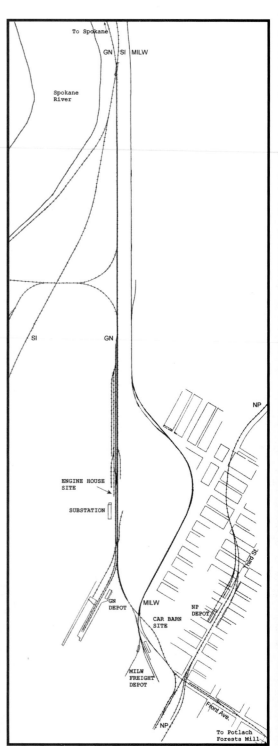

Coeur d'Alene railroads circa 1940. (Author's collection)

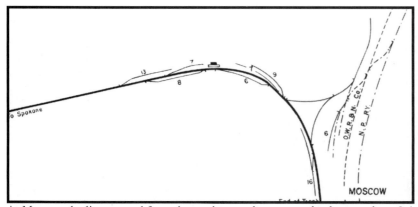

At Moscow the line entered from the north, turned west past the depot and ran 0.4 mile west to a wye, the tail of which connected to interchange tracks with the UP and NP and extended to industry spurs. (Great Northern Railway)

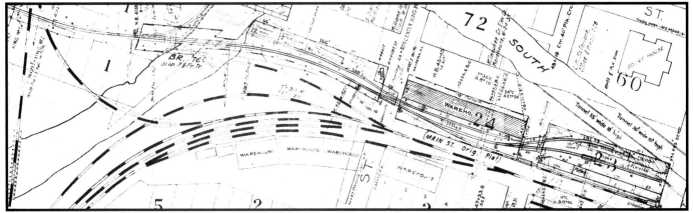

Plan of the Colfax terminal area. Dashed lines are UP/OWR&N tracks. (Great Northern Railway)

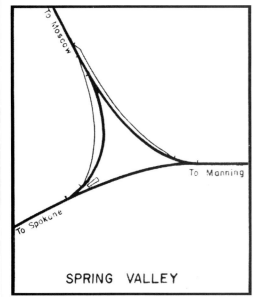

Spring Valley track arrangement.
(Great Northern Railway)

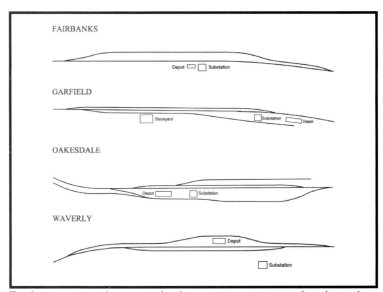

Tracks at many stations were simple arrangements, even at locations where a depot was required, as at Fairbanks, Garfield, Oakesdale and Waverly. (Traced from Great Northern Railway drawings)

Sources

Interstate Commerce Commission. Bureau of Valuation. Spokane, Coeur d'Alene and Spokane Railway - Engineering Field Notes. 1929.

Great Northern Railway President's Subject File No.9128. Spokane & Inland Empire Railroad History of Properties – Operating Property. 1919.

Maps and plats relating to stations on the Spokane & Inland Empire Railroad and successors.

Electric Railway Review, February 2, 1907, 27: 148. "The Spokane Electric Terminal".

Electric Railway Review, December 7, 1907: 891. "Spokane & Inland Shops".

Electric Railway Journal, October 8, 1910, 36: 639.

Street Railway Review, May 15, 1906, 16: 279. "The Freight & Express Traffic of the Coeur d'Alene &Spokane Ry."

Mattson, James C., private communication.

President Blackwell informed the Spokesman Review in early June 1904 of the imminent arrival of six more cars from the same source: two motor baggage and passenger cars and four passenger trailers. While similar in style to their predecessors, power was increased by 50% to 300 hp (four 75hp motors) and the trailer cars were extended to hold 44 passengers.

An order was placed in November 1904 for two 2-car sets, a motor combine and trailer for each. Their design set the pattern for future orders, the manufacturer presenting numerous alternatives before final selection. Brill delivered the four cars in June 1905 at a price of $50,000. They were larger than the previous series, being nearly 50 feet long and five inches wider. Arched pairs of windows gave the cars a modern appearance, this style being recently adopted by the Pullman Company. While the semi-convertible system was applicable to the new style windows, only the lower sash was partially contained in the roof, the upper sash being stationary. Underframes were reinforced by 3/8-inch thick steel plate in the side sills. Power output was unchanged from the previous order with combination cars getting four 75 hp motors (later replaced by a 90 hp version). The larger size allowed for an 8 foot 4 inch baggage compartment in the combination cars and a small toilet was provided in the center. Seats in the smoking and passenger compartments of the two combination cars were spring cane and the interior finish was golden oak. Trailer cars had 52 plush-upholstered seats and enclosed entrances at both ends. One end of the trailer cars was subsequently modified to provide an observation platform to match cars built later.

Notable innovations for the new power cars were multiple unit control, giving the motorman command over all motors in the train, and, for safety, automatic air brake application when the motorman removed his hand from the controller lever. Only New York subway cars were said to have such capabilities. The new features were so foreign to the Coeur d'Alene shops staff that a manufacturer's representative was called in, delaying service introduction by two weeks. Ensuing orders for rolling stock specified these devices.

Table 6.1. Passenger Rolling Stock Delivered.

Initial Owner	Built	Brill Order No.	Type	Length-Framing	Power	Motors	Total Cars	Running Numbers Original	Assigned c. 1914	Notes
CdA&S Railway	1903	12930	MBP	39'4"	DC	4-50 hp	3	1-3	201-214 series	To Traction Division c. 1910.
"	1904	13521	MBP	~40'	DC	4-75 hp	2	4-5	201-214 series	No. 4 to Traction Division c. 1910; No. 5 rebuilt 1910 to MBE No.44.
"	1903	12932	MBE	40'1"	DC	2-75 hp	3	151-152	25-26	Re-numbered 41-42 (c. 1905); No.42 rebuilt 1907 with 10 foot RPO compartment.
"	1903	12931	TP	38'	-	-	3	50-52	201-214 series	To Traction Division c. 1910.
"	1904	13320	TP	~44'	-	-	4	53-56	201-214 series	To Traction Division c. 1910.
"	1905	14082	MBP	50'9"	DC	4-75 hp	2	8-9	40-41	To Traction Division 1910.
"	1905	14084	TP	49'8"	-	-	2	61-62	320-321	90 hp motors by 1919.
S&IE Railroad (CdA&S Railway)	1907	15567	MBP	56'3"	DC	4-90 hp	2	10-11	42-43	Re-numbered 17-18 (1909).
S&IE Railroad (CdA&S Railway)	1907	15569	MP	56'3½"	DC	4-90 hp	2	15-16	60-61	Re-numbered 63-64 (1909).
"	1907	15571	TP	55'9"	-	-	2	17-18	322-323	
"	1907	15573	TL	56'	-	-	2	See Notes	360-361	Named "Kootenai" and "Shoshone"; sold 1919 to Pacific Northwest Traction Company.
"	1907	15575	TP	55'9"	-	-	2	12, 14-16	44-47	Rebuilt with 15 foot 8 inch RPO compartment.
S&IE Railroad (CdA Division)	1909	16904	MBP	56'3"	DC	4-90 hp	4	65-68	324-327	
S&IE Railroad (CdA Division)	1909	16906	TP	55'9"	-	-	4			
S&IE Railroad	Rebuilt		MBE	~40'	DC	4-75 hp	1	200	-	Rebuilt 1910 from MBP No. 5; to Traction Division 1913; destroyed by fire 1918.
S&I Railway	1906	14737	MBP	58'2"	AC	4-100 hp	6	100-105	80-86 series	Re-numbered c. 1909 in 80-86 series.
S&I Railway	1906	14739	MP	55'5"	AC	4-100 hp	6	106-111	70-74 series	No. 107 rebuilt 1908 to MBP and re-numbered in 80-86 series; the rest renumbered c. 1909 in 87-91 series.
"	1906	14741	TP	57'6"	-	-	4	300/2/3/5	300-303	Nos. 302/3/5 re-numbered 301-303 in sequence.
"	1906	14743	MBE	49'8"	AC	4-100 hp	3	301/4	310-311	Rebuilt 1910 with 16 foot RPO compartment.
"	1906	"	MP		AC	4-100 hp	2	25-26, 30	1-3	Rebuilt 1908 to Day Coach and Parlor.
"	1906	"	MBE		AC	4-100 hp	2	27	20	Rebuilt 1908 for regular DC service with 4-90 hp motors and 15 foot 9 inch RPO compartment.
S&IE Railroad	1906	"			AC	4-100 hp	2	28-29	10-11	
S&IE Railroad	?	Officer		50'4"	-	-	1	101	500	Purchased 1911 from Grand Rapids & Indiana Railroad; 6-wheel trucks; classified as work equipment 1917.

Notes

Cars built 1903-4 constructed by American Car Company on Brill trucks; constructed by Brill from 1905

MP: Motor Passenger
MBE: Motor Baggage and Express
MBP: Motor Baggage and Passenger
TP: Trailer Passenger
TL: Trailer Parlor

On May 18, 1907, two new three-car sets, along with two parlor cars, arrived in Spokane. Transit from Brill's Philadelphia manufacturing plant was over the Canadian Pacific Railway and the new Spokane International Railway. Letterboards proclaimed "Inland Empire System" with "Cd'A&S Ry." in smaller letters at the ends. Both sets consisted of a motor baggage and passenger car, motor passenger car and a trailer car. A parlor car could be attached to the rear for specific trips such as boat expresses. Power cars had four 100 hp motors, so the motorman controlled 800 hp. Brill-type 27-E2 trucks were used. These new cars were 56 feet in length, larger than their two-year-old sisters although quite similar in exterior appearance. Extra space in the combination cars allowed for more passengers (56) on cane seats, and a 10 foot 9 inch baggage compartment. Motor passenger cars held 45 passengers in high backed plush-upholstered seats. The 75-seat trailer cars had an extra seating bay and a 7 foot 9 inch observation platform. Oak was the interior finish.

Parlor cars could be recognized by their distinctive window arrangement and observation platform surrounded by a heavy brass railing. In Pullman fashion, the cars were named "Kootenai" and

Coeur d'Alene & Spokane Railway's passenger equipment order in 1903 included a pair of 40-foot motor baggage and express cars. (Author's collection)

One of the pair of 40-foot motor baggage and express cars was rebuilt with an RPO compartment in 1907 for mail service between Spokane and Coeur d'Alene. (Warren Wing Collection)

Motor baggage and express car No. 43 built in 1907 was also converted for the Railway Mail Service. The rebuilt 40-foot car is shown re-numbered as No. 21. (D. Cozine Collection)

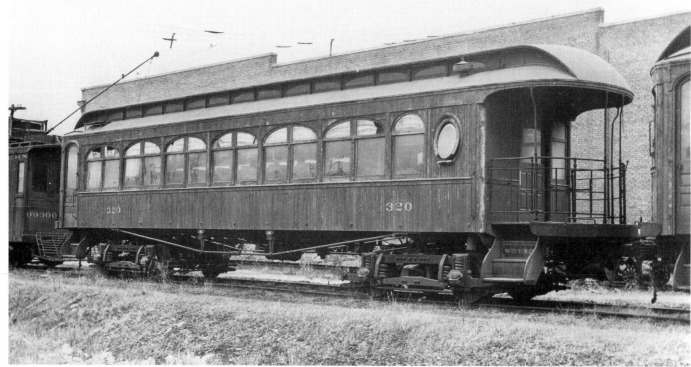

Fifty-foot passenger trailers Nos. 61 and 62 were renumbered to 320 and 321. No.320 is shown from the observation platform end. (Harold Hill; Warren Wing collection)

"Shoshone"; numbers were added several years later. Interiors, finished in vermillion wood, were elegantly fitted out and comparable to Pullman drawing room coaches, according to a *Spokesman Review* reporter. Two dozen wicker chairs, upholstered in leather, sat on Axminster carpet. Smokers got a similarly lavish 6-seat compartment. Separate lavatories for men and women were considered prudent.

The last series of cars to arrive, two years later, were four pairs of 56-foot combination motor cars and passenger trailers. Overall, they were identical to the 1907 batch. They went to the Coeur d'Alene Division, the merged companies by then functioning as divisions of the S&IE.

All twelve of the passenger cars built in 1903-4 were transferred around 1910 to the Traction Division. Arrival of the last batch of new (56-foot) cars probably made the older cars redundant. Another possibility is that the Gibbs collision (Chapter 10), where the body of a 40-foot motor car was destroyed, prompted their reassignment for lighter duty. At least six were converted to streetcars for work on the city lines; two trailers were fitted with motors for the Opportunity line and two remained as trailers. One

Interior of trailer No. 321, photographed in 1939. (Harold Hill, Warren Wing Collection)

The next eight cars supplied for the Coeur d'Alene line in 1907 were 56 feet in length. Eight more were delivered two years later. Summarizing, there were six motor baggage and passenger cars, two motor passenger cars and eight trailer cars in the 1907 and 1909 batches. Motor baggage and passenger car No.42 at the Spokane car barn in 1938 and the next several illustrations depict individual 56-foot cars carrying their post-1914 running numbers. (Harold Hill; Warren Wing collection).

Motor passenger and baggage car No. 45 was found outside the Spokane machine shop in 1937.
(Warren Wing Collection)

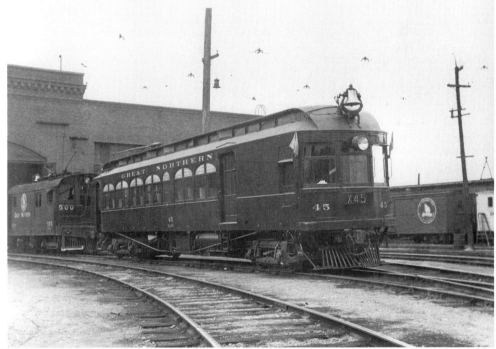

Interior of car No. 45 in 1938, looking towards the smoking compartment.
(Warren Wing Collection)

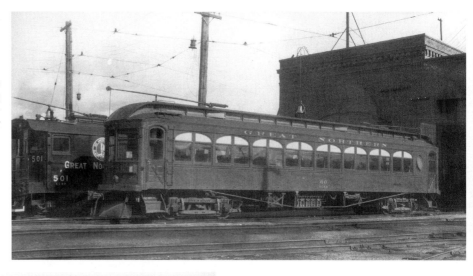

Motor passenger cars Nos. 60 and 61 were equipped to run in either direction, having a control stand at each end and two trolley poles. Car No. 60 was reputedly the last car in service. (Richard Yaremko Collection)

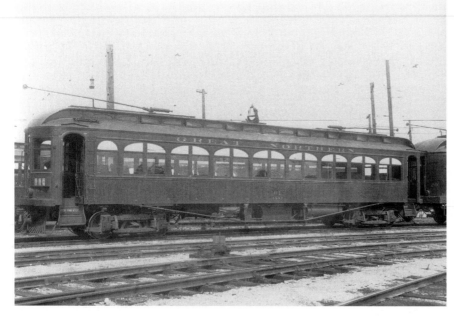

Sister motor passenger car No. 61 illustrates the opposite side.
(Harold Hill, Warren Wing Collection)

Six passenger trailers delivered in 1907 and 1909 became Nos. 322-327 after the 1914 renumbering. No. 322 is shown here in 1938. The inboard oval window was for the toilet and the outboard window for the seven-foot observation platform. Sometimes the painters added a period after the Great Northern title in the letterboard. (Harold Hill, Warren Wing Collection)

Interior of trailer No. 323 as it existed in 1936. Bare electric light bulbs provided illumination. (Warren Wing Collection)

View towards the rear of "Shoshone" showing the individual chairs, carpet and light fixtures. (Warren Wing Collection)

of the motor cars was rebuilt and enlarged in 1914 after fire damage. After the Gibbs collision in 1909, the underframe and trucks from the wrecked vehicle were used to construct a 40-foot motor baggage and express car for the Opportunity line.

An AC powered 50-foot motor baggage car was transferred from the Inland Division in 1908 to fulfill mail contract requirements. Modifications included a 15 foot 9 inch RPO compartment, appropriate electrical equipment and Brill trucks.

Parlor trailer "Kootenai" at the rear of the "Shoshone Flyer," near the Spokane terminal. (Warren Wing Collection)

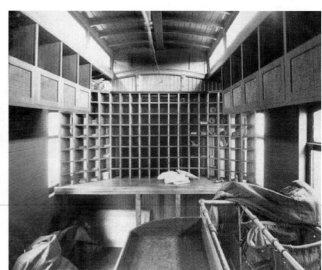

This 50-foot car No. 20, originally AC motor baggage and express car No. 27, was transferred to the Coeur d'Alene Division when two years old and modified for DC operation and mail duty. Modification included a change to Brill trucks, as in this late 1930s view. Otherwise, it was similar externally to the AC version except for the absence of a pantograph. (Harold Hill, Warren Wing Collection)

A 50-foot motor baggage and express car compartment modified to an RPO. (Museum of N. Idaho Trr-1-95)

Alternating Current Lines

Spokane & Inland Railway ordered 18 passenger carrying cars from J.G. Brill Company for service between Spokane and Moscow/Colfax. Six 58 foot 2 inch motor baggage and passenger cars arrived on August 21, 1906, followed two months later by six 55 foot 5 inch motor passenger cars and six 57 foot 6 inch trailers in November 1906. All were carried on Baldwin double equalizer beam trucks. Body style followed the pattern established the previous year by the Cd'A&S. Motor cars had four 100 hp motors and electrical equipment similar to the locomotives described below. A pantograph and a trolley pole were fitted to each car for operation on three different electrical systems: 6,600 volts AC, 700 volts AC (required by some small towns) and at the 600 volts DC mandatory within Spokane.

Combination cars had 56 seats in smoking and passenger compartments. Their baggage compartment was unusually cramped at about five feet in length without exterior access. Remedial action in 1909-10 removed part of the smoking room to gain a 20 foot 6 inch baggage compartment with a door on each side, the redundant arch windows being paneled over. One motor passenger car was rebuilt to motor passenger and baggage configuration at the same time.

Motor passenger cars held 62 passengers. Great Northern acquired one of the cars in 1929 to work temporarily over its new 11,000 volt AC Cascade tunnel main line. In addition to electrical equipment changes, modification included a 16 foot 6 inch baggage room with a door on each side, but leaving the arch windows uncovered.

Passenger trailers had the same seating capacity as the motor passenger cars. A rear 7 foot 6 inch vestibule functioned as an observation room with space for twelve chairs. Two trailers were rebuilt into day coach-parlor cars, furnishing a parlor compartment with individual seats and a smoking compartment in place of the observation room. Spokane shops were directed in 1909 to rebuild the other four trailers with open observation ends.

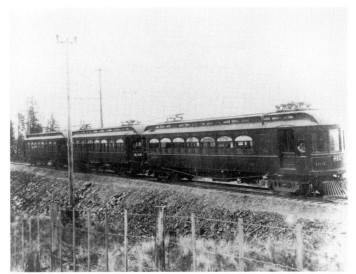

Spokane & Inland Railway passenger cars duplicated the body style established by the Cd'A&S as shown by this three-car train near Valley Ford station soon after opening. The train consisted of motor passenger and baggage car No. 104, motor passenger car No. 111 and a passenger trailer car. Both motor cars were equipped with a pantograph for AC operation and a trolley pole to work under the Spokane city DC wires. Note the small baggage compartment behind the motorman's cab. Cars were lettered "Spokane & Inland Railway" when delivered. (Warren Wing Collection)

Combination motor passenger and baggage car No. 80 with the destination board in the front window labeled Moscow and Colfax. Passenger services to the two towns were combined in 1914 as an economy measure. (Inland Empire Railway Historical Society Collection)

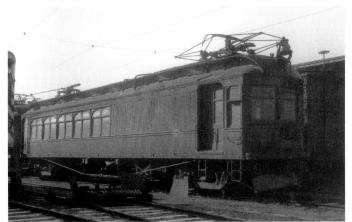

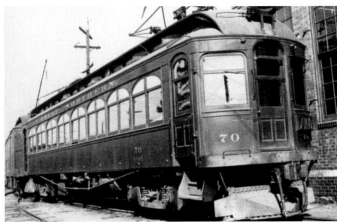

The baggage compartment of the motor passenger and baggage cars had to be enlarged as shown by No. 83, the passenger compartment losing two windows on each side. (Harold Hill, Warren Wing Collection)

Motor passenger car No. 70 equipped in the conventional way for DC and AC power collection with a trolley and a pantograph. (Sheldon Perry Collection)

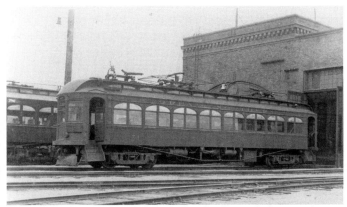

Motor passenger car No. 73 looked to be in good shape as late as 1939 when photographed outside Spokane Shops. (Harold Hill, Warren Wing Collection)

Interior of car No. 73 in 1937. (Warren Wing Collection)

Great Northern modified motor passenger car No. 74 in 1929 to operate over its newly electrified 11,000 volt AC main line. The electrical system was altered, a second pantograph and baggage compartment added and the car given the number 2400 in the GN series. The modified car returned to SC&P in mid-1930 becoming No. 90. (Harold Hill, Warren Wing Collection)

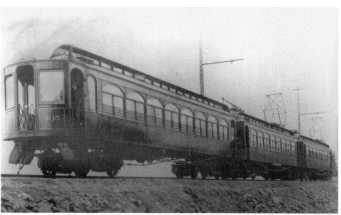

Six trailers, Nos. 300-305, were delivered to the Spokane & Inland Railway. No. 305 is shown at work behind a motor passenger car and baggage car. An enclosed observation compartment was provided at the car rear when built. (Warren Wing Collection)

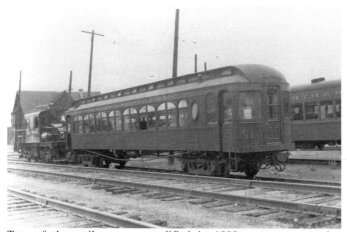

Two of the trailers were modified in 1909 to create a parlor compartment with individual seats and a smoking compartment instead of the observation room. No. 310 was one of the cars modified. (Harold Hill, Warren Wing Collection)

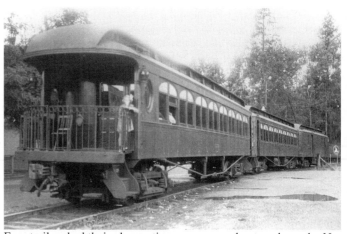

Four trailers had their observation room opened out as shown by No. 323. (Harold Hill, Warren Wing Collection)

Six AC motor baggage & express cars Nos. 25-30 delivered to the Spokane & Inland in 1906 are illustrated here by No. 30. (Sheldon Perry Collection)

Delivery of six 50-foot motor baggage and express cars to the S&I began in November 1906. Powered by four 100 hp motors, the cars had two doors on each side. Three cars were given a 16-foot RPO compartment in 1910 for the Railway Mail Service and, "as previously noted, another was transferred to the Coeur d'Alene Division for such work.

As the size of the railway system grew, management decided an officer car was appropriate for business purposes. A motor baggage and passenger car from the AC fleet got this assignment for a couple of years followed by a motor passenger car. The secondhand market was searched for a car, about 56 foot long, suitable for conversion to this role. Northern Pacific suggested a coach, converted earlier from an old

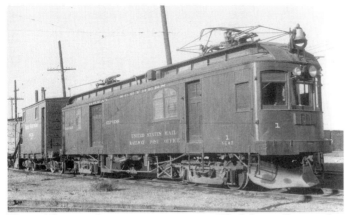

Three AC motor baggage cars were modified for mail operation in 1910. One of them became motor baggage and mail car No. 1, originally No. 25. (Harold Hill, Warren Wing Collection)

Opposite side of No. 1. (Harold Hill, Warren Wing Collection)

Motor baggage and mail car No. 3 had lost its mail exchange equipment by the 1920s and was used in electric line repair service. It was later re-numbered into the work equipment series. (P. Walden, D. Cozine Collection)

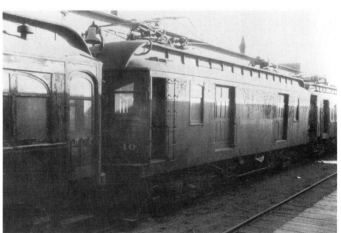

Car No.10 remained a motor baggage car as in this late 1930s photograph. There was no central window by this time and sister car No. 11 had no side windows. (Harold Hill, Warren Wing Collection)

sleeper, while the Grand Rapids and Indiana Railroad offered a 50 foot 4 inch private car on 6-wheel trucks. The S&IE purchased the latter vehicle in February 1911 for $5,400. Six years later, it was converted for outfit service at a cost of $6,082.

Changes were made to the cars to improve safety or to meet operating needs:
- The pair of DC motor passenger cars had controllers at both ends, and two trolley poles, so that they could be driven in either direction. Such capability would have been needed for local runs to stations where no turning facilities existed.
- Some, if not all, of the five AC motor passenger cars were similarly equipped, getting a controller and trolley pole at each end and the pantograph moved inboard. Technical journals made no mention of dual-end controls for either the new AC or DC cars, so modification was apparently done by the railway's shops rather than delivered in this way.
- Automatic couplers replaced the inherently dangerous link and pin couplers in 1910 as required by federal law.
- Service experience showed that horizontal flat pantograph shoes tended to rub the trolley wire in one spot. The company developed a larger, gently curved, shoe with turned down ends that wore more evenly over the surface and improved wire contact, even over rough track.

- Headlamps went through several iterations. Five high wattage lamps arranged in a circle on a simple reflector were not satisfactory. Arc headlamps blinked with pantograph bounce. Incandescent lamps gave the desired performance, after the reflector had been modified from metal to glass to prevent deterioration.
- During the winter months, front windows of the cars were partially covered by metal slats about four inches wide and spaced an inch or two apart, except directly in front of the motorman. They were adopted after a train hit a snowdrift.
- Locomotive-type, air-activated bells were fitted to power cars for warning purposes.
- Inland Division passenger cars were modified in 1908-9 to enable four-car trains to divide at Spring Valley into two two-car trains for Moscow and Colfax, respectively.

Running Numbers

Numbering information for all rolling stock was drawn primarily from Official Railway Equipment Register publications. Coeur d'Alene & Spokane Railway numbered new passenger-carrying motor cars in the 1 to 18 series and trailers as 50 to 68; both series were discontinuous. Corresponding Spokane & Inland Railway series were 100 to 111 for motor cars, altered around 1909 to 80 to 91 and 300 to 305 for trailers. Motor baggage cars carried two digit numbers, the S&I series being 25 to 30 and Cd'A&S cars were numbered 41 to 44. For some reason, the first two Cd'A&S baggage cars were delivered as Nos. 151 to 152, but were soon changed to Nos. 41 to 42.

A new scheme was introduced in 1914 and most of the fleet re-numbered. In general, new numbers were assigned in the same sequence as the old series, with the exception of the AC passenger motor cars.

The small cars transferred to the Traction Division were immediately re-numbered into the new owner's series. Re-numbered again under the 1914 scheme, they went into the 200 to 214 series. Definitive correlation to their original Cd'A&S numbers could not be established.

When the S&IE was reorganized in 1920 into two companies, the Spokane & Eastern Railway & Power Company acquired the (1) Coeur d'Alene Division fleet, (2) two Inland Division trailer cars Nos. 310 to 311 and (3) the small cars previously transferred to the Traction Division. Inland Empire Railroad Company got the rest of the Inland Division fleet (Table 6.2). No number changes were made at that time, or later by the Spokane, Coeur d'Alene & Palouse Railway.

Livery

The description of the new DC powered three-car sets by the *Spokesman Review* noted that they were dark red, similar to cars then in use. Later, a reporter mentioned that cars for the new Opportunity line were painted red, like suburban cars on the S&IE system.

Authorization in November 1908 to paint S&I Division passenger cars in Inland Empire red, with gold leaf for lettering and numbering, implies that they were painted a different color. This prior scheme may well have been green, an olive shade being favored at the time the cars were ordered. Livery for both Divisions' cars eventually became dark green, SP&S management conceivably implementing the change.

Retirement

Prior to acquisition by SC&P, several cars departed the passenger car roster. They included demotion of the officer car and a motor baggage and express car to the work equipment roster. The two named parlor cars were sold in 1919 to Pacific Northwest Traction Company. Motors and trolley collectors were added to them, to run between Seattle and Everett. After retirement in

Running Number	Type	Owner 1920-7*	Built	Length-Framing	Motors	Retired	Notes
							Table 6.2. Passenger Rolling Stock From 1920.
1	MBE RPO	IE	1906	49' 8"	4-100 hp	c. 1941	
2	MBE RPO	IE	1906	49' 8"	4-100 hp	c. 1941	
3	MBE RPO	IE	1906	49' 8"	4-100 hp	1935	Used as line car No. 3 c. 1920-7; to line repair car No. 99303 in 1935.
10	MBE	IE	1906	49' 8"	4-100 hp	1938	
11	MBE	IE	1906	49' 8"	4-100 hp	1938	To line repair car No. 99305 c. 1938.
20	MBE RPO	S&E	1906	49' 8"	4-90 hp	1941	
21	MBE RPO	S&E	1907	40' 3"	4-75 hp	1940	
25	MB	S&E	1903	40' 1"	4-75 hp	1927	
26	MB	S&E	1903	40' 1"	4-75 hp	1927	
40	MBP	S&E	1905	50' 9"	4-90 hp	c. 1939	
41	MBP	S&E	1905	50' 9"	4-90 hp	c. 1939	
42	MBP	S&E	1907	56' 3"	4-90 hp	c. 1939	
43	MBP	S&E	1907	56' 3"	4-90 hp	1940	
44	MBP	S&E	1909	56' 3"	4-90 hp	1940	
45	MBP	S&E	1909	56' 3"	4-90 hp	1940	
46	MBP	S&E	1909	56' 3"	4-90 hp	1940	
47	MBP	S&E	1909	56' 3"	4-90 hp	1940	
60	MP	S&E	1907	56' 3½"	4-90 hp	c. 1942	
61	MP	S&E	1907	56' 3½"	4-90 hp	1940	
70	MP	IE	1906	55' 5"	4-100 hp	c. 1942	
71	MP	IE	1906	55' 5"	4-100 hp	c. 1939	Retired by 1927; reinstated c. 1930, without motors.
72	MP	IE	1906	55' 5"	4-100 hp	c. 1939	
73	MP	IE	1906	55' 5"	4-100 hp	1940	
74	MP	IE	1906	55' 5"	4-100 hp	1940	Rebuilt January 1929 by GNR as MBP for 11,000 volts AC & r/n 2400; returned May 1930 to SC&P as No. 9...
80	MBP	IE	1906	58' 2"	4-100 hp	1940	
81	MBP	IE	1906	58' 2"	4-100 hp	by 1927	
82	MBP	IE	1906	58' 2"	4-100 hp	c. 1939	
83	MBP	IE	1906	58' 2"	4-100 hp	c. 1939	
84	MBP	IE	1906	58' 2"	4-100 hp	1940	
85	MBP	IE	1906	58' 2"	4-100 hp	1924	
86	MBP	IE	1906	55' 5"	4-100 hp	c. 1928	
202	TP	S&E		39' 6½"	-	1927	
203	TP	S&E		39' 6½"	-	1927	
204	MP	S&E		40' 6"	4-75 hp	1927	
206	MP	S&E		38'	2-75 hp	1927	
207	MP	S&E		40'	4-35 hp	1927	
208	MP	S&E		40'	2-45 hp	1927	
209	MP	S&E		44'	2-50 hp	1927	
210	MP	S&E		52' 7"	4-50 hp	1927	Rebuilt 1914 with increased length by Niles Manufacturing Company after fire damage.
211	MP	S&E		40'	2-50 hp	1927	
212	MP	S&E		40'	2-75 hp	1927	
214	MP	S&E		40'	2-100 hp	1927	
300	TP	IE	1906	57' 6"	-	1927	To GN No. 572 4/23/27.
301	TP	IE	1906	57' 6"	-	1927	To GN No. 573 3/29/27.
302	TP	IE	1906	57' 6"	-	1928	To GN No. 574 5/25/28.
303	TP	IE	1906	57' 6"	-	c. 1928	
310	TP	S&E	1906	57' 6"	-	c. 1939	
311	TP	S&E	1906	57' 6"	-	1938	
320	TP	S&E	1905	49' 8"	-	c. 1939	
321	TP	S&E	1905	49' 8"	-	c. 1939	
322	TP	S&E	1907	55' 9"	-	c. 1940	
323	TP	S&E	1907	55' 9"	-	c. 1942	
324	TP	S&E	1909	55' 9"	-	1928	To GN No. 575 5/24/28.
325	TP	S&E	1909	55' 9"	-	c. 1940	
326	TP	S&E	1909	55' 9"	-	c. 1940	
327	TP	S&E	1909	55' 9"	-	c. 1940	

* Owned by Spokane, Coeur d'Alene & Palouse from 1927.

MBP: *Motor Baggage & Passenger*
MBE: *Motor Baggage & Express*
MP: *Motor Passenger*
TP: *Trailer Passenger*

S&E: *Spokane & Eastern Railway and Power Co.*
IE: *Inland Empire Railroad*

1932, the two bodies were used as restaurants.

New owner SC&P immediately reduced the fleet to nearly half of its pre-1919 size. All the 1903-1904 built cars were sold for scrap. Four trailers moved to the Great Northern Railway to partner gas-electric cars. By late 1928, the following remained in service: 18 motor cars, nine trailers and seven baggage and express, or mail, cars.

Few changes were made to the passenger car fleet during the next decade. One motor baggage car was transferred to work equipment to replace a line repair car. Its crew had attempted to cross a burning trestle that collapsed under the car and its regular load of a catenary maintenance tower car. Most of the stock was retired in 1940, following the abandonment of passenger service, the last half dozen being disposed of during the next couple of years.

LOCOMOTIVES

Electric

A total of 13 electric locomotives, equipped for multiple unit operation, were purchased (Table 6.3). Baldwin erected them and Westinghouse supplied the electrical equipment. With the exception of the last locomotive delivered, all were four-axle, B-B, box cab units that could run on either 6,600 (or 700) volt single phase AC or 600 volts DC. Both pantograph and wheel trolleys were fitted for current collection, the wheel trolley being for operation under the lower voltage AC or DC supply. Significant weight was added by the two auto-transformers carried on each locomotive for AC operation; motors were controlled by voltage variation. When operated on DC, current was fed directly to the motors. Two motors were mounted on each truck, geared to the axles. A blower cooled the transformers and motors. Both straight and automatic air brakes were standard, fed by a pair of electric motor-driven air compressors. The steel cab housed the auxiliary equipment.

Six locomotives, representing three models, were delivered in 1906: one 360 hp, one 500 hp and four 600 hp; a second 360 hp locomotive was supplied in 1907. The three models had similar appearance. Cab length of the 600 hp version was 24 foot 10 inches, four inches longer than the other two models. Weight was close to 50 tons except the 360 hp locomotives weighed 38 tons. All were lettered "Spokane & Inland Railway" when delivered. General Manager J.B. Ingersoll said that he had designed the locomotives. Haulage capacity of the 600 hp units was reported as seven loaded freight cars at 30 mph on level track.

The AC system was not ready when the first three (600 hp) locomotives arrived. So, in late August 1906 one was tried out, hauling freight on the Coeur d'Alene line. Performance was reported as most satisfactory. The line to Waverly was switched on two months later. The GN converted two 600 hp locomotives for operation on the 11,000 volts AC Cascade Tunnel main line in 1929. They returned to SC&P the following year and continued to work in modified form.

At the time of the first deliveries, The New York, New Haven & Hartford Railroad had started to receive four-axle locomotives equipped for multiple unit operation of passenger trains over single-phase AC and third rail DC lines. The body style resembled the S&I units, but they operated at 11,000 volts AC and differed in size, performance characteristics and drive system.

Three larger locomotives rated at 1160 hp arrived from Baldwin in 1907. Their cab had four windows on each side compared to two for their predecessors. An additional 1,160 hp pair was acquired in 1910. The last locomotive delivered in 1912 was a 500 hp steeple cab. Intended purely for yard work, it was equipped for DC operation only.

Table 6.3. Electric Locomotives.

Model	Built	Construction Number	Frame Length	Running Numbers 1906	1907	1910-12	Disposition
360 hp	4/1906	27927	28' 6"	B2	M4	500	Sold 1940 to WallaWalla Valley Railway (No.500); scrapped in 1950.
360 hp	7/1907	31244	,,	-	M99	501	Sold 1940 to Tacoma Municipal Belt Railway (No.1628); later moved to Skagit River Railway.
500 hp	2/1912	37513	29' 5"	-	-	502	Sold 1940 to Bamberger Railroad (No.502); scrapped in 1952.
500 hp	3/1906	27735	28' 6"	A1	M1	503	Sold 1940 to Bamberger Railroad (No.503); scrapped in 1952.
600 hp	3/1906	27823	28' 10"	B1	M3	603	Scrapped in 1941.
60 0hp	4/1906	27926	,,	A2	M2	604	Scrapped in 1941.
600 hp	4/1906	27885	,,	C1	M5	605	Scrapped in 1941.
600 hp	4/1906	27928	,,	C2	M6	606	Scrapped in 1941.
1160 hp	7/1907	31371	36' 2"	-	M7	701	Scrapped in 1941.
1160 hp	7/1907	31372	,,	-	M8	702	Scrapped in 1941.
1160 hp	8/1907	31435	,,	-	M9	703	Scrapped in 1941.
1160 hp	3/1910	34397	,,	-	M10	704	Scrapped in 1941.
1160 hp	3/1910	34398	,,	-	M11	706	Scrapped in 1941.

All locomotives constructed by Baldwin-Westinghouse. The 1160 hp locomotives had 50-inch drivers the others had 38-ich drivers.

Three running number schemes had been employed by 1912. The first two were alphanumeric: a prefix letter of A, B or C was used to start with, succeeded by a prefix M scheme. The final scheme identified the 600 hp locomotives as 603 to 606 and assigned numbers 701 to 706 (705 not used) to the largest units; lower hp units were numbered 500 to 503.

Employee timetable No.1 issued by SC&P in 1927 listed maximum tonnage limits handled in road or switching service:
Locomotive Tons
No. 500   450
No. 501   450
No. 502   700
No. 503   700
Class 600   150
Class 700   300

The limits accounted for gradients encountered in their areas of operation. Double the tonnage was permitted for pairs of 600 and 700 class locomotives.

When the Spokane & Eastern was formed, three locomotives were assigned to the new company: the 500 hp steeple cab and two 360 hp box cabs. The latter pair had been modified around 1910 for regular DC operation to replace steam power on Coeur d'Alene freight trains. The AC locomotives naturally went to the Inland Empire Railroad and the 500 hp box cab was transferred to the S&E in 1923.

All four DC locomotives were sold in 1940. Two survived a dozen years under their new owners, thus achieving nearly a half-century of service. There were no buyers for the AC locomotives and they were scrapped in 1941.

Comparison of maintenance costs in 1926 showed AC locomotives were more expensive, costing 7.7 cents per mile versus 4.5 cents per mile for DC. One reason was that AC motor commutators needed turning at one third of the mileage experienced with DC locomotives. Average life of brake shoes and pantograph strips, for all equipment, was 121,244 and 171,886 miles, respectively. Similar trends were found with passenger cars: 4.3 cents per mile for AC cars compared to 3.1 cents for DC power. Commendably high availability of 96.5% for 20-year-old equipment was attributed to regular maintenance.

Publicity photo of S&I electric Locomotive No. C1 with a string of company boxcars all in new condition. (Sheldon Perry Collection)

Locomotives numbered in the 500 series were eventually assigned to the DC lines. No. 500, standing outside Spokane Shops' storehouse in 1938, illustrates that a trolley pole had replaced the pantograph. (Harold Hill, Warren Wing Collection)

No. 503, the last locomotive transferred to the DC lines, is shown in action at Coeur d'Alene. (Ted Holloway Collection)

Locomotive Nos. 501 and 503 show off their new ownership. (D. Cozine Collection)

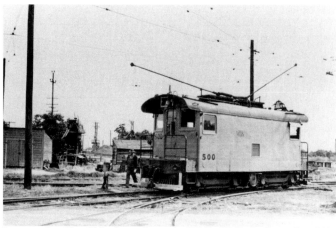

Locomotive No. 500 after sale to the Walla Walla Railway in 1940. (Sheldon Perry Collection)

Locomotive Nos. 605 and 606 illustrate the Nos. 603-606 series of AC locomotives delivered in 1906. (Harold Hill, Warren Wing Collection)

Locomotive Nos. 603 and 604 were altered to operate on the GN 11,000 volts AC main line in 1929. They are shown in this modified form with dual pantographs. (Harold Hill, Warren Wing Collection)

Larger locomotives with more power were purchased, three in 1907 and a pair in 1910. Compared to the smaller versions, they had an additional pair of windows on each side, a central pantograph and were equipped for a trolley pole at each end. No. 701 is shown here hauling a freight train in multiple with two similar locomotives. (Harold Hill, Warren Wing Collection)

Locomotive No. 702 was the second of the trio delivered in 1907. (Sheldon Perry Collection)

Locomotive No. 704 with its front facing to the right. (Harold Hill, Warren Wing Collection)

Locomotive No. 706 at Spokane Shops. (Harold Hill, Warren Wing Collection)

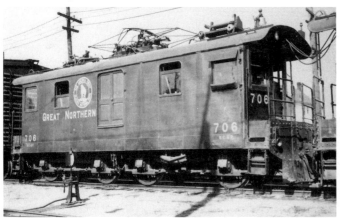

Opposite side of Locomotive No. 706 to that shown in the previous illustration. (Sheldon Perry Collection)

The last locomotive purchased by the S&IE was No. 502 in 1912. This DC steeple cab was for local switching exclusively. (Harold Hill, Warren Wing Collection)

Steam

Two steam locomotives, a 2-6-0 and a 4-6-0, were delivered to the Cd'A&S in 1903 and 1904, respectively. Three secondhand 4-4-0 locomotives acquired by the S&I, to assist in road construction, and a secondhand 2-8-0 brought the total to six by 1907. The S&IE Annual Report for 1908 to the State of Washington showed an additional locomotive acquired during that year, but balanced by the disposal of another, the total was unchanged. By 1912 only two steam locomotives remained on the roster. One was sold in 1915 and the other in November 1918. Available information is given Table 6.4. At least one locomotive was leased, from a logging company, to help with construction work.

Although this circa 1906 rudimentary steam engine facility is believed to be in Spokane, the exact location is unclear. Identifiable are Locomotive Nos. 1, 4 and 5 along with an engine lettered Northern Pacific on the tender and a small 0-4-0. (Sheldon Perry Collection)

This enlarged photograph shows the tender of a Cd'A&S 2-6-0 carrying No. 2. This number was also carried by a 4-6-0, so there had been some re-numbering or a temporary exchange of tenders. (Sheldon Perry Collection)

Coeur d'Alene & Spokane Railway 2-6-0 steam Locomotive No. 1. (D. Cozine Collection)

This considerably enlarged view of 4-4-0 locomotives Nos. 4 and 5 is the only image found of either. (Sheldon Perry Collection)

Number	Wheels	Delivered	Builder-Date, Serial Number	Prior Ownership	Disposition
Cd'A&S 1	2-6-0	1903	?	New.	Off roster c1906.
S&IE 1	4-4-0	c1906	Baldwin-1870, 2145.	McGoldrick L. No. 1, ex-SP 1203.	?
Cd'A&S 2	4-6-0	1904	Baldwin - 1904, 23931	New.	To S&IE No. 2 1906. Sold July 1911 to SP&S as No. 156.
S&IE 3	4-4-0	1905	Portland - 1883, 486	NP No. 771, ex-No. 248.	?
S&IE 4	4-4-0	1906	Baldwin - 1883, 6972	NP No. 337, r/n 1897 to 739.	Sold 1915 to Brooks Scanlon Lumber Company via SP&S.
S&IE 5	4-4-0	1906	Portland - 1883, 476	NP No. 238, r/n 1897 to 761.	Sold 1918 to City of Prineville as No. 1.
S&IE 6	2-8-0	1905	Baldwin - 1890, 11217	Central New England RR. No. 27.	Sold 1913 to Pacific & Eastern Railroad as No. 5.

Table 6.4. Steam Locomotives.

Coal and water were available at Spokane and Coeur d'Alene. Water was accessible at several points on the Inland during line construction and a water tank remained at Spring Valley Junction for the next decade.

Diesel-Electric

In 1942 three 1,000 hp model NW2 4-axle diesel-electric locomotives were purchased from the Electromotive Division of General Motors to handle traffic on the Inland lines. Financial analysis made by the GN accounting department to justify procurement is reproduced in Table 6.5.

Ordered as SC&P Nos. 800-802 (EMD construction Nos.1711-1713), their running numbers were amended to GN Nos. 5334-5336 before delivery as a result of the ownership change. Great Northern re-numbered the units two years later to 134-136. Assigned to Spokane's Hillyard engine facility for at least a dozen years, two had moved to other divisions by the 1960s. But No. 136 remained home, getting GN blue livery. Burlington Northern sold the trio, as BN Nos. 479-481 in 1982.

Several more Great Northern NW2 units were assigned to Spokane during the 1940s along with a number of Alco 1,000 hp and 1,500 hp model diesel-electrics. In fact, Alco models RS2 and RS3 were commonly used on the Inland system during most of the 1950s. Model 1,500 hp GP-7 and 1,750 hp GP-9 units had started appearing on these duties by 1958. They became the primary source of power for the next quarter century. Heavier four-axle units introduced by Burlington Northern were barred from certain parts of the Inland lines, whereas 2,000 hp GP-38-2 and 2,350 hp GP-39 units eventually became common power to Coeur d'Alene.

Table 6.5 Financial Analysis Made by GN Accounting Department.

Great Northern 1,000 hp road switcher diesels built by EMD and Alco were commonly used on the old SC&P system following their introduction in the 1940s. Alco Model RS1 No. 183 heads a freight train over Viola trestle on May 12, 1947.
(Phillip Johnson Collection, Museum N. Idaho Trr-3-1)

EMD model GP-9 became a popular choice for the Moscow line, BN No. 1753 being shown at work there. (Ted Holloway Collection)

Visiting Colfax in July 1954 were this pair of 1600 hp Alco class FA units. (Howard Hill, Warren Wing collection)

FREIGHT CARS AND CABOOSES

The Cd'A&S bought twenty new flat cars in 1903, using them for construction work. Twenty more went into traffic the following year, accompanied by the same quantity of boxcars now that the line was in operation. Similar orders were placed by the Spokane & Inland. Almost 450 cars belonged to the S&IE by 1908: 210 flat cars, 225 boxcars and ten stock cars as listed in Table 6.6. No more were bought. Renumbering of the fleet into a homogeneous system began in 1912.

				Original		Original	1912
Type	**Total**	**Builder**	**Built**	**Owner**	**Length**	**Numbers**	**Numbers**
Flat	20	AC&F	1903	Cd'A&S	36'	200-219	811-825
Flat	20	Fitz-Hugh Luther	1904	Cd'A&S	36'	220-239	826-845
Flat	10	Fitz-Hugh Luther	1906	Cd'A&S	40'	301-310	974-1003
Flat	40	AC&F	1905	S&I	36'	400-439	846-885
Flat	20	Fitz-Hugh Luther	1906	S&I	40' 3¾"	441-460	801-810
Flat	80	Fitz-Hugh Luther	1907	S&IE	41'	900-979	900-999
Flat	20	AC&F	1906	S&I	40'	980-999	980-999
Box	20	AC&F	1904	Cd'A&S	36' 8"	400-419	1501-1519
Box	30	AC&F	1905	IE	40' 7½"	1000-1029	2001-2028
Box	75	Seattle Car Co.	1907	S&IE	36' 10"	1600-1674	1600-1673
Box	25	Fitz-Hugh Luther	1907	S&IE	40'	1901-1925	1901-1925
Box	25	Seattle Car Co.	1907	S&IE	40'	1926-1950	1926-1950
Box	50	Fitz-Hugh Luther	1907	S&IE	40'	1951-2000	1951-2000
Stock	10	Fitz-Hugh Luther	1906	IE	40'	2001-2010	3001-3009
Refrigerator	6	Rebuilt by S&IE*		S&IE	36' 6"	4000-4005	4000-4005
Caboose	6		c.1906	S&I	14' 10"	A1-A6	**
Caboose	1			Cd'A&S		301	**
Caboose	3	Seattle Car Co.	1910	S&IE	24'	C1-C3	751-753
Caboose	2	S&IE	c.1911	S&IE	24'	C4-C5	754-755

Table 6.6. Freight Cars 1903-1919

* *Rebuilt 1908 from 16XX and 19XX series boxcars.*
** *Retired circa1910-1911.*

Cd'A&S 36-foot boxcar No. 401 acquired in 1905. (Author's collection)

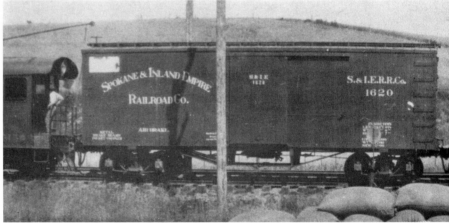

A 36 foot boxcar, No. 1620 delivered in 1906, shows S&IE markings. (Michael J. Denuty, Ted Holloway collection)

Boxcar No. 1941 marooned in the flooded yard at Rosalia. (D. Cozine Collection)

Flat car No. 222, which probably spent most of its revenue life carrying logs, illustrates the lettering style used by the Cd'A&S. (Ted Holloway Collection)

A post-1920 log-loading scene illustrates several flat cars. At least two carried S&E markings. (Ted Holloway Collection)

Six refrigerator cars for local work were converted from boxcars in 1908 and another pair of boxcars modified in 1918 to carry automobiles. Other changes made by the S&IE included dismantling flat cars in the Nos. 801-825 series during 1916, since they had the lowest load capacity. Fifteen flats were converted to gondolas around the time of receivership.

The freight car fleet was equally divided between the S&E and IE companies in 1920. Distribution of individual types was made according to the needs of each company (Table 6.7). When handed over to SC&P in 1927 there were 287 cars. Their condition did not impress the new owner and half were immediately retired. Survivors were assigned numbers in the GN series and planned for remarking as Great Northern and stenciled "SC&P Ry." By 1933, only 51 cars remained. Just one, a boxcar, existed by 1942.

With regard to cabooses, the S&I owned five, whereas Cd'A&S reported only one. No doubt they were the four-wheel type, which became obsolete by 1911 because of non-compliance with new state laws. To replace them, Seattle Car Company supplied three new 25-foot cars and S&IE shops built two of the same size. Contractor-built cars went to the S&E in 1920, the IE getting the homemade pair. Although four cabooses were assigned numbers in the GN series in 1927, only one was listed in the official roster by 1929 and remained there for a dozen years. Great Northern cabooses were used instead. Caboose No. X198 was actually assigned to SC&P when new in 1941. Caboose No. X175, converted from an outside-braced boxcar in 1962, regularly worked Spokane/Coeur d'Alene trips until the BN era.

Table 6.7. Freight Car Numbering and Distribution from 1920.							
				Total Cars			
		Running Numbers		1920	1920	1927	
Type	Length	S&IE Series*	GN Series**	S&E	IE	SC&P	Obsolete
Flat	36'	826-885	99100-99106	0	51	7	1937
Flat	40'	974-1003	99111-99122	6	16	12	c. 1939
Flat	41'	901-973	99123-99173	61	0	51	c. 1941
Gondola	36'	See Note 1.	-	0	5	0	1927
Gondola	40'	See Note 2.	99180-99184	2	2	5	c. 1939
Gondola	41'	See Note 3.	99190-99196	6	0	7	1937
Box	36' 8"	1501-1519	99000-99001	0	17	2	c. 1939
Box	36' 10"	1600-1673	-	10	63	0	1927
Box	40'	1901-2000	99010-99043	95	0	34	After 1941
Box-Auto	40'	1980-1981	-	1	1	0	c. 1925
Box	40' 7½"	1990-2028	99044-99053	1	27	10	1937
Stock	40'	3001-3009	99090-99098	5	4	9	1937
Refrigerator	36' 6"	4000-4005	99080-99085	3	3	6	1928-Sold
Caboose	25'	751-753	99200-99201	3	0	2	c. 1928
Caboose	25'	754-755	99205-99206	0	2	2	c. 1941
				193	191	147	
* S&IE series running numbers. Unchanged by S&E and IE.							
** GN series running numbers assigned in 1927 to SC&P cars.							
Notes							
1. Converted c. 1920 from flat car Nos. 826, 829, 831, 833 and 834.							
2. Converted c. 1920 from flat car Nos. 975, 979, 995 and 998; Nos.984 and 991 converted c. 1925.							
3. Converted c. 1920 from flat car Nos. 919, 932, 942, 955, 959 and 967; No. 939 converted c. 1925.							
4. Flat car running numbers were unchanged when converted to gondolas.							

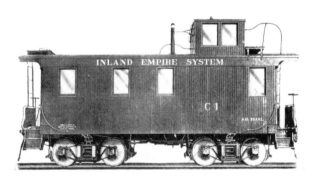

Four-wheel caboose No. A3 built circa 1906 for the Spokane & Inland Railway by Seattle Car Company. Dimensions were 14 feet 10 inches over body, 18 feet 10 inches over platforms and 9 feet 1½ inches width over side sills. The S&I had six four-wheel cabooses; all were gone by 1911, being outlawed by Washington state law. (Seattle Car and Foundry)

Eight-wheel caboose No. C1 (later 751) was one of a three built circa 1910 for the S&IE by Seattle Car Company to replace four-wheel versions. Length over body was 24 feet, over platforms 29 feet and width over side sills 9 feet 1½ inches. (Seattle Car and Foundry)

WORK EQUIPMENT

In addition to the customary vehicles found in this category, there were special vehicles for maintenance of overhead wiring and for snow removal (Table 6.8). To support sporadic haulage of freight by steam on the S&I, a 9,000-gallon water tank was built on a flat car to operate behind the locomotive and so avoid the cost of constructing water facilities along the line. Two such cars were built, the first in 1909.

Some work cars carried four numbers, at different times, final renumbering being into the GN series from 1927. The GN augmented the fleet at that time, supplying fifteen converted boxcars for various duties.

Table 6.8. Work Equipment						
	S&IE Number			**GN**	**Off**	
Type	**Pre-1912**	**1912-14**	**Post-1914**	**Number***	**Roster**	**Notes**
Derrick	-	-	X773	99221	c. 1928	Acquired c. 1923.
Steam Shovel	1	X1	X775	-	c. 1920	
Ditcher	-	-	X775	99222	c. 1929	Acquired c. 1923.
Steam Shovel	2	X2	X776	99223	c. 1928	Built Marion 1907.
Steam Shovel	3	-	-	-	c. 1910	
Water Tank	948	X5	X780	99231	c. 1936	Tank carried by flat car ex-No. 948.
Water Tank	979	X6	X781	-	c. 1927	Tank carried by flat car ex-No. 979 and flat car ex-No. 968 after c. 1920.
Pile Driver	-	-	X784	99211	c. 1936	Acquired c. 1913 and carried by flat car ex-No. 991.
Tower	212	X8	X785	99230	c. 1939	Carried on flat car; renumbered X858 c. 1918.
Tower	-	-	-	99231	> 1941	Acquired c. 1940.
Flanger	201	X9	X788	-	c. 1915	
Snow Plow (Russell)	-	-	X789	99235	> 1941	Acquired c. 1913 and carried by flat car ex-No. 976.
Wrecking	218	X11	X790	99212	c. 1936	Flat car.
Outfit	-	-	X785	99240	c. 1934	Rebuilt 1917 from 50' 4" Officer car No. 101; 6-wheel trucks.
Outfit	-	-	X797	99251	> 1941	Acquired c. 1917.
Outfit	-	-	X798	99252	> 1941	Acquired c. 1917.
Outfit	-	-	X799	-	c. 1927	Acquired c. 1917.
Line	-	-	3	99303	c. 1938	Motor Baggage and Mail No.3 converted c. 1920.
Line			-	99305	> 1941	Motor Baggage and Express No. 11 converted c. 1938.
Line	-	-	X201	99300	c. 1939	Built 1907, 4-wheels; from Traction Division c. 1922.
Line			561	-	> 1932	Northwestern "Casey Jones", 4-wheels; from Traction Division c. 1922.
Snow Sweeper	-	-	X204	99301	> 1941	Built 1908 McGuire Cummings, 2 motors. From Traction Div. c.1922.
Work (City)	-	-	X206	99302	> 1941	Built 1908, 4 motors; from Traction Division c. 1922.
Office	-	-	-	99265	c. 1939	Ex-GN 36 foot No. 096, 1927.
Commissary	-	-	-	99270	c. 1939	Ex-GN 36 foot No. 0376, 1927.
Diner	-	-	-	99275	c. 1939	Ex-GN 40 foot No. 0568, 1927.
Cook	-	-	-	99280	c. 1939	Ex-GN 40 foot No. 0752, 1927.
Cook & Diner	-	-	-	99285	c. 1939	Ex-GN 40 foot No. 0843, 1927.
Cook & Diner	-	-	-	99286	c. 1939	Ex-GN 40 foot No. 0844, 1927.
Tool	-	-	-	99290	c. 1939	Ex-GN 36 foot No. 01192, 1927.
Tool	-	-	-	99291	c. 1939	Ex-GN 36 foot No. 01193, 1927.
Tool	-	-	-	99292	> 1941	Acquired c. 1940.
Bunk	-	-	-	99253	c. 1939	Ex-GN 40 foot No. 02454, 1927.
Bunk	-	-	-	99254	c. 1939	Ex-GN 40 foot No. 02455, 1927.
Bunk	-	-	-	99255	c. 1936	Ex-GN 36 foot No. 02456, 1927.
Bunk	-	-	-	99256	c. 1936	Ex-GN 36 foot No. 02457, 1927.
Bunk	-	-	-	99257	c. 1939	Ex-GN 36 foot No. 02458, 1927.
Bunk	-	-	-	99258	c. 1939	Ex-GN 36 foot No. 02559, 1927.
* GN running numbers assigned from 1927.						

This line repair car, carried on a single truck, was used by the Traction Division until 1922 and survived another twenty years, being re-numbered into the GN work equipment series as No. 99300. (Harold Hill, Warren Wing Collection)

Snow sweeper No. 99301, built by McGuire Cummings in 1908, had also belonged to the Traction Division. A center door was absent from the opposite side. (Harold Hill, Warren Wing Collection)

Work car No. 99302 was homemade to carry materials around Spokane Shops and to negotiate a particularly tight curve. A reversible trolley pole attached to the car center collected current for the motor. (Harold Hill, Photographer; Warren Wing Collection)

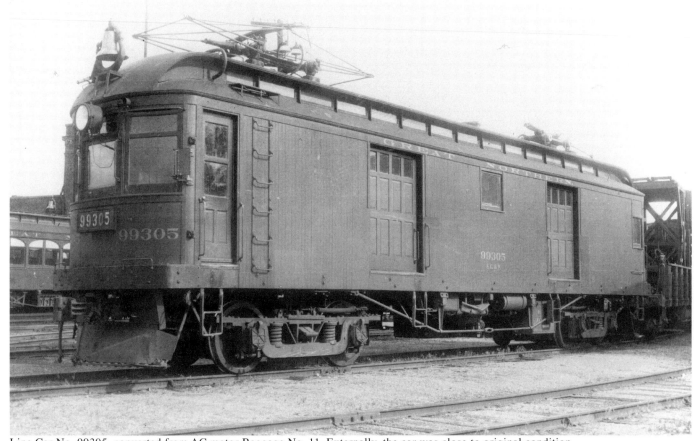

Line Car No. 99305, converted from AC motor Baggage No. 11. Externally, the car was close to original condition. (Harold Hill, Warren Wing Collection)

Sources

Spokane, Coeur d'Alene & Palouse Railway. Annual Report to the Interstate Commerce Commission. 1905-1906.

Spokane & Inland Empire Railroad. Annual Report to Stockholders. 1907-1918.

Spokane, Coeur d'Alene & Palouse Railway. Annual Report to Washington State. 1927-1942.

Great Northern Railway. Classification and Numbering of Locomotives and Equipment. 1927, 1929, 1930, 1938, 1940 and 1942.

Great Northern Railway Vice President – Operations File. Spokane, Coeur d'Alene & Palouse Railway Diesel Locomotives.

Official Railway Equipment Register. 1905-1942, various issues.

Brill's Magazine, June 15, 1907; 97, "Additional Equipment for the Inland Empire System."

Electric Railway Journal, March 12, 1910; 36: 439. "Inland Empire Mail Services."

Electric Railway Journal, December 1912; 40: 1264, New Electric Locomotive for Spokane.

Electrical World, March 31, 1906; 47: 310, "Electrification of the New York, New Haven & Hartford Railroad."

Electrical World, August 25, 1906; 48: 373, "The Spokane & Inland Railway."

Street Railway Journal, February 6, 1904; 23: 223, "Cars for the New Coeur d'Alene-Spokane Line."

Street Railway Journal, June 30, 1905; 25: 996, "Interurban Cars for the Coeur d'Alene & Spokane Railway."

Street Railway Journal, August 25, 1906; 25: 294, "The Spokane & Inland Railway."

Street Railway Journal, November 10, 1906; 28: 951, "Rolling Stock for the New Palouse-Spokane Line Washington."

Street Railway Journal, August 31, 1907; 30: 321. "Extending the Inland Empire System."

Street Railway Review, February 20, 1904; 14: 113, "Fast Express Cars for Coeur d'Alene."

Mayham, A. J. "Twenty Four Years' Operation on the Spokane, Coeur d'Alene & Palouse," Railway Age, April 4, 1931; 90: 676.

Spokane Spokesman Review.

A Coeur d'Alene train of four 56-foot cars, two motor cars and two trailers collects passengers along a Spokane city street.
(Museum of North Idaho Trr-1-94)

Chapter 7

TRAIN SERVICES

PASSENGER

Coeur d'Alene Lines

Regular passenger service between Spokane and Coeur d'Alene began on December 28, 1903. Passenger equipment had not arrived, so a small streetcar was borrowed temporarily from Washington Water Power Company to inaugurate the service. This car was an older type, with sixteen seats and open ends, displaced from WWP's city lines. Two round trips made from Spokane on the first day carried about 170 passengers, the afternoon run to Coeur d'Alene carrying 53. Business was considered so satisfactory by the general manager that he borrowed a second car from WWP to go into service on the last day of the year. Under a two-car schedule, four trains departed daily from both ends of the line, two in the morning and two in the afternoon.

The Cd'A&S issued timetable No.1 on January 8, 1904. Trains departed from Spokane at 8:00 and 9:40 a.m. and 2:20 and 4:20 p.m. Westbound departures were 9:40 a.m., 12:00 noon, 4:00 and 6:40 p.m. There were 13 stations between the termini and trains could be boarded at cross streets in Spokane. Running times varied from one hour 50 minutes to two hours for the 34-mile trip, cars passing at Greenacres or Spokane Bridge. Long journey times resulted from delayed commissioning of substations needed to feed power to the line. New passenger stock ordered by the railway finally went into traffic on February 5, 1904. Each train consisted of a motor baggage and passenger car and a trailer.

Full electric supply became available by the end of May 1904. This enabled the fastest of six trains each way, introduced with the June 1904 timetable, to make the run in one hour. Trains subject to station flag stops required an hour and twenty minutes. Delivery of more stock allowed three-car consists when appropriate. On summer Sundays as many as twenty trains operated each way. Following the acceleration in timings, passenger loads increased, so that later that year the number of daily trains each way increased to nine. Local service between Spokane and Greenacres started in 1906. Several trains served Hayden Lake from Coeur d'Alene each day following the opening of this 8.2-mile extension on August 15, 1906. Motor baggage and express motorcars, which made three round trips per day to carry less than car-load merchandise to stations, accepted passengers during the first couple of years of operation – loose chairs were provided.

The Cd'A&S Railway and the Coeur d'Alene & St. Joe Transportation Company (the "Red Collar" line) jointly established rail/steamer service and fares between Spokane and Harrison and other steamer destinations from February 1, 1904. Journey time and fares were considerably less than competitors. The railway-owned, deep-water dock at Coeur d'Alene allowed railside access to the boat. The name "Shoshone Flyer" was given to the Spokane-Coeur d'Alene boat train in May 1904. Leaving Spokane at 9:00 am, it connected with the 10:00 a.m. lake steamer to Harrison to meet the OR&N train to Wallace. Once clear of Spokane, the train ran 31 miles

Before entering the cars ask the Ticket Agent or Conductor whether the train stops at the station to which you may be ticketed. There are stations at which some trains do not stop.

Freight is dispatched daily, except Sunday, from our freight depot, Market and Ferry, Spokane, at 11:15 a. m. and 5:20 p. m., for all points on Coeur d'Alene Lake, St. Maries and St. Joe. Freight should be at our depot 30 minutes before time for train to leave. No freight received after 5:00 p. m. Express business is carried on all passenger trains from the passenger depot.

Trains leaving or entering Spokane follow Main Avenue and will stop at the NEAR CROSSING of the following streets ONLY—Post, Howard, Washington, Division, Front, Sheridan, Perry and Crestline.

Fares Cannot be Adjusted by Conductors.—In the event of any disagreement with a conductor relative to tickets required, privileges allowed, etc., passengers should pay the conductor, take his receipt, and refer the case to the General Manager for adjustment. The conductor is governed by rules he cannot change.

Baggage Regulations. — Personal baggage not exceeding 150 pounds in weight will be checked to and from all stations, except East Spokane, upon presentation of one full passage ticket, 75 pounds on half ticket.

Personal baggage in excess of 150 pounds will be charged for in accordance with tariff furnished Agents, but no piece of baggage weighing more than 250 pounds will be received.

Bicycles and baby cabs will be checked when accompanied by owners. Each bicycle or carriage will be charged for at the rate of 25 cents, excepting locally within the State of Washington, where Bicycles only will be carried as other baggage and subject to charge for weight in excess of free allowance. Lamps and cyclometers must be removed before wheels will be checked.

Dogs will be carried in baggage cars at owner's risk, at a charge the same as for a passenger, but not to exceed 25 cents each.

Loaded firearms or guns not taken apart may not be taken into the passenger cars, but guns may be carried free in the baggage car, when accompanied by a passenger.

Large and cumbersome packages cannot be taken in the cars, but must be sent by freight or express.

FROM THE MOTORMAN'S WINDOW, SIX MILE TANGENT, IN THE SPOKANE VALLEY

The "SHOSHONE FLYER"

Leaving Spokane at 7:50 a. m. every day in the year, one of the fastest electric trains in the United States, makes the 34 miles in one hour and five minutes, and connects with the Steamers of the Coeur d'Alene & St. Joe Transportation Co. for Harrison and points on the O. R. & N. Ry. Co.'s lines in the famous Coeur d'Alene Mining Country. Also for St. Maries and St. Joe and all points on the Coeur d'Alene and St. Joe rivers. Returning it leaves Coeur d'Alene at 5:30 p. m., arriving at Spokane at 6:30 p. m. This train makes only one stop—at Post Falls.

In effect 5 a. m. Thursday, March 8, 1906.

PASSENGER TIME TABLE

This Folder, giving train time, is printed for general use and the utmost care is taken to keep it revised to date of issue; but the Company cannot guarantee perfect accuracy or hold itself responsible for any error, and reserves the right to deviate from or change the figures herein given without published notice.

For pamphlets, folders or information regarding special cars, etc., apply to the Traffic Department, Spokane Terminal Bldg., Lincoln and Main streets, Spokane, Wash.

R. F. BLACKWELL, Gen'l Mngr.
WALDO G. PAINE, Traffic Mngr.

Every day in the year, 7:50 a. m., to Harrison, Wardner, Wallace, Burke, Gem, and all points in the Coeur d'Alene Country. "Shoshone Flyer"

Coeur d'Alene & Spokane Ry. Co. Passenger Time Card No. 12

IN EFFECT 5 A.M. THURSDAY, MARCH 8TH, 1906.

WEST BOUND PASSENGER TRAINS. Leave Daily—Read Down   EAST BOUND PASSENGER TRAINS. Leave Daily—Read Up

17	33	15	19	11	31	9	7	5	3	1	STATIONS	2	4	6	8	10	30	12	14	32	16	18
9 15	5 30	4 35	3 15		1 15	11 25	10 00	8 30	6 20		lv COEUR d'ALENE ar	7 45	8 55	10 20	12 20	2 10		4 20	6 30		8 32	12 35
f 9 19		f 4 39	f 3 19		f 1 19	f 11 29	f 10 04	f 8 34	f 6 24		LA CROSSE	f 7 41		f 10 16	f 12 16	f 2 06		f 4 15	f 6 25		8 28	12 31
f 9 22		f 4 43	f 3 22		f 1 23	f 11 33	f 10 07	f 8 38	f 6 28		HUETTER	f 7 38		f 10 12	f 12 12	f 2 02		f 4 12	f 6 21		8 25	12 28
f 9 26		f 4 47	f 3 26		f 1 27	f 11 37	f 10 14	f 8 42	f 6 32		ROSS	f 7 34		f 10 08	f 12 08	Y 1 58		f 4 08	f 6 18		8 22	12 25
9 31	5 44	4 52	3 31		s 1 32	11 42	f 10 18	8 51	6 37		POST FALLS	7 29	8 41	10 03	12 03	1 53		4 03	6 13		8 17	12 20
f 9 34		f 4 55	f 3 34		f 1 35	11 45	f 10 21	8 54	6 40		McGUIRES	f 7 25		f 9 59	f 11 59	1 48		3 59	6 09		8 13	12 16
f 9 37						11 48			6 42		CUROE	f 7 22							6 06		8 10	12 13
f 9 41		f 5 02	f 3 40		f 1 41	11 50	f 10 27	f 9 00	6 46		SPOKANE BRIDGE	f 7 19		f 9 53	f 11 53	f 1 43		3 53	6 03		8 07	12 10
s 9 51	7 05	s 5 07	f 3 45		f 1 49	11 58	f 10 32	f 9 05	6 51		LIBERTY LAKE	f 7 14		f 9 47	f 11 47	f 1 38		3 47	5 52		8 01	12 05
9 54	7 09	s 5 12	s 3 53	2 15		s 12 03	10 37	s 9 10	6 56		GREENACRES	s 7 09		9 42	11 42		2 01	3 42	5 47	6 50	7 56	12 00
f 9 57	7 13	f 5 15	f 3 56	f 2 19		f 12 07	f 10 40	f 9 13	7 05		CARDERS	f 7 05		f 9 38	f 11 38		f 1 52	f 3 37	f 5 43	f 6 46	7 52	11 56
f 10 01	7 16	s 5 19	f 4 00	f 2 23		12 10	f 10 43	f 9 17	7 09		TRENT ROAD	f 7 02		f 9 34	f 11 34		f 1 48	f 3 33	f 5 39	f 6 42	7 48	11 52
f 10 03	7 18	s 5 23	f 4 04	f 2 26		12 12	f 10 46	f 9 21	7 12		N. P. SUBWAY	f 6 59		f 9 30	f 11 30		f 1 44	f 3 29	f 5 35	f 6 38	7 44	11 48
f 10 05	7 20	s 5 25	f 4 06	f 2 28		12 17	f 10 48	f 9 23	7 14		WOODWARDS	f 6 57		f 9 28	f 11 28		f 1 42	f 3 27	f 5 33	f 6 36	7 42	11 46
f 10 07	7 22	f 5 27	f 4 08	f 2 30		12 19	f 10 50	f 9 25	7 16		ORCHARD AVE	f 6 56		f 9 26	f 11 25		f 1 40	f 3 25	f 5 31	f 6 34	7 40	11 44
f 10 09	7 24	f 5 33	f 4 10	f 2 32		12 21	f 10 52	f 9 28	7 18		PARK AVE	f 6 53		f 9 24	f 11 23		f 1 38	f 3 23	f 5 28	f 6 32	7 38	11 42
f 10 12	7 27	f 5 35	f 4 12	f 2 34		12 23	f 10 54	f 9 30	7 20		WATERWORKS	f 6 51		f 9 22	f 11 21		f 1 36	f 3 21	f 5 26	f 6 30	7 35	11 40
		f 5 38	f 4 15	f 2 37		12 26	f 10 57	f 9 34	7 22		EAST SPOKANE	f 6 47		f 9 18	f 11 17		f 1 33	f 3 17	f 5 22	f 6 27	7 32	11 37
10 30	7 50	5 55	4 35	2 55	2 25	12 45	11 15	9 40	7 40	ar	lv SPOKANE	6 30	7 50	9 00	11 00		1 00	1 15	3 00	5 05	6 10	7 15	11 20
											Main and Lincoln											

WHERE NO TIME IS SHOWN, TRAINS DO NOT STOP.   THE COMPANY RESERVES THE RIGHT TO VARY FROM THE ABOVE SCHEDULE.   F—FLAG STATION.

Passenger timetable issued by Coeur d'Alene & Spokane Railway, March 8, 1906.

in 34 minutes, an average of 55 mph. Passengers for an earlier steamer to St. Joe river towns caught the 8:00 a.m. train from Spokane. The 1:10 p.m. train from Spokane connected with a third steamer, to Harrison and St. Maries. Matching connections between boat and train were made in the westbound direction. These integrated arrangements generated considerable revenue for the railway over several years.

New cars went into the "Shoshone Flyer" in June 1907: two motor coaches (200 hp each), a trailer coach and a parlor coach at the rear. Extra charge was made for travel in the parlor coach in a reserved seat attended by a uniformed porter. The 4-car consist made two daily round trips, running in the afternoon to Hayden Lake as the "Campers' Limited." During the winter months the load was reduced to three cars.

To connect with lake steamers, trains ran past the depot onto the dock at Coeur d'Alene. The "Idaho," owned by the Coeur d'Alene & St. Joe Transportation Company, made the morning sailing to Harrison for a number of years. Soon after the railway opened, two passenger trailer cars were inadvertently pushed over the end of the dock and into the lake. They were quickly rescued and sand bumpers installed.
(Museum of North Idaho Trr-1-5)

Thirteen trains ran daily from Spokane to Coeur d'Alene in 1907, practically making an hourly interval service between 8:00 a.m. and 7:00 pm, leaving Spokane mostly on the hour. Typical consists were a motor baggage and passenger car and one or two trailers, usually the latter. Seven made connections to Hayden Lake during the summer months, but reduced in number during the winter. Fares at that time were 2½ cents per mile for single journeys, compared to 3 cents on steam railroads, and commuter tickets reduced the fare by half.

The Liberty Lake branch extended 2.1 miles from Liberty Lake Junction, midway between Greenacres and Spokane Bridge stations. Opening day on June 15, 1907 coincided with the inauguration of the summer schedule on the Coeur d'Alene Division. Three trains ran from Spokane to Liberty Lake station; otherwise passengers changed at Liberty Lake Junction. Completion of the second track from Greenacres to Spokane Bridge allowed expansion of through services. In summer 1909 there were eight daily trains each way between Spokane and Liberty Lake and ten to Coeur d'Alene, several of which served Hayden Lake. During the winter months fewer trains ran to the resorts: three making the daily run to Liberty Lake, others turning around at Greenacres instead. The Annual Report for 1910 noted that the daily number of trains (including the Inland Division) increased from 50 to 60 during the summer months.

The Cd'A&S won a Railway Mail Service contract for railway post office operation between Spokane

COEUR D'ALENE & SPOKANE DIVISION
PASSENGER TIME CARD.

EAST BOUND — Sept. 15, 1912 — **READ DOWN**

STATIONS	No. 2 Lv AM	No. 8 Lv AM	No.10 Lv AM	No.12 Lv AM	No.14 Lv AM	No.16 Lv PM	No.18 Lv PM	No. 20 Lv PM	No. 22 Lv PM	No. 24 Lv PM	No. 26 Lv PM	No. 28 Lv PM	No. 30 Lv PM	No. 32 Lv PM
Spokane	*5 50	7 30	8 00	9 00	10 30	12 15	1 00	2 35	3 15	4 29	5 40	6 20	7 00	11 20
Spokane (Main & Wash.)	5 53	7 33	8 03	9 03	10 33	12 18	1 03	2 38	3 18	4 23	5 43	6 23	7 03	11 28
Waterworks	f 6 06	f 7 46		f 9 16	f10 47		f 1 17		f 3 32	f 4 36	f 5 37	f 6 37	f 7 16	f11 36
Del Monte	f 6 08	f 7 48		f 9 18	f10 49		f 1 19		f 3 34	f 4 38	f 5 58	f 6 38	f 7 18	f11 38
Orchard Ave.	f 6 10	f 7 49		f 9 20	f10 51	f 1 21		f 3 36	f 4 40	f 6 00	f 6 40	f 7 20	f11 40
Millwood	f 6 12	f 7 51		f 9 22	f10 53	[12 36	f 1 23		f 3 38	f 4 42	f 6 02	f 6 42	f 7 22	f11 43
N. P. Subway	f 6 18	f 7 52		f 9 23	f10 54		f 1 24		f 3 40	f 4 43	f 6 03	f 6 43	f 7 23	f11 45
Sullivan	f 6 15	f 7 54		f 9 25	f10 56		f 1 26		f 3 42	f 4 45	f 6 05	f 6 45	f 7 25	f11 47
Pinecroft	* 6 17	f 7 56		f 9 27	f10 58		f 1 28		f 3 44	f 4 47	f 6 07	f 6 47	f 7 27	f11 49
Carders	Ar AM	f 8 00		f 9 31	f11 02		f 1 32		f 3 49	f 4 51	f 6 11	f 6 51	f 7 31	f11 53
Flora		f 8 02		f 9 33	f11 05		f 1 35		f 3 52	f 4 53	f 6 13	f 6 53	f 7 33	f11 55
Greenacres		s 8 04		s 9 35	s11 07	f12 48	f 1 37		s 3 54	s 4 55	s 6 15	s 6 55	s 7 35	s11 57
Tolido				f 9 37	f11 09		f 1 40		f 3 56	f 4 58	f 6 18	f 6 58	f 7 36	f11 59
Liberty Lake Jct.				s 9 40	f11 11		f 1 42		4 00	f 5 00	f 6 20	7 00	f 7 40	f12 02
Seaton		f 8 09		Ar AM	f11 13		f 1 43		Ar PM	f 5 03	f 6 23	Ar AM	f 7 43	f12 05
Spokane Bridge		f 8 12			f11 15	f 1 00	f 1 45		s 5 07	s26 27		s 7 47	s12 08
Curoe		f 8 16			s11 20		f 1 49		f 5 09	f 6 30		f 7 49	f12 11
Signal Point		f 8 18			f11 23		f 1 52		f 5 12	f 6 33		f 7 53	f12 14
McGuires		f 8 22			f11 26		f 1 56		f 5 14	f 6 34		f 7 54	f12 16
Post Falls		f 8 23			f11 27		f 1 57		f 5 18	f 6 37		f 7 57	s12 19
Alan		f 8 26	s 8 45		s11 30	s 1 10	s 2 00	s 8 19	f 5 21	f 6 41		f 8 01	f12 23
Ross		f 8 30			f11 35		f 2 04		f 5 22	f 6 42		f 8 02	f12 24
Huetter		f 8 31			f11 36		f 2 05		f 5 25	f 6 45		f 8 05	f12 26
Atlas		f 8 36			f11 41		f 2 10		f 5 27	f 6 47		f 8 07	f12 28
Gibbs		f 8 38			f11 44		f 2 13		f 5 29	f 6 49		f 8 09	f12 30
Coeur d'Alene		f 8 41			f11 47		f 2 16		f 5 31	f 6 51		f 8 11	f12 32
		8 45	9 00		11 50	1 25	2 20	3 35	5 35	6 55		8 15	12 35
	No. 2	No. 8	No.10	No.12	*r AM	No 16	Ar PM	No. 20	Ar PM	Ar PM	No. 28	Ar PM	Ar AM
					No.14		No.18		No. 22	No. 24	No. 26		No. 30	No. 32

*Daily except Sunday. All other trains daily.
Nos. 10 and 20 make connections daily for Wallace, Wardner Burke and all points in Coeur d'Alene mines and St. Joe River country. Nos. 8, 13, 18, 23 carry U. S. Mail and Express. Nos. 10, 15, 20 and 29 carry a chair car.

COEUR D'ALENE & SPOKANE DIVISION
SEPT. 15, 1912
PASSENGER TIME CARD

WEST BOUND — Sept. 15, 1912 — **READ UP**

STATIONS	No. 1 Ar AM	No. 3 Ar AM	No. 9 Ar AM	No.11 Ar AM	No.13 Ar AM	No.15 Ar AM	No.17 Ar PM	No.21 Ar PM	No. 23 Ar PM	No. 25 Ar PM	No. 27 Ar PM	No. 29 Ar PM	No.31 Ar PM	No. 33 Ar PM
Spokane	* 6 45	7 45	9 00	10 35	11 15	11 55	2 15	3 45	4 55	6 15	6 30	7 40	7 55
Spokane (Main & Wash.)	6 40	7 40	8 55	10 30	11 10	11 50	2 10	3 40	4 40	4 50	6 10	6 25	7 35	7 50
Waterworks	f 6 29	f 7 28	f 8 43	f10 19		f 1 59	f 3 29		f 4 39	f 5 59		f 7 39
Del Monte	f 6 27	f 7 26	f 8 42	f10 17	f10 56	f 1 57	f 3 27		f 4 37	f 5 57		f 7 37
Orchard Avenue	f 6 25	f 7 25	f 8 40	f10 15	f10 55	f 1 55	f 3 25		f 4 36	f 5 56		f 7 35
Millwood	f 6 23	f 7 23	f 8 38	f10 13	f10 53	f 1 53	f 3 23		f 4 33	f 5 54		f 7 32
N. P. Subway	f 6 22	f 7 22	f 8 37	f10 12	f10 52	f 1 52	f 3 22		f 4 32	f 5 53		f 7 30
Sullivan	f 6 20	f 7 20	f 8 35	f10 10	f10 50	f 1 50	f 3 20		f 4 30	f 5 51		f 7 30
Pinecroft	* 6 18	f 7 18	f 8 33	f10 08	f10 48	f 1 48	f 3 19		f 4 28	f 5 49		f 7 28
Carders	Lv AM	f 7 14	f 8 29	f10 04	f10 44	f 1 44	f 3 15		f 4 24	f 5 45		f 7 24
Flora		f 7 12	f 8 27	f10 02	f10 42	f 1 42	f 3 13		f 4 22	f 5 42		f 7 22
Greenacres		s 7 10	s 8 25	s10 00	s10 40	s 1 40	s 3 11	s 4 14	f 4 20	s 5 41	s 7 07	f 7 21
Tolido		f 7 07	f 8 22	f 9 57	f10 37	f 1 37	f 3 08		f 4 17	f 5 38		f 7 17
Liberty Lake Jct.		f 7 05	f 8 20	s 9 55	f10 35	f 1 35	f 3 06		4 15	f 5 36		7 15
Seaton		f 6 50	f 8 17	Lv AM	f10 32	f 1 32	f 3 03	f 4 06	Lv PM	f 5 32		f 6 59
Spokane Bridge		s 6 47	s 8 13		s10 28	s 1 28	s 3 00	s 4 03		s 5 29		f 6 56
Curoe		f 6 44	f 8 10		f10 24	f 1 25	f 2 57	f 3 59		f 5 22		f 6 53
Signal Point		f 6 40	f 8 05		f10 21	f 1 22	f 2 54	f 3 56		f 5 21		f 6 48
McGuires		f 6 40	s 8 02		f10 21	f 1 21	f 2 53	f 3 55		f 5 21		f 6 48
Post Falls		f 6 37	s 8 02		s10 18	s11 13	f 1 18	s 2 50	s 3 52		s 5 18	s 5 47	f 6 45
Alan		f 6 33			f10 14		f 1 14	f 2 45	f 3 48		f 5 14		f 6 41
Ross		f 6 32	f 7 57		f10 13		f 1 13	f 2 44	f 3 47		f 5 13		f 6 37
Huetter		f 6 27	f 7 52		f10 08		f 1 08	f 2 38	f 3 42		f 5 08		f 6 35
Atlas		f 6 25	f 7 50		f10 06		f 1 06	f 2 36	f 3 40		f 5 05		f 6 35
Gibbs		f 6 23	f 7 48		f10 03		f 1 03	f 2 33	f 3 38		f 5 03		f 6 32
Coeur d'Alene		6 20	7 45		10 00	11 00	1 00	2 30	3 35		5 00	5 35	6 30
	Lv AM	Lv AM	Lv AM		Lv AM	Lv AM	Lv PM	Lv PM	Lv PM		Lv PM	Lv PM
	No. 1	No. 3	No. 9	No.11	No.13	No.15	No.17	No.21	No. 23	No. 25	No. 27	No. 29	No.31	No. 33

*Daily except Sunday. All other trains daily.

Timetable issued for Coeur d'Alene line passenger services, September 1912.

Mail train leaving Greenacres consisted of motor baggage and mail car No .27, motor baggage and passenger car No. 11 and trailer No. 68. (Ted Holloway Collection)

and Coeur d'Alene. Contract requirements called for similar service to that on steam lines, with a post office clerk in charge. Service began on June 3, 1907 with two round trips daily, operating as passenger trains hauled by a motor baggage and mail car. Departures from Spokane were 6:40 a.m. and 1:10 p.m., returning from Coeur d'Alene at 9:40 a.m. and 6:40 p.m. Based on data for 1925, the morning trip required a motor baggage and mail car with a 15-foot RPO compartment while a shorter RPO sufficed for the afternoon duty. Between July 1915 and April 1917, an RPO car worked through to Hayden Lake. Mail cranes were installed at Millwood and Spokane Bridge for nonstop mail exchange.

Following double tracking between Spokane and Spokane Bridge, the feasibility of reducing the journey time to 40 minutes was examined. Faster time by the OWR&N to Harrison was the stimulus, the S&IE boat train having to leave Spokane at least an hour earlier to make connection. The best time that resulted was 55 minutes, made by two trains from Coeur d'Alene.

Passenger loads began to diminish on the main line as road competition increased. The timetable began to reflect this lower demand. Thus, in summer 1917 there were seven departures daily from Spokane to Coeur d'Alene and a similar number to Liberty Lake. By 1919 the service had decreased to five and six, respectively. Most of the Coeur d'Alene trains earned an average of less than $1 per mile and the rest of them generated little more.

After Spokane & Eastern management assumed control, they increased the number of trains in an attempt to attract passengers. There were eleven round trips daily to Coeur d'Alene, five of which served Hayden Lake. Nevertheless, by the time SC&P took over, introduction of regular

FIRST SUBDIVISION—HAYDEN LAKE AND SPOKANE

WESTWARD — FIRST CLASS | Time Table No. 1 — Effective May 29, 1927 | **EASTWARD** — FIRST CLASS

15	13	11	9	7	5	3	1	Car Cap. of Sidings	Station Numbers	STATIONS	Dist. from Spokane	Tel. Calls	Signs	2	4	6	8	10	12	14	16
Pass.	Pass.	Pass.	Pass.	Pass.	Pass.	Pass.	Pass.							Pass.	Pass.	Pass.	Pass.	Pass.	Pass.	Pass.	Pass.
Daily	Daily	Daily	Daily	Daily	Daily	Daily	Daily Ex. Sun.							Daily Ex. Sun.	Daily	Daily	Daily	Daily	Daily	Daily	Daily
			L 8.45					18	C40	HAYDEN LAKE	39.70	HN	D Loop		A 8.45						
			f 8.48					10	C39	HONEYSUCKLE FARMS	38.18				f 8.41						
			f 8.51					17	C37	DALTON	36.45				f 8.38						
			f 8.57						C34-A	WOODLAWN	33.56				f 8.33						
		L 4.20	9.05					66	102	C32	COEUR D'ALENE	31.74	CA Agent	D Y K		8.25 / 8.20		A 2.20				
		f 4.24	f 9.09					36	C31	GIBBS	30.94		O K		f 8.16		f 2.16				
		f 4.26	f 9.11					86	C30	ATLAS	29.15		K		f 8.14		f 2.13				
		f 4.28	f 9.13					10	C29	HUETTER	27.91				f 8.12		f 2.11				
		f 4.30	f 9.15					9	C28	McCLELLAN	27.56				f 8.11		f 2.10				
		f 4.33	f 9.18					9	C26-A	ROSS	26.75				f 8.07		f 2.07				
		f 4.34	f 9.19					27	C26	ALAN	26.14				f 8.06		f 2.06				
		f 4.37	f 9.22					16	C24	POST FALLS	23.27	PF			f 8.02		f 2.03				
		f 4.39	f 9.24					21	C22	McGUIRES	21.73		K		f 7.59		f 2.01				
		f 4.41	f 9.26						C21	SIGNAL POINT	20.59				f 7.57		f 1.59				
		f 4.43	f 9.28						C20	CUROZ	19.48				f 7.55		f 1.57				
		f 4.45	f 9.30					26	18	C19	SPOKANE BRIDGE	18.39				f 7.53		f 1.55				
		f 4.48	f 9.32						C17	SEATON	16.76				f 7.50		f 1.52				
									L2	LIBERTY LAKE	16.86	B Y	Loop							
		f 4.53	f 9.35						C16	LIBERTY LAKE JCT.	14.92		Y		f 7.47		f 1.49				
		f 4.57	f 9.39					20	C15-B	GREENACRES	12.65	SubSta. G R			f 7.41		f 1.44				
		f 4.58	f 9.40					9	C13	FLORA	11.93				f 7.38		f 1.43				
		f 5.00	f 9.42					5	C12	CARDERS	10.90				f 7.36		f 1.41				
L 6.50	5.45	f 5.03	L 4.14	9.45	L 8.21	L 7.15		5	C10	PINECROFT	8.88			A 7.13	7.32	A 8.21	f 1.38	A 4.12	A 5.44	A 6.48
f 6.51	f 5.46	f 5.04	f 4.15	9.46	8.22	7.16			C9	SULLIVAN	8.07			f 7.11	7.30	8.19	f 1.36	4.10	f 5.42	6.46
f 6.53	f 5.48	f 5.06	f 4.17	9.48	8.24	7.18	L 6.27		C8	N. P. SUBWAY	7.15		A 6.26	f 7.10	7.28	8.18	f 1.34	4.09	f 5.41	6.45
f 6.54	f 5.49	f 5.09	f 4.18	9.50	8.26	7.21	6.30	2	C7	MILLWOOD	6.60			6.24	7.09	7.27	8.17	f 1.33	4.08	f 5.40	6.44
f 6.55	f 5.51	f 5.11	f 4.20	9.52	8.28	7.24	6.33	15	C6	ORCHARD AVE.	5.59			f 6.21	7.06	7.24	8.15	f 1.31	4.06	f 5.38	6.42
f 6.57	f 5.52	f 5.13	f 4.21	9.54	8.30	7.26	6.35		C3-A	DEL MONTE	4.80			6.18	7.04	7.22	8.14	f 1.30	4.05	f 5.36	6.41
f 6.59	f 5.53	f 5.16	f 4.23	9.56	8.32	7.29	6.37	3	C3	PARKWATER	4.17			f 6.17	7.03	7.20	8.13	f 1.28	4.04	f 5.34	6.39
								100	C2	O.-W. R. & N. CROSSING	1.69		1 K								
f 7.07	f 6.00	5.24	f 4.30	10.04	f 8.40	7.38	6.43	30	N2	INLAND JCT.	.94		Y	6.11	6.56	7.12	8.06	1.20	3.56	f 5.26	6.31
f 7.08	f 6.01	5.25	f 4.31	10.05	8.41	7.39	6.44	25		SHOPS	.80		Y	6.10	6.55	7.11	8.05	1.19	3.55	5.25	6.30

TRAINS WILL BE GOVERNED BY SPOKANE DIV. TIME TABLE BETWEEN CONNECTION WITH G. N. RY. TRACKS AND PASSENGER DEPOT

A 7.15	A 6.05	A 5.30	4.35	A 10.15	A 8.45	A 7.45	A 6.50	Yard	B O	SPOKANE	0.00	DS	DN K	L 6.05	L 6.50	L 7.05	L 8.00	L 1.10	L 3.50	L 5.20	L 6.25
15	13	11	9	7	5	3	1							2	4	6	8	10	12	14	16
Daily	Daily	Daily	Daily	Daily	Daily	Daily	Daily Ex. Sun.			Time Over District / Average Speed per Hour				Daily Ex. Sun.	Daily	Daily	Daily	Daily	Daily	Daily	Daily
0.25 / 22.90	0.20 / 26.40	1.10 / 27.70	0.21 / 25.14	1 / 36.90	0.24 / 23.94	0.30 / 19.10	0.23 / 24.93							0.21 / 25.14	0.22 / 26.40	1.40 / 22.90	0.21 / 23.14	1.10 / 27.70	0.22 / 21.30	0.24 / 23.94	0.22 / 24.93

SPECIAL RULES
Eastward trains are superior to Westward trains of the same class.

All Passenger Trains will stop on flag at:

Crestline Street .... Mile Post 1.69	Wilbur Road .... Mile Post 8.48	Pennsylvania Avenue, Coeur d'Alene
Nelson Street .... Mile Post 2.25	Mount View .... Mile Post 9.75	Homes .... Mile Post 30.75
Union Stock Yards .... Mile Post 2.77	Tolido .... Mile Post 13.94	Johnsons .... Mile Post 34.58
Esperance .... Mile Post 3.66	Green Ferry Road .... Mile Post 24.80	Gun Club Grounds .... Mile Post 35.60
Air Port .... Mile Post 4.54	Fourth Street, Coeur d'Alene	South Dalton .... Mile Post 36.11
Regon .... Mile Post 6.10	Eighth Street, Coeur d'Alene	North Dalton .... Mile Post 37.11
	Sherman Street, Coeur d'Alene	

FOURTH SUBDIVISION—SPOKANE AND LIBERTY LAKE

WESTWARD — FIRST CLASS | Time Table No. 1 — Effective May 29, 1927 | **EASTWARD** — FIRST CLASS

117	115	113	111	109	107	105	103	Cap. of Sidings, Wyes, Loop	Telep. Rings	Telg. Calls	STATIONS	Dist. from Station	Station No.	102	104	106	108	110	112	114	116
Pass.	Pass.	Pass.	Pass.	Pass.	Pass.	Pass.	Pass.							Pass.	Pass.	Pass.	Pass.	Pass.	Pass.	Pass.	Pass.
Daily	Daily	Daily	Daily Ex. Sat. & Sun.	Daily	Daily	Daily	Daily Ex. Sun.							Daily Ex. Sun.	Daily	Daily	Daily	Daily Ex. Sat. & Sun.	Daily	Daily	Daily
		L 5.02			L 7.50			Loop 8	oo-	By	LIBERTY LAKE	16.70	V 17		A 7.45				A 5.00		
		f 5.04			f 7.52						LIBERTY HOME	16.16			f 7.43				f 4.58		
		f 5.07			f 7.55			Y			LIBERTY LAKE JCT.	14.76	V 15		f 7.40				f 4.55		
		f 5.09			f 7.57						TOLIDO	13.78			f 7.38				f 4.53		
L 7.18	L 6.18	f 5.13	L 4.02	N 9.00	8.00	L 7.00		20	-ooo	G R	GREENACRES	12.49	V 13	A 6.50	7.35	A 8.49	A 3.50	4.50	A 6.06	A 7.08	
f 7.20	f 6.20	f 5.14	f 4.04	f 9.03	8.02	f 7.02	L 5.53	Y			FLORA	11.75	V 12	5.50	f 6.48	7.33	8.47	3.48	4.48	6.04	7.06
f 7.23	f 6.23	f 5.18	f 4.07	f 9.05	8.05	f 7.05	5.56	20			VERA	10.35	V 11	5.47	f 6.45	7.30	8.44	3.45	4.45	6.01	7.03
f 7.25	f 6.25	f 5.20	f 4.09	f 9.07	8.07	f 7.07	5.58				MANCHESTER	9.51		5.46	f 6.44	7.29	8.43	3.44	4.44	6.00	7.02
f 7.27	f 6.27	f 5.22	f 4.11	f 9.09	8.09	f 7.09	6.00				STATION 16	9.03		5.44	f 6.42	7.27	8.41	3.42	4.42	5.58	6.59
f 7.28	f 6.28	f 5.24	f 4.12	f 9.11	8.11	f 7.11	6.02	20		Y	OPPORTUNITY	8.52	V 9	5.42	f 6.40	7.25	8.39	3.40	4.40	5.56	6.57
f 7.30	f 6.30	f 5.26	f 4.14	f 9.12	8.13	f 7.13	6.04				BOWDISH	8.05		5.41	f 6.38	7.23	8.37	3.38	4.38	5.54	6.55
f 7.32	f 6.32	f 5.28	f 4.16	f 9.14	8.15	f 7.15	6.05	8			APPLE CENTER	7.51	V 8	5.39	f 6.36	7.21	8.35	3.36	4.36	5.52	6.53
f 7.34	f 6.34	f 5.30	f 4.18	f 9.16	8.17	f 7.17	6.07				FARR	6.89		5.37	f 6.34	7.19	8.33	3.34	4.34	5.50	6.51
f 7.35	f 6.35	f 5.32	f 4.19	f 9.18	8.18	7.18	6.08	11			DISHMAN	6.44	V 7	5.36	6.33	7.18	8.32	3.33	4.33	5.49	6.50
f 7.37	f 6.37	f 5.34	f 4.21	f 9.21	8.20	7.20	6.10	19			SPEAR	5.75	V 6	5.34	6.31	7.16	8.30	3.31	4.31	5.47	6.48
f 7.38	f 6.38	f 5.35	f 4.22	f 9.22	8.21	7.21	6.11				EDGECLIFF	5.45		5.33	6.30	7.15	8.29	3.30	4.30	5.46	6.47
f 7.40	f 6.40	f 5.37	f 4.24	f 9.24	8.23	7.23	6.13				KAY	4.67		5.31	6.28	7.13	8.27	3.28	4.28	5.44	6.44
f 7.42	6.42	f 5.42	f 4.26	f 9.26	8.25	7.25	6.15	4			GRANITE POINT	2.90		5.29	6.26	7.11	8.25	3.26	4.26	5.42	6.42
f 7.44	f 6.44	f 5.44	f 4.28	f 9.28	8.27	f 7.27	6.17				NEW STOP	3.40		5.27	6.24	7.09	8.20	3.24	4.24	5.41	6.41
f 7.47	f 6.47	f 5.47	f 4.31	f 9.31	8.30	7.30	6.21				GREEN STREET	2.55		6.21	7.06	8.17	3.21	4.21	5.38	6.38	
L 7.52	L 6.52	L 5.52	f 4.39	f 9.39	f 8.38	7.38	6.27	80			SHOPS	.80		L 6.15	6.13	6.58	8.07	3.13	4.13	5.30	6.30

TRAINS WILL BE GOVERNED BY SPOKANE DIV. TIME TABLE BETWEEN CONNECTION WITH G. N. RY. TRACKS AND PASSENGER DEPOT

A 7.57	A 6.57	A 5.57	4.45	A 9.45	A 8.43	A 7.46	A 6.35	Loop Yard	—	DS	SPOKANE	0.00	B O	L 6.05	L 6.50	L 8.00	3.05	4.05	L 5.25	L 6.25	
117	115	113	111	109	107	105	103							102	104	106	108	110	112	114	116
Daily	Daily	Daily	Daily Ex. Sat. & Sun.	Daily	Daily	Daily	Daily Ex. Sun.			Time Over District / Average Speed per Hour				Daily Ex. Sun.	Daily	Daily	Daily	Daily Ex. Sat. & Sun.	Daily	Daily	Daily
0.39 / 21.19	0.39 / 21.19	0.55 / 18.95	0.43 / 17.30	0.43 / 17.30	0.50 / 15.61	0.46 / 17.16	0.52 / 17.74							0.55 / 18.75	0.45 / 17.55	0.55 / 18.95	0.49 / 15.20	0.58 / 17.55	0.58 / 18.95	0.41 / 17.85	0.43 / 17.55

Eastward trains are superior to Westward trains of the same class.

Spokane, Coeur d'Alene & Palouse employee timetable May 29, 1927
for the Coeur d'Alene and associated DC lines

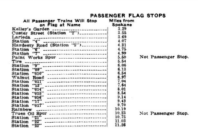

PASSENGER FLAG STOPS

All Passenger Trains Will Stop on Flag at Name	Miles from Spokane	
Kelley's Garden	2.25	
Custer Street (Station "2")	2.55	
Larieda	2.69	
Station "4"	4.07	
Hardesty Road (Station "5")	4.31	
Station "6"	4.75	
Station "8"	4.99	
Paint Works Spur	5.50	Not Passenger Stop.
Tire	5.54	
Station "9"	6.06	
Station "89"	6.12	
Station "010"	6.54	
Walnut Road	6.97	
Station "011"	7.64	
Station "12"	7.94	
Station "014"	8.01	
Station "015"	8.54	
Station "034"	9.14	
Station "17"	9.43	
Station "017"	9.70	
Rainbow	10.19	
Truex Oil Spur	10.23	Not Passenger Stop.
Station "21"	10.75	
Station "22"	11.02	
Station "23"	11.26	

Last passenger service on the Coeur d'Alene line at Helena Street, Spokane on July 13, 1940. (Clyde Parent, Michael J. Denuty Collection)

bus service had practically wiped out the railway passenger business. Coeur d'Alene service was soon reduced to two daily trains each way, rerouted to the GN depot in Spokane instead of the terminal at Lincoln and Main. Several local trains operating in the Spokane area were eliminated. Liberty Lake lost its passenger service on June 20, 1927. Hayden Lake line passenger trains were withdrawn March 31, 1929, although a few excursions ran afterwards.

Starting in 1935 the number of Coeur d'Alene daily round trips increased to three for a while – two sufficed by 1940. A consist of a motor baggage and mail car and trailer was all that was usually required to carry the meager loads during the final years; a motor passenger car was added when necessary. In rejecting protests against notice of abandonment of passenger service on the Coeur d'Alene Division, the Washington Department of Public Service concluded that it was not a public necessity and that discontinuance would cause little, if any, inconvenience to the traveling or shipping public. The last SC&P passenger train ran July 13, 1940, the 4:30 p.m. from Coeur d'Alene arriving 5:40 p.m. at the Spokane GN depot. Motor baggage and mail car No. 20 headed the train with engineer C.L. Jones and conductor Tom R. Smith.

Coeur d'Alene-Spokane

Read Down — Read Up

11 Daily	9 Daily	7 Daily	Mls	STATIONS	8 Daily	10 Daily	12 Daily	Fares to Spokane 1way	Rtrn
3:55	9:05	6:20	.0	Lv Coeur d'Alene Ar	8:50	2:20	6:20	$.45	$.70
3:59	9:09	6:24	1.5	Gibbs	8:46	2:16	6:16	.43	.65
4:01	9:11	6:26	2.6	Atlas	8:44	2:13	6:13	.42	.65
4:03	9:13	6:28	3.8	Huetter	8:42	2:11	6:11	.40	.60
4:05	9:15	6:30	4.1	McClellan	8:41	2:10	6:10	.39	.60
4:08	9:18	6:33	6.0	Ross	8:37	2:07	6:07	.37	.60
4:09	9:19	6:34	6.6	Alan	8:36	2:06	6:06	.36	.55
s4:12	s 9:22	s6:37	8.5	Post Falls	s8:32	s2:03	s6:03	.33	.50
4:14	9:24	6:39	10.0	McGuires	8:29	2:01	6:01	.31	.50
4:16	9:26	6:41	11.1	Signal Point	8:27	1:59	5:59	.30	.45
4:20	9:30	6:45	13.5	Spokane Bridge	8:23	1:55	5:55	.27	.45
4:22	9:32	6:47	15.0	Seaton	8:20	1:52	5:52	.24	.40
s4:30	s 9:39	s6:55	19.1	Greenacres	s8:11	s1:44	s5:44	.19	.30
4:31	9:40	6:56	19.8	Flora	8:08	1:43	5:43	.18	.30
4:33	9:42	6:58	20.9	Garders	8:06	1:40	5:40	.16	.25
4:36	9:45	7:01	22.9	Pinecroft	8:02	1:37	5:37	.13	.20
4:36	9:45	7:01	23.3	Wilbur Road	8:02	1:37	5:37	.13	.20
4:37	9:46	7:02	23.7	Sullivan	8:00	1:34	5:34	.12	.20
4:39	9:48	7:04	24.6	N. P. Subway	7:58	1:32	5:32	.12	.20
4:42	9:50	7:07	25.1	Millwood	7:57	1:31	5:31	.10	.15
4:43	9:51	7:08	25.6	Regon	7:56	1:30	5:30	.10	.15
4:44	9:52	7:09	26.2	Orchard Ave.	7:54	1:29	5:29	.10	.15
4:46	9:54	7:11	27.0	Del Monte	7:52	1:27	5:27	.10	.15
4:47	9:55	7:12	27.2	Air Port	7:51	1:26	5:26	.10	.15
4:49	9:56	7:14	27.6	Parkwater	7:50	1:25	5:25	.10	.15
4:50	9:57	7:15	28.1	Esperence	7:49	1:24	5:24	.10	.15
5:05	10:15	7:30	32.0	Ar Spokane Lv	7:35	1:10	5:10		

Lightface type A. M.
Blackface type P. M.

S—Regular Stop.
All other stations are flag stops.

Return Tickets carry final limit of 25 days.
Children 5-12 years, half fare.
150 lbs. of free baggage.

SPOKANE-COLFAX

Mls	STATIONS		Mls	STATIONS	
.0	Spokane, Wn.		58.2	Cashup	
39.4	Spring Valley		60.4	Bankson	
40.9	Rollins		63.0	Steptoe	
44.1	Rosalia		64.9	Blackwell	
46.5	Early		68.0	Rye	
48.9	Balder		69.5	Manning	
49.3	Harris		73.1	Lincoln	
50.7	Stoneham		75.1	Colfax	
53.7	Thornton				

Spokane, Coeur d'Alene & Palouse Railway April 1935 timetable.

On the Opportunity/Vera line, the Traction Division offered hourly service between 6:05 a.m. and 7:05 pm, less frequently at later hours. Small cars transferred from the Coeur d'Alene Division usually performed these duties and a motor baggage car made three round trips over the branch to carry express merchandise. Following the sale of the Traction Division in 1922, the S&E retained the Vera/Opportunity tracks and ran the trains through to Liberty Lake. This gave unprecedented service frequency to this station, although the numerous stops on this route incurred a journey time of one hour, a 15-minute penalty compared to the main line route. However, the ICC found that few passengers used the trains. Passenger service over the line was abandoned on June 20, 1927.

Inland Lines

Spokane & Inland Railway lines opened incrementally as detailed in Chapter 3. The system was finally complete on September 15, 1908, when the Palouse-Moscow section opened to traffic. Three services were provided each way between Spokane and Moscow and the same number to Colfax. In addition, there was an early morning train from Rosalia to Spokane, balanced by an evening return. Fastest time for the 90 miles to Moscow was 3 hours 5 minutes. Corresponding time to Colfax (76.7 miles) was two hours 40 minutes. Expresses ran nonstop over the Spokane-Spring Valley section, but the practice ceased by 1912. Four local trains supplemented the service to communities along a 19-mile stretch between Spokane and Freeman. Commuters to Spokane were adequately served with a morning train and three evening departures from Spokane between 5:00 p.m. and 6:15 p.m.

A circa 1909 view of S&I train No. 10 passing Spokane frequency reduction station. The three-car consist was a motor baggage and passenger car, motor passenger car and a trailer. (D. Cozine Collection)

SPOKANE & INLAND DIVISION
PASSENGER TIME CARD

SOUTH BOUND   Daily   Read Down   SEPT. 15, 1912   **NORTH BOUND**   Daily   Read Up

No. 76 Lv PM	No. 74 Lv PM	No. 72 Lv PM	No. 70 Lv PM	No. 68 Lv PM	No. 66 Lv AM	No. 64 Lv AM	No. 62 Lv AM	STATIONS	No. 63 Ar AM	No. 65 Ar AM	No. 67 Ar AM	No. 69 Ar AM	No. 71 Ar PM	No. 73 Ar PM	No. 75 Ar PM	No. 77 Ar PM
6 15	5 10	4 15	12 55	12 10	10 05	8 30	8 00	*Spokane	7 48	10 30	11 25	11 50	2 58	3 22	6 35	6 50
s 6 29	s 5 22	s 4 28	s 1 08	s12 23	s10 17	s 8 42	s 8 12	Third Ave	s 7 34	s10 15	s11 13	s11 38	s 2 46	s 3 10	s 6 22	s 6 42
f 6 35	f 5 28	f 4 34	f 1 12	....	f10 21	....	f 8 16	Tudor	f 7 29	f10 10	....	f11 33	f 2 41	....	....	f 6 38
f 6 38	f 5 30	f 4 37	f 1 14	....	f10 24	....	f 8 18	Pantops	f 7 27	f10 08	....	f11 31	f 2 39	....	....	f 6 36
f 6 39	f 5 32	f 4 39	f 1 16	....	f10 26	....	f 8 19	Glenrose	f 7 26	f10 07	....	f11 30	f 2 35	....	....	f 6 35
f 6 41	f 5 34	f 4 41	f 1 18	....	f10 28	....	f 8 20	Pine Grove	f 7 25	f10 05	....	f11 29	f 2 37	....	....	f 6 34
f 6 44	f 5 38	f 4 44	f 1 20	....	f10 31	....	f 8 23	Moran	f 7 22	f10 02	....	f11 26	f 2 34	....	....	f 6 31
f 6 46	f 5 40	f 4 46	f 1 21	....	f10 33	....	f 8 24	Piedmont	f 7 20	f10 00	....	f11 24	f 2 32	....	....	f 6 30
f 6 48	f 5 42	f 4 48	f 1 23	....	f10 35	....	f 8 26	Park View	f 7 18	f 9 58	....	f11 22	f 2 30	f 2 59	....	f 6 28
f 6 50	f 5 45	f 4 50	f 1 26	....	f10 36	....	f 8 28	Hillby	f 7 16	f 9 56	....	f11 20	f 2 28	....	....	f 6 26
f 6 51	f 5 46	f 4 51	f 1 27	....	f10 37	....	f 8 29	Willow Springs	f 7 15	f 9 55	....	f11 19	f 2 27	....	....	f 6 25
f 6 52	f 5 48	f 4 53	f 1 29	....	f10 38	....	f 8 31	Silver Hill	f 7 13	f 9 53	....	f11 17	f 2 25	....	....	f 6 24
s 6 54	s 5 51	s 4 55	s 1 32	f12 42	s10 41	....	s 8 33	Kiesling	s 7 11	s 9 50	....	s11 15	s 2 22	....	....	s 6 22
f 6 56	f 5 54	f 4 57	f 1 34	....	f10 42	....	f 8 35	Sharon	f 7 08	f 9 48	....	f11 12	f 2 20	....	....	f 6 20
f 6 58	f 5 56	f 4 59	f 1 36	....	f10 45	....	f 8 37	Belair	f 7 05	f 9 46	....	f11 10	f 2 18	....	....	f 6 18
f 6 59	f 5 57	f 5 00	f 1 37	....	f10 46	....	f 8 38	Kennerwood	f 7 04	f 9 45	....	f11 09	f 2 17	....	....	f 6 17
f 7 00	f 5 59	f 5 01	f 1 38	....	f10 47	....	f 8 39	Excelsior	f 7 03	f 9 44	....	f11 08	f 2 16	....	....	f 6 16
s 7 04	s 6 03	s 5 05	s 1 41	f12 50	s10 51	....	s 8 43	Valleyford	s 7 00	s 9 40	....	s11 05	s 2 13	....	f 5 56	f 6 13
f 7 05	f 6 04	f 5 07	f 1 42	....	f10 52	....	f 8 44	Larkin	f 6 58	f 9 39	....	f11 03	f 2 11	....	....	f 6 11
f 7 06	f 6 05	f 5 09	f 1 43	....	f10 53	....	f 8 46	Rubeck	f 6 57	f 9 37	....	f11 02	f 2 10	....	....	f 6 10
f 7 09	s 6 08	s 5 11	s 1 46	f12 54	10 55	....	s 8 48	*Freeman	s 6 55	s 9 35	s10 38	11 00	s 2 08	....	....	s 6 08
f 7 13	f 6 13			f12 58		f 9 19		Ochlare	f 6 50		f10 33	Lv AM	f 2 35	f 2 39	s 5 52	f 6 03
s 7 20	s 6 19	f 5 23	f 1 57	s 1 05		s 9 25	f 8 59	Mt. Hope	s 6 43	f 9 25	s10 26		s 2 29	s 2 29	f 5 41	s 5 56
f 7 23	f 6 22			f 1 07		f 9 28		Treat	f 6 41		f10 23		f 2 26	f 2 26		f 5 53
f 7 26	f 6 24			f 1 11		f 9 31		Rattlers Run	f 6 38		f10 20		f 2 24	f 2 24		f 5 49
f 7 28	f 6 26			f 1 14		f 9 33		Lenox	f 6 36		f10 18		f 2 22	f 2 22		f 5 48
f 7 31	f 6 29	f 5 32		f 1 16		f 9 36	f 9 10	W. Fairfield	f 6 33	f 9 10	f10 15		f 2 20	f 2 20		f 5 45
f 7 34	f 6 32			f 1 19		f 9 39		Saline	f 6 30		f10 12		f 2 18	f 2 18		f 5 42
f 7 35	f 6 34			f 1 21		f 9 42		Russ	f 6 28		f10 09		f 2 16	f 2 16		f 5 40
s 7 38	s 6 36	f 5 38	f 2 14	s 1 24		s 9 43	f 9 19	Waverly	s 6 26		s10 08		s 2 14	s 2 14		s 5 38
f 7 40	f 6 38							Clifton	f 6 24							
f 7 43	f 6 41			f 1 28		f 9 48		Jefferson	f 6 21		f10 02			f 2 07		f 5 33
7 50	6 48	5 50	2 25	1 35		9 55	9 33	Spring Valley	6 13	8 50	9 55		1 25	1 58	6 13	5 25
	5 50			1 35			9 33	Spring Valley			9 55			1 55		
	f 5 55			f 1 39			9 39	Konah			f 9 49			f 1 49	f 5 07	
	s 6 01			s 1 44			9 45	Fairbanks			s 9 45			s 1 44	s 5 02	
	f 6 05			f 1 48			9 50	Seabury			f 9 40			f 1 40	f 4 58	
	f 6 10			f 1 52			9 55	Geary			f 9 34			f 1 35	f 4 53	
	f 6 12			f 1 55			9 58	Dan			f 9 31			f 1 30	f 4 48	
	s 6 17			s 1 58			s10 02	Oakesdale			s 9 27			s 1 28	s 4 46	
	f 6 20			f 2 02			f10 06	Davidson			f 9 22			f 1 22	f 4 40	
	f 6 24			f 2 04			f10 08	Robinson			f 9 20			f 1 20	f 4 38	
	f 6 26			f 2 06			f10 11	Sokulk			f 9 17			f 1 18	f 4 36	
	f 6 30			f 2 10			f10 16	Elmer			f 9 12			f 1 14	f 4 32	
	f 6 32			f 2 12			f10 18	Crabtree			f 9 09			f 1 12	f 4 29	
	f 6 33			f 2 13			f10 19	Coberly			f 9 02			f 1 11	f 4 28	
	s 6 40			s 2 20			s10 26	Garfield			s 9 01			s 1 04	s 4 22	
	f 6 50			f 2 30			f10 35	Ladow			f 8 52			f12 55	f 4 14	
	f 6 54			f 2 34			f10 40	Grinnell			f 8 47			f12 50	f 4 09	
	f 6 59			f 2 39			f10 44	Horn			f 8 42			f12 45	f 4 04	
	s 7 05			s 2 45			s10 50	Palouse			s 8 37			s12 40	s 3 59	
	f 7 06			f 2 46			f10 51	Pottery			f 8 31			f12 39	f 3 54	
	f 7 11			f 2 51			f10 56	Ringo			f 8 30			f12 33	f 3 53	
	f 7 12			f 2 52			f10 58	Cove			f 8 27			f12 31	f 3 51	
	f 7 18			f 2 58			f11 03	Viola			f 8 22			f12 26	f 3 46	
	f 7 21			f 3 01			f11 06	Poe			f 8 19			f12 23	f 3 43	
	f 7 24			f 3 04			f11 10	Ayer			f 8 15			f12 20	f 3 40	
	f 7 27			f 3 07			f11 13	Estes			f 8 11			f12 17	f 3 37	
	f 7 29			f 3 09			f11 15	Ferris			f 8 09			f12 13	f 3 33	
	7 35			3 15			11 20	Moscow			8 05			12 10	3 30	

No. 76	No. 74	No. 72 Ar PM	No. 70 Ar PM	No. 68	No. 66	No. 64 Ar AM	No. 62 Ar AM		No. 63	No. 65 Lv AM	No. 67	No. 69	No. 71 Lv PM	No. 73 Lv PM	No. 75 Lv PM	No. 77
7 50	6 48	Ar PM	2 25		9 55	Ar AM		Spring Valley	6 13	8 50	Lv AM		1 25	Lv PM	Lv PM	5 25
f 7 55	f 6 53	f 2 30		f10 00				Rollins	f 6 06	f 8 43			f 1 18			f 5 18
8 02		s 2 36		s10 07				Rosalia	6 00	s 8 36			s 1 11			s 5 10
Ar PM	f 7 02	f 2 38		f10 09				Broadview Farms	Lv AM	f 8 30			f 1 09			f 5 07
	f 7 05	f 2 41		f10 11				Earley		f 8 25			f 1 06			f 5 03
	f 7 09	f 2 45		f10 16				Balder		f 8 20			f 1 02			f 4 59
	f 7 10	f 2 47		f10 17				Harris		f 8 19			f 1 01			f 4 57
	f 7 13	f 2 49		f10 20				Stoneham		f 8 17			f12 58			f 4 56
	f 7 16	f 2 52		f10 22				Trestle Creek		f 8 14			f12 55			f 4 53
	s 7 19	s 2 55		s10 26				Thornton		s 8 11			s12 52			s 4 49
	f 7 25	f 3 01		f10 32				Barnes		f 8 04			f12 45			f 4 42
	f 7 28	f 3 04		f10 35				Cashup		f 8 02			f12 43			f 4 40
	f 7 30	f 3 05		f10 36				Lynn		f 8 00			f12 42			f 4 38
	f 7 33	f 3 08		f10 40				Bankson		f 7 58			f12 39			f 4 36
	f 7 38	f 3 13		f10 45				Steptoe		s 7 53			s12 34			s 4 31
	f 7 42	f 3 17		f10 49				Blackwell		f 7 48			f12 29			f 4 20
	f 7 48	f 3 23		f10 54				Rye		f 7 43			f12 23			f 4 20
	f 7 51	f 3 26		f10 57				Manning		f 7 40			f12 20			f 4 17
	f 7 52	f 3 28		f10 59				Harpole		f 7 39			f12 19			f 4 16
	f 7 58	f 3 34		f11 04				Lincoln		f 7 34			f12 14			f 4 10
	8 05	3 40		11 10				Colfax		7 30			12 10			4 05

No. 76	No. 74	No. 72	No. 70	No. 68	No. 66	No. 64	No. 62		No. 63	No. 65	No. 67	No. 69	No. 71	No. 73	No. 75	No. 77
	Ar PM	Ar PM	Ar PM		Ar AM					Lv AM			Lv PM	Lv PM	Lv PM	

*Saturday only, special train will leave Spokane at 11:15 p. m., arriving at Freeman at 12:05 a. m. Leave Freeman Sunday only at 12:05 a. m., arriving Spokane at 12:45 a. m., making all intermediate stops on flag.

All trains entering or leaving Spokane will follow Main avenue and stop at the near crossing of the following streets only: Post, Howard, Washington, Division, Front and Sheridan. Local trains only also stop at Olive avenue and Nelson street on flag or to discharge passengers. The Company reserves the right to vary from the above schedule.

Passenger timetable issued September 15, 1912 by Spokane & Inland Empire Railroad for the Spokane & Inland Division.

Colfax was the county seat and a good deal of business was conducted there. Convenient connections for Colfax were arranged at Spring Valley for passengers coming from towns on the Moscow branch. In addition, Washington, Idaho and Montana Railway trains made connections with the electric service at Palouse as demonstrated by 1913 eastbound schedules:

Spokane (leave)	7:30 a.m.	11:50 a.m.
Palouse (leave)	10:25 a.m.	4:20 p.m.
Potlatch (arrive)	10:50 a.m.	6:15 p.m.
Bovill (arrive)	12:20 p.m.	

Stairs connected the SI and lower level WI&M depots; an electrically-powered elevator assisted freight and baggage transfer.

Parlor car service between Spokane and Moscow was introduced to on January 7, 1909. Colfax got the same amenity on June 15, 1909, leaving Spokane at 12:30 p.m. and returning from Colfax at 5:00 p.m. Spokane shops upgraded the interior of two trailer cars for this work.

Spokane-Moscow train No. 68 arriving at Palouse. The train consisted of motor baggage and mail car No. 26, a motor passenger car and a trailer. The boxcar on the right carried Inland Empire Railroad markings. (Ted Holloway Collection)

An RPO mail service to Colfax was inaugurated December 1, 1909, a motor, baggage and mail car leaving with the 12:20 p.m. train and returning north at 5:00 p.m. Moscow got an equivalent service several months later. The Colfax RPO was withdrawn in February 1911. Mail cranes were erected at Kiesling, Sharon, Valleyford, Freeman and Waverly because certain mail trains did not stop there. Part of the mail load on the morning RPO to Moscow was for towns along the WI&M and mail for Elk River, Idaho, was forwarded in a Chicago, Milwaukee, St. Paul & Pacific Railroad RPO from Bovill. By 1925, the Mail Service required mail transfer on the northbound run at Garfield to the OWR&N Spokane and Pendleton RPO and at Spokane to the Northern Pacific's eastbound Miles City RPO.

The S&I planned on using three-car consists of a motor passenger and baggage car, motor passenger car and passenger trailer, accommodating 180 passengers. Apparently, this capacity was excessive. By 1911, daily train consists were a motor car and trailer (close to 120 seats) supplemented by a motor baggage/express and RPO car for mail service (Table 7.1). Each Moscow and Colfax train made one round trip daily. One motor car would have worked the local turns to Freeman. Trailer cars were cut from the Moscow trains in the mid-1920s due to reduced traffic; two motor cars per train usually became the norm.

Table 7.1.Inland Division Passenger Train Consists in 1911.

Route	Round Trips	Equipment
Spokane-Freeman	4	Motor passenger car (double ended)
Spokane-Rosalia	1	2 motor cars
Spokane-Moscow	1	Motor baggage/express & mail car, motor passenger & baggage car, trailer
Spokane-Moscow	2	Motor passenger & baggage car, trailer
Spokane-Colfax	1	Motor baggage/express & mail car, motor passenger & baggage car, trailer
Spokane-Colfax	2	Motor passenger & baggage car, trailer

Data from G. B. Kirker and L.S. Haskins, Electric Journal, October 1911.

The Spokane *Spokesman Review* chartered a special train to Moscow that departed about 11:30 p.m. on Saturday nights to deliver newspapers along the line. Usually one baggage and passenger consist made the trip, a trailer being omitted to reduce the journey time since passenger loads were light.

Moscow and Colfax services were combined to and from Spokane in 1915 to reduce operating expenses. Under the new arrangement, trains continued to leave Spokane at the traditional times to Moscow (8:00 a.m., noon and 5:00 p.m.). Possibly, through-cars for Moscow and Colfax ran combined to Spring Valley junction where they were divided (rolling stock had been modified for such operation a few years earlier). The timetable was not clear in this respect, a separate train shuttling between Colfax and Spring Valley to connect with the Moscow service being a potential alternative.

Representatives of the S&IE, NP and OWR&N railroads jointly agreed to reduce service in September 1918, having concluded that the Palouse territory had too few passengers chasing too many passenger trains. The S&IE cut Moscow to one daily round trip. A mixed train was substituted to maintain the Colfax-Spring Valley connection as passenger trains on the branch were generating, on average, only 23 cents per mile. Trips between Colfax and Spokane now took five hours in each direction.

The newly appointed S&IE receiver objected to these changes. He and the traffic manager considered better passenger service essential – even at a loss – to attract freight business. They believed that the associated increase in passenger revenue with improved service would enhance the net income. Services were restored in February 1919 to the previous level, but their operational costs outweighed the gain in revenue. When the Inland Empire Railroad was incorporated it went even further, reinstating a third daily train to Moscow/Colfax in 1920 and the Freeman local train. Meanwhile, the RPO service had continued to operate to Moscow.

Train 67 after arrival at Moscow from Spokane. The consist of a motor baggage and mail car and trailer was typical of daily service on the Inland line during the final years of operation. (Sheldon Perry Collection)

Westward   SECOND SUBDIVISION—SPOKANE AND MOSCOW   Eastward

Second Class 93	FIRST CLASS 67	FIRST CLASS 65	FIRST CLASS 63	Passing Tracks	Other Tracks	Station Numbers	STATIONS	Distances from Spokane	Telephone and Telegraph Calls	Signs	FIRST CLASS 62	FIRST CLASS 64	FIRST CLASS 66	Second Class 92
Freight Daily Ex. Sun.	Passg'r Daily	Passg'r Daily	Passg'r Daily Ex. Sun.				Time Table No. 1 Effective May 29, 1927				Passg'r Daily Ex. Sun.	Passg'r Daily	Passg'r Daily	Freight Daily Ex. Sat.
L 4.15AM	L 3.45PM	L 8.10AM		10	98	B90	MOSCOW	89.00	MO o--o	D Y K		A11.15AM	A 8.30PM	A 3.20AM
							3.42							
4.26	f 3.52	f 8.17			13	B87	ESTES	85.58				f11.06	f 8.23	3.05
							2.98							
4.34	f 3.58	f 8.23			5	B84	POE	82.60				f10.59	f 8.17	2.52
							1.60							
4.40	f 4.02	f 8.26		18	13	B82	VIOLA	81.00				f10.56	f 8.14	2.45
							3.70							
4.50	f 4.10	f 8.34			8	B79	RINGO	78.30				f10.47	f 8.07	2.30
							2.78							
5.00	s 4.15	s 8.40		16	111	B76	PALOUSE	75.52	PA oo—o	D Y K		s10.40	s 8.01	2.08
							4.86							
5.20	f 4.25	f 8.49		30	9	B71	GRINNELL	70.66				f10.31	f 7.51	1.57
							2.09							
5.28	f 4.29	f 8.53		37	4	B69	LADOW	68.57				f10.27	f 7.47	1.48
							3.61							
							N. P. & O. W. R. & N. CROSSINGS	64.98						
							0.36							
5.45	s 4.37	s 9.01		23	25	B65	GARFIELD	64.30	GF ooo—	D		s10.19	s 7.39	1.31
							4.03							
6.00	f 4.45	f 9.09		27	8	B61	CRABTREE	60.27				f10.11	f 7.31	1.18
							3.60							
6.17	f 4.52	f 9.16		21	8	B57	SOKULK	56.67				f10.04	f 7.24	12.59
							2.39							
6.25	f 4.57	f 9.21				B55	DAVIDSON	54.28				f10.00	f 7.20	12.49
							0.98							
							N. P. CROSSING	53.30						
							0.18							
							O.-W. R. & N. CROSSING	53.12						
							1.63							
6.33	s 5.02	s 9.25		37	60	B53	OAKESDALE	52.49	OD o—	D K		s 9.56	s 7.16	12.41
							3.23							
6.47	f 5.08	f 9.31		27	1	B50	GEARY	49.26				f 9.49	f 7.09	12.27
							2.19							
6.55	f 5.12	f 9.35			12	B48	SEABURY	47.07				f 9.45	f 7.05	12.18
							2.46							
7.05	f 5.17	f 9.40 (64)		27		B45	FAIRBANKS	44.61				9.40 (63)	f 7.00	12.07AM
							5.24							
8.00	s 5.30	s 9.51		18 17		B40	SPRING VALLEY	39.37	S ooo	D Y		s 9.30	s 6.50	11.30
							1.91							
8.06	5.33	9.56		15		B38	DURKEE	37.46				9.26	6.45	11.25
							1.60							
8.12	f 5.36	f 9.59			5	B37	JEFFERSON	35.86				f 9.23	f 6.42	11.20
							2.48							
8.20	s 5.40	s10.04		18	20	B34	WAVERLY	33.38	W — —	D		s 9.17	s 6.39	11.13
							2.10							
8.27	f 5.44	f10.08			6	B32	SALINE	31.28				f 9.12	f 6.34	11.06
							1.51							
8.32	f 5.47	f10.11		38		B30	WEST FAIRFIELD	29.77				f 9.09	f 6.31	11.01
							1.43							
8.37	f 5.50	f10.15			3	B29	LENOX	28.34				f 9.06	f 6.28	10.57
							1.38							
8.42	5.52	10.18			9	B28	LOKE	26.96				9.04	6.25	10.53
							0.96							
8.47	f 5.54	f10.20			5	B27	TREAT	26.00				f 9.02	f 6.23	10.49
							1.55							
8.59 (64)	s 5.57	s10.23		32	18	B25	MT. HOPE	24.45	— — oo			s 8.59 (93)	s 6.20	10.45
							3.37							
9.11	f 6.04	f10.30			7	B22	OCHLARE	21.08				f 8.52	f 6.14	10.34
							2.33							
9.19	f 6.09 (66)	f10.35	L 6.50AM (62)	18	94	B19	FREEMAN	18.75			A 6.50AM (63)	f 8.47	f 6.09 (67)	10.28
							1.14							
9.24	f 6.11	f10.38	f 6.52			B18A	RUBECK	17.61			f 6.47	f 8.45	f 6.06	10.23
							1.41							
9.30	s 6.14	s10.41	s 6.55	32	6	B17	VALLEY FORD	16.20	V oo —		s 6.44	s 8.42	s 6.03	10.18
							1.65							
9.35	f 6.17	f10.45	f 6.58	23		B15	EXCELSIOR	14.55			f 6.41	f 8.39	f 6.00	10.13
							1.90							
9.41	f 6.21	f10.50	f 7.02		5	B13	SHARON	12.65			f 6.38	f 8.35	f 5.55	10.07
							0.92							
9.45	f 6.23	f10.52	f 7.04		14	B12	KIESLING	11.73			f 6.36	f 8.33	f 5.53	10.04
							1.80							
9.51	f 6.27	f10.56	f 7.07		6	B11	WILLOW SPRINGS	9.93			f 6.32	f 8.29	f 5.47	9.59
							1.26							
9.55	f 6.29	f10.59	f 7.10	20	11	B 9	PARKVIEW	8.67			f 6.30	f 8.26	f 5.44	9.55
							1.49							
10.01	f 6.32	f11.02	f 7.13	18	9	B 8	MORAN	7.18			f 6.27	f 8.23	f 5.41	9.50
							1.35							
10.05	f 6.34	f11.05	f 7.16		18	B 7	PINE GROVE	5.83			f 6.24	f 8.20	f 5.38	9.47
							1.62							
10.12	6.37	11.09	7.19		25	B 5	GRAVEL PIT	4.21			6.21	8.17	5.34	9.42
							2.68							
10.27	s 6.44	s11.16	s 7.25			B 2B	THIRD AVE.	1.53			f 6.17	f 8.11	f 5.28	9.33
							0.33							
A10.30AM	6.45	11.17	7.26	28		B 2A	SPRAGUE AVE.	1.20			6.16	8.10	5.27	9.32
							0.26							
	6.46	11.18	7.27				INLAND JCT.	0.94		Y	6.15	8.09	5.26	9.31
							0.14							
	f 6.47	f11.19	f 7.28				SHOPS	0.80			f 6.14	f 8.08	f 5.25	L 9.30AM

TRAINS WILL BE GOVERNED BY SPOKANE DIV. TIME TABLE BETWEEN CONNECTION WITH G. N. RY. TRACKS AND PASSENGER DEPOT

93	67	65	63				STATIONS			Signs	62	64	66	92
A 7.00PM	A11.30AM	A 7.40AM	Yard	Yard	B.O.		0.80 SPOKANE	0.00	DS	DNK	L 6.05AM	L 8.05AM	L 5.20PM	
Daily Ex. Sun.	Daily	Daily	Daily Ex. Sun.								Daily Ex. Sun.	Daily	Daily	Daily Ex. Sat.
6.15 14.16	3.15 27.81	3.20 27.11	0.50 23.3				Time Over Subdivision Average Speed per Hour				0.45 25.9	3.10 28.10	3.15 27.81	5.50 15.24

Eastward trains are superior to Westward trains of the same class.
Train Nos. 63 and 66 will stop on flag at the second crossing east of Kiesling Depot to receive and discharge passengers.

Spokane, Coeur d'Alene & Palouse Railway employee timetable May 29, 1927 for the Inland lines.

Second Class 95	FIRST CLASS 83	FIRST CLASS 81	Car Capacity of Sidings Passing Tracks	Car Capacity of Sidings Other Tracks	Station Numbers	Time Table No. 1 Effective May 29, 1927 STATIONS	Distances from Spring Valley	Telephone and Telegraph Calls	Signs	FIRST CLASS 80	FIRST CLASS 82	Second Class 94
Freight Daily Ex. Sun.	Passg'r Daily	Passg'r Daily								Passg'r Daily	Passg'r Daily	Freight Daily Ex. Sun.
L 4.30 AM	L 4.05 PM	L 8.10 AM		53	W77	COLFAX	35.74	CX —o—	D I	A 11.10 AM	A 8.10 PM	A 2.45 AM
						O.-W. R. & N. CROSSING 0.29	35.45					
					W75-A	COLFAX WYE 1.23	34.22		Y			
4.40	f 4.09	f 8.14			W75	LINCOLN 0.52	33.70			f 11.05	f 8.05	2.35
4.58	f 4.17	f 8.22		7	W71	MANNING 3.62	30.08			f 10.58	f 7.58	2.18
5.05	f 4.20	f 8.25		14	W70	RYE 1.47	28.61			f 10.54	f 7.54	2.13
5.20	f 4.28	f 8.32	17	8	W67	BLACKWELL 3.12	25.49			f 10.47	f 7.47	1.58
5.30	s 4.32	s 8.36	38	29	W65	STEPTOE 1.87	23.62	Q o———	D	s 10.43	s 7.43	1.50
5.42	f 4.37	f 8.41			W62	BANKSON 2.59	21.03			f 10.37	f 7.37	1.38
5.53	f 4.42	f 8.46		32	W60	CASHUP 2.19	18.84			f 10.32	f 7.32	1.28
6.14	s 4.52	s 8.55	25	9	W55	THORNTON 4.56	14.28	R N —o—o—	D	s 10.22	s 7.22	1.08
						O.-W. R. & N. CROSSING 0.57	13.71					
6.30	f 4.58	f 9.01		5	W52	STONEHAM 2.39	11.32			f 10.16	f 7.16	12.53
6.36	f 5.01	f 9.04	23		W51-A	HARRIS 1.36	9.96			f 10.12	f 7.12	12.49
6.38	f 5.02	f 9.05		13	W51	BALDER 0.46	9.50			f 10.11	f 7.11	12.47
6.50	f 5.07	f 9.10		8	W48	EARLY 2.35	7.15			f 10.08	f 7.08	12.37
6.57	f 5.10	f 9.13		3	W47	BROADVIEW FARMS 1.37	5.78			f 10.05	f 7.05	12.30
7.01	s 5.12	s 9.15	13	20	W46	ROSALIA 1.02	4.76	R O —oo	D K	s 10.03	s 7.03	12.25
7.17	f 5.18	f 9.21		12	W43	ROLLINS 3.23	1.53			f 9.56	f 6.56	12.12
A 7.30 AM	A 5.25 PM	A 9.27 AM	32 37		B40	SPRING VALLEY 1.53	0.00	S ooo	D Y	L 9.51 AM	L 6.51 PM	L 12.01 AM
95	83	81								80	82	94
Daily Ex. Sun.	Daily	Daily								Daily	Daily	Daily Ex. Sun.
3.00 12.2	1.20 27.8	1.17 27.84				Time Over Subdivision Average Speed per Hour				1.19 27.9	1.19 27.9	2.45 13.3

SPECIAL RULES

Eastward trains are superior to Westward trains of the same class.
Exception: Trains No. 81 and 83 are superior to trains No. 80 and 82.

All Passenger Trains will stop on flag at:

Tudor	Mile Post 3.85
Pantops	Mile Post 4.65
Glenrose	Mile Post 5.07
Foch	Mile Post 7.74
Hillby	Mile Post 9.66
Silver Hill	Mile Post 10.73
Belair	Mile Post 13.63
Kennerwood	Mile Post 14.07
Sand St.	Mile Post 15.35
Larkin	Mile Post 16.95
Ingersoll	Mile Post 19.76
Rock Creek	Mile Post 22.05
Rattlers Run	Mile Post 27.48
Bound Brook	Mile Post 32.61
Clifton	Mile Post 34.41
Konah	Mile Post 42.59
Dan	Mile Post 50.65
Robinson	Mile Post 55.63
Elmer	Mile Post 59.12
Coberly	Mile Post 61.45
Hampshire	Mile Post 63.05
Horn	Mile Post 72.75
Pottery	Mile Post 66.35
Cove	Mile Post 79.50
Ayer	Mile Post 85.05
Ferris	Mile Post 77.48
Trestle Creek	Mile Post W 53.05
Barnes	Mile Post W 57.59
Lynn	Mile Post W 60.23
Harpole	Mile Post W 71.11

Spokane, Coeur d'Alene & Palouse Railway employee timetable May 29, 1927 for the Inland lines.

Spokane-Palouse-Moscow

Read Down   Read Up

64 Daily	Mls	STATIONS	67 Daily	Fares from Spokane 1way	Rtrn
8:15	.0	Lv...Spokane, Wn...Ar	6:30	$......	$......
8:18	1.0	Ar... Shops ...Lv	6:24	.10	.15
8:21	1.8	Third Ave.	6:20	.10	.15
8:30	6.0	Pine Grove	6:10	.10	.15
8:33	7.0	Moran	6:08	.14	.25
8:36	8.9	Parkview	6:05	.17	.30
8:39	10.1	Willow Springs	6:03	.20	.30
8:43	12.0	Kiesling	5:59	.24	.40
8:45	12.9	Sharon	5:56	.24	.40
8:49	14.8	Excelsior	5:53	.27	.45
s 8:52	16.4	Valley Ford	s5:50	.30	.45
8:57	19.0	Freeman	5:45	.37	.60
9:02	21.5	Ochlare	5:40	.44	.70
s 9:09	24.7	Mt. Hope	s5:34	.47	.75
9:12	26.2	Treat	5:31	.50	.75
9:15	28.6	Lenox	5:27	.57	.90
9:17	30.0	W. Fairfield	5:24	.60	.90
9:19	31.5	Saline	5:21	.60	.90
s 9:24	33.6	Waverly	s5:17	.67	1.05
9:28	36.1	Jefferson	5:13	.70	1.05
s 9:35	39.6	Spring Valley	s5:07	.70	1.05
9:45	44.9	Fairbanks	4:56	.80	1.20
9:49	47.3	Seabury	4:51	.84	1.30
9:52	49.5	Geary	4:47	.90	1.35
s 9:58	52.7	Oakesdale	s4:41	.94	1.45
10:05	56.9	Sokulk	4:33	1.04	1.60
10:12	60.5	Crabtree	4:26	1.10	1.65
s10:20	64.5	Garfield	s4:19	1.17	1.80
10:29	68.5	Ladow	4:12	1.24	1.90
10:34	70.6	Grinnell	4:07	1.27	1.95
s10:45	75.5	Palouse (WI&M Jct.)	s4:00	1.37	2.10
10:52	78.2	Ringo	3:48	1.44	2.20
11:01	81.9	Viola	3:42	1.54	2.35
11:11	86.5	Estes	3:35	1.60	2.40
11:20	89.9	Ar...Moscow, Ida. ...Lv	3:30	1.67	2.55

W. I. & M.

Tu., Th., Sa. |Tu.,Th.,Sa|

4:30	11:05	.0	Lv...... Palouse ...Ar	3:52	9·00	....
4:55	11:41	11.0	Potlatch	3:26	8:35	....
....	11:51	14.0	Princeton	3:04	....	....
....	12:04	20.0	Harvard	2:51	....	....
....	12:43	34.0	Deary	2:17	....	....
....	1:13	47.0	Ar...... Bovill ...Lv	1:45	....	....

Lightface type A. M.—Blackface P. M.
S—Regular stop. All other stations are flag stops.
Return tickets carry final limit of 25 days.
150 lbs. baggage free.

Passenger services for Moscow line, April 1935.

Services remained this way until SC&P made revisions with its first timetable, limiting Spokane/Moscow to two round trips, morning and afternoon. From March 1931 only one daily round trip was made. Colfax maintained a passenger train connection until November 1930 when one round trip by a mixed train was substituted. The Colfax train class changed from mixed to freight between consecutive issues of the April 14, 1935 and November 14, 1937 employee timetable.

The last day an electric passenger train went to Moscow was April 1, 1939, Washington Department of Public Service having dismissed protests filed against passenger service abandonment. In making its case at the hearing, SC&P cited average passenger earnings, including mail, milk, etc., of 31 cents per mile compared with the cost of rendering the service of 50 cents per mile, while residents of that territory were served by seven round trips by Union Pacific Stages (road bus) and two air-conditioned trains by the Northern Pacific.

FREIGHT

Coeur d'Alene Lines

The Cd'A&S used steam locomotives to haul heavy freight. At night, a steam train operated in both directions between Spokane and Coeur d'Alene terminal points. Typical loads were 10 to 20 cars carrying logs, sawed lumber, cordwood, hay, mill feed and vegetables. Refrigerator car service began on July 15, 1909, and was available daily except Sunday. Less-than-carload traffic was handled by motor baggage cars making three daily round trips.

By 1910, freight trains ran twice daily each way except Sunday, leaving Spokane at 4:35 a.m. and 11:00 a.m. Electric locomotive haulage appears to have replaced steam around this time. One round trip was sufficient by 1918 and became common practice. Thus, the GN Spokane Division's Seventh Subdivision 1950 employee timetable called for a Monday through Friday third class train: No. 95 departed Spokane at 8:00 a.m. and arrived at Coeur d'Alene at 10:50 a.m.; No. 96 departed for Spokane at 3:00 p.m., arriving at 5:00 p.m. Intermediate stations were flag stops. Reassignment of the line to the Kalispell Division in 1956 had negligible effect on the timings.

Burlington Northern continued to operate in a similar way, although by 1976 the scheduled departure was from the ex-NP Spokane Erie Street yard at 9:00 a.m. as train No. 842. Ten years later, the train, by then identified as Coeur d'Alene Local 51846, departed Yardley terminal at 8:00 a.m. and traveled via the ex-NP main line to Hauser Junction and the branch to Post Falls before reaching the ex-GN and Milwaukee Road joint line to Coeur d'Alene. By 2006, the train occasionally turned around at Hauser Junction and on some days at Huetter along the branch. Traffic had been lost due to sawmill closures.

Inland Lines

Spokane & Inland timetable No.1, when issued in November 1906, did not identify freight service on the new line to Waverly. After further track extension, a freight train had started to run

Burlington Northern GP-7 No. 1636 switching at Coeur d'Alene. (Ted Holloway Collection)

regularly between Spokane and Garfield by June 1907, making a connection at Spring Valley for Colfax. Once the Inland system was completed, a regular pattern for daily (except Sunday) freight trains was established. Departure, around midnight, from Spokane to Moscow assured morning deliveries to the terminals on the Moscow and Colfax branches, the latter being served by a freight train from Spring Valley. A balancing freight train ran from Moscow in the opposite direction, the Spokane-based crew of conductor, motorman and two brakemen making the 178-mile round trip within the sixteen-hour legal limit.

Refrigerator car service was made available from July 15, 1909, operating three days per week to and from Colfax and Moscow. Cars departed both towns in the morning (on Monday, Wednesday and Friday) and returned from Spokane the same night.

About 18 cars of less-than-carload freight (l.c.l.) were loaded daily at Spokane by 1914. Freight received up to 5:00 p.m. was delivered the following morning. Solid cars were loaded for Colfax, Moscow, Palouse, Coeur d'Alene and a pair for points on the WI&M. Generally, three cars of l.c.l. traffic were delivered daily for the boats at Coeur d'Alene, the S&IE securing 90% of the business there. Additional cars served points on the Vera/Opportunity line.

As time went on, the Moscow freight train departed Spokane progressively earlier in the evening:

Station	1919	1927	1935
Spokane (leave)	12:15 a.m.	9:30 p.m.	6:45 p.m.
Moscow (arrive)	5:25 a.m.	3:20 a.m.	1:40 a.m.
Colfax (arrive)	6:00 a.m.	2:45 a.m.	12:50 a.m.

Additional freight trains were dispatched as extras whenever necessary and particularly at wheat harvest time. For example, in 1914 an average of three trains ran daily during the fall wheat rush. Pairs of 700 class electric locomotives worked the Moscow freight trains while class 600 pairs were normally assigned to the Colfax line.

A daily Spokane-Moscow round trip still remained in operation in 1953, now re-routed over UP rails between Spokane and Fairfield as discussed in Chapter 12. Colfax was limited to a bi-weekly

Electric locomotives Nos. M2 and M5 hurried a Sells-Loto special train for the next circus performance. (D. Cozine Collection)

Two 700 class locomotives hauling a freight train on the Inland line within Spokane City limits. Note the pantograph on the second unit was deployed, this being the normal practice. (Clyde Parent, Richard Yaremko Collection)

Freight train of a dozen boxcars crossing Rock Creek Bridge headed by an Alco locomotive. Over half of the cars were GN-owned. (Ted Holloway Collection)

local freight from Spokane by that time and the service was cut back to Manning after closure of the tunnel there. By 1968, the Moscow train ran two or three times a week.

Analysis of one hundred freight cars carried on the Inland lines in 1967-69 revealed that covered hoppers and boxcars were employed to the same extent (50:50 ratio). Over 95% of the covered hoppers were owned by the GN, most of the modern classes on the roster being represented. Of the boxcars recorded, 70% were owned by the GN, the remainder coming from a variety of railroads. A mix of both types of car was supplied to most elevator stations, although orders by Balder and Spring Valley shippers favored boxcars at that time.

Burlington Northern truncated the Inland tracks, leaving the remaining segments as branches from the ex-NP Spokane-Moscow line (Chapter 12). Certain branches could not carry the jumbo hopper cars commonly used for grain haulage due to bridge or track limitations and were subject to a 220,000 pound car gross loaded weight restriction. For several years the branches were served by the "Rosalia Local" train, which had the following duties:

· Train No. 865, Monday, Wednesday and Friday – Rosalia to Viola and return, with side trips to Grinnell and Crabtree as required.
· Train No. 866, Tuesday, Thursday & Saturday – Rosalia to Manning and return, Rosalia to Seabury and return with a side trip to Mount Hope as required. Operated as train No. 866 which depart 6:30 a.m.

Both trains departed at 6:30 a.m. Estes was served (Mondays, Wednesdays and Fridays) by the "Pullman switcher" which started from its namesake and ran to Palouse on Tuesdays, Thursdays and Saturdays.

After the Balder-Manning and Fairbanks-Seabury segments were abandoned in late 1980, the "Pullman switcher" served the Fairbanks and Mount Hope branches three days per week (Tuesdays, Thursdays and Saturdays). Almost all the trains on the Mount Hope branch terminated at Waverly since there was little traffic beyond there. From February 1982, a local train from Spokane (normally hauled by a model GP-7) served Waverly and Fairbanks and Balder two days per week on an "as needed" basis. Grinnell operated on a similar schedule from Pullman, normally worked by a model GP-9.

Operational Aspects

Burlington Northern diesels Nos. 1741 and 1744 head the "Rosalia Local" freight over the P&L line steel bridge north of Rosalia in April 1980. (Clyde Parent, Jim Davis Collection)

"Rosalia Local" getting ready to return from Mount Hope. The shell of the substation remains in the background as a reminder of earlier days on the line. (Clyde Parent, Jim Davis Collection)

The S&IE railroad system operated entirely under steam railroad rules and regulations. All motormen and conductors were required to have a minimum of three years of steam road practice, motormen previously being locomotive engineers. Train orders were issued by telephone when the Cd'A&S Railway opened, changing to telegraph several years later. A block system was introduced on April 4, 1905, semaphores being erected at several stations to signal motormen to stop for further orders. A similar system was adopted for the Inland lines.

Employee timetables listed special rules and instructions. A selection taken from several issues, released between 1915 and 1935, provides insight as to operating practices during that period:
- Employees must not, under any circumstances, touch any part of either trolley or other electric connections, or climb on top of motorcars or electric locomotives unless pantograph and trolley poles are securely fastened down so that it is impossible to come up within four feet of trolley wire.
- Vestibule doors between coaches made up in trains must be kept locked and under no circumstances will passengers be permitted to pass from one coach to another.
- Conductors must see that window guards on left side of passenger cars are securely fastened up while moving in either direction on double track in Spokane.
- When passenger cars are added or taken off passenger trains, trolley poles or pantograph, or both of them must be lowered from trolley wire before bus line is coupled or uncoupled.
- Trolley and span wires will not clear man on top of boxcar or any car of equal height, also that poles are close to track and that many poles will not clear a man on side of car.
- Train register stations are: Spokane Terminal, Inland Junction, Greenacres (trains originating or terminating only), Liberty Lake Junction (Liberty Lake trains only), Spokane Bridge, Coeur d'Alene, Hayden Lake, Liberty Lake, Flora, Spring Valley, Moscow, Freeman (certain trains) and Colfax.
- Maximum speed of trains at any point on these lines must not exceed 50 mph (in 1915). Passenger trains limit 40 mph and freight trains 30 mph by 1919. Passenger trains limited

This instance of Coeur d'Alene passenger and freight depots under water was almost certainly in the winter of 1933 when the lake experienced the greatest flooding ever recorded. The snow sweeper at the right-hand side wasn't of help under these conditions.
(Ted Holloway Collection)

Sources

Great Northern Railway President's Subject File No.8758, Spokane & Inland Empire Railroad Train Service.

Employee timetables issued by Spokane & Inland Empire Railroad, its predecessors and successors, various issues.

Public timetables issued by Spokane & Inland Empire Railroad, its predecessors and successors, various issues.

Division of Transportation, Washington Department of Public Service, Cause No. F.H. 7210, 1939, In the Matter of Proposed Abandonment of Passenger Train Service on the Inland Division by the Spokane, Coeur d'Alene & Palouse Railway Company.

Division of Transportation, Washington Department of Public Service, Cause No. F.H. 7345, 1940, Ex-rel. Patrons v. Spokane, Coeur d'Alene & Palouse Railway Company. In Re: Discontinuance of Passenger Service between Spokane and Coeur d'Alene Idaho.

Interstate Commerce Commission, Finance Docket AB-6, Sub Nos. 39, 134 and 146, 1975-1983, Application of Burlington Northern Inc. to Abandon Line of Railroad…. State of Washington.

Railway Mail Service, Thirteenth Division, Schedule of Mail Trains No.87, July 16, 1925.

Official Guide of the Railways, National Railways Publications Company, New York, various issues.

Electric Railway Journal, April 10, 1909; 33: 706, "Inland Empire Extends Parlor Car Service."

Electric Railway Journal, August 7, 1909; 34: 238, "Refrigerator Service on the Inland Empire System".

Electric Railway Journal, March 12, 1910; 35: 439, "Inland Empire Mail Service."

Flagg, Charles E. "Parlor Car Service – Inland Empire System", Electric Railway Review, December 28, 1907; 18: 977.

Electric Railway Review, 28: 278. "Mail Service on the Inland Empire System."

Kirker, G. B. and Haskins, L.S. "The Spokane and Inland Empire Railroad." Electric Journal, October 1911; 8: 859.

Railway Age Gazette, September 4 1914: 423, "Hill System Electric Lines in the Northwest."

Spokane Spokesman Review.

Looking north along the transfer track (1) that connected the GN and NP freight yards in Spokane in 1928. Track (2) was the connection from the SC&P freight yard to the transfer track. The electric main line, running parallel to Trent Avenue (E), crossed the transfer track at D. One truss of S&IE bridge No. 1-3 cane be seen on the east side. Structure on the left belonged to Schade brewery at that time.
(Northern Pacific Railway; Walt Ainsworth collection)

Chapter 8

COMPETITION AND COLLABORATION

To provide access to countrywide markets for its customers, the S&IE interchanged traffic with other railroads. Interchange locations are listed in Table 8.1. Many were installed within the first few years of operation. Latecomers included a connection with the OWR&N at Oakesdale in 1923, and Palouse, where interchange with the NP took place over tracks belonging to the Washington, Idaho & Montana Railway until direct interchange was instituted in 1946. The S&IE did not conduct interchange at Colfax, where the UP had a significant presence, until 1967 when permanent closure of the nearby tunnel forced the GN to make such arrangements.

Most of the cars were exchanged at Spokane, facilitated by close proximity of a transfer track that connected the GN and NP freight yards. This was accessed from the east end of the S&IE freight yard via a switch. Diagrams of interchange arrangements at Spokane and several other points are included in this chapter.

The company was in the unusual position of competing with four interchange partners for business within its area of operation. Northern Pacific Railway and Oregon Railroad & Navigation were long established there before the electric line opened, with the Chicago, Milwaukee & St. Paul Railroad and Spokane International Railway arriving afterwards. Aspects of the relationship between the S&IE and the four companies are outlined below.

Table 8.1. Interchange Points

Location	GN	NP	SP&S	CM&StP	OWR&N	SIR	WI&M
Spokane	X	X	X	X	X	X	
Millwood						X	
McGuires				X*			
Huetter		X**					
Atlas		X					
Gibbs						X	
Coeur d'Alene		X		X			
Oakesdale					X		
Palouse		X					X
Moscow		X			X		
Rosalia		X		X			

*X – Interchange tracks; *I&WN until 1916; ** circa 1908-1918.*

0801		"SCP" Main Line	0855	03	Taylor Edwards, Warehouse #2 - Track #2
0802		Old "NP" - "SCP" Inter-change Track	0859	03	Corrugated Metals
0805	06	City of Spokane (salt)	0859	07	Spokane Distributors
0810		Old "GN" Transfer Track	0859	08	Floor Supply
0811		Short Rip	0860		"SCP" Wye - West Leg
0820	20	Gulf Atlantic, Warehouse #1 - Track #1	0860	90	3rd Avenue Team Track
0820	35	F. O. Berg	0865		"SCP" Wye - East Leg
0821		"SCP" South Main	0867	06	"SCP" Steel Spur - Overhead Ramp
0822	06	Inland Metals (North)	0869	04	Roundup Grocery
0825	90	South Rip Team Track	0893	01	Centennial Mills #4 (Storage)
0826	14	Inland Metals (South)			
0828		"SCP" North Main	0895	01	Centennial Mills #3 (Storage)
0830	04	Gulf Atlantic, Warehouse #1 - Track #2	0897	12	Centennial Mills #5 (Empties for loading)
0850		"SCP" Passing Track			
0852	09	Mid Mountain Masonry	0898	33	Centennial Mills #6 (Wheat to unload)
0854	09	Taylor Edwards, Warehouse #2 - Track #1			

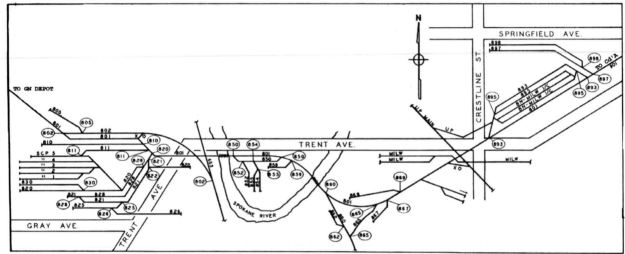

Burlington Northern schematic diagram dating from 1972 of SC&P tracks in Spokane. Little had changed during the previous forty years. Track 801 from the GN depot extended through the freight yard and over the two Spokane River bridges to reach Inland Junction. Transfer track 802 provided for interchange with the GN and NP freight yards which now belonged to BN. Interchange tracks with the UP and Milwaukee Road are evident at the right-hand side of the diagram.

Northern Pacific Railway

Northern Pacific was the first railroad to serve Coeur d'Alene. The Spokane Falls & Idaho Railroad, headed by Daniel C. Corbin, built the line in 1886 and leased the company to the NP the following year. Known as the Fort Sherman branch, the right-of-way extended 13.5 miles from the NP main line at Hauser Junction through Post Falls. At that time, the main function was to carry ore shipped over the lake from the Coeur d'Alene mining district.

Consequently, Northern Pacific had been the sole operator for sixteen years when the Cd'A&S electric railway opened. To say the least, the NP management was displeased at the newcomer entering their territory. President Mellen decided that, "without appearing too prominently in the matter, he would like the [NP] attorneys to put up as good a fight as possible to kill this [Spokane] franchise, or at least it should be modified so as to prevent the use of steam."

In the Palouse country, the NP had begun construction of a 101-mile long branch south from Spokane in 1888, reaching Lewiston ten years later. Towns along this "Palouse & Lewiston" (P&L) route included Rosalia, Oakesdale, Garfield, Palouse, Pullman and Moscow; except for Pullman, the S&I served all. Announcement of S&I plans to build a parallel railroad were greeted with dismay at NP headquarters. An electric railroad expert, hired by parties with potential financial interests in the line, appraised NP management of the proposed route and financing, noting that Graves

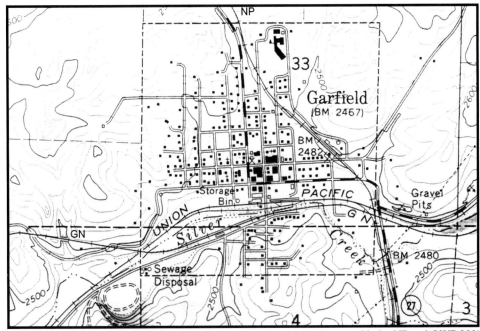

Three railroads served Garfield. The electric railroad did not interchange with the NP and OWR&N/UP here, but Burlington Northern installed a connection between the NP and GN tracks to serve local customers when the Inland line through here was abandoned in 1972. (USGS map)

had discussed the plans with James J. Hill. Howard Elliot, NP's new president, expressed the opinion that it was a bad scheme for his company's interests and, in his judgment, would be a bad scheme for anyone to put money into because the territory could not support three railroads – an accurate prophecy, as it turned out. He requested banking friends to discourage the bond company actively engaged with the S&IE.

Elliot later told Hill that the electric railroad was getting to be of such a size as to become a menace to the interests of the NP. His concern was that if the S&IE built all the lines talked about, they would give the Canadian Pacific and Milwaukee access to traffic in the Palouse-Lewiston country. Elliot's proposed solution was to gain indirect control of the entire enterprise and let it be managed by outside parties. He was unaware that Hill already held a significant amount of S&IE stock and thus influence in the company.

Spokane and Inland right-of-way crossed the P&L line at three points: Rosalia, Oakesdale and Garfield. The NP demanded separate grades at the first two. At Rosalia the S&I built a bridge to carry their line over the NP. Negotiation resulted in a grade crossing at Oakesdale, primarily because the NP lawyers were unlikely to force a grade separation here. A grade crossing for Garfield was acceptable to both parties. It was agreed that the S&I would install interlocking systems at both crossings when traffic levels made it necessary, but that was never implemented.

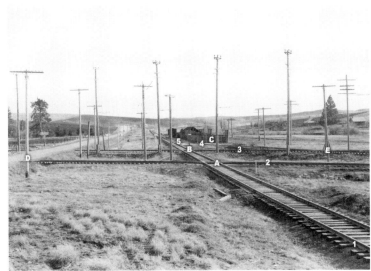

This 1928 photograph of Garfield shows the SC&P track (3) paralleled the OWR&N (2), crossing both the NP (1) at B and a NP-OWR&N connection at E. (Northern Pacific Railway; Walt Ainsworth collection)

Once the S&I line was built, relations between the two managements became more amicable, although Elliot still resented its presence. Graves sometimes asked Elliot's advice. However, when the NP requested a share of traffic that the S&IE generated at Spokane, this was bluntly refused. At the instigation of the S&IE, a connecting track between the electric line and NP line was proposed at Huetter near Coeur d'Alene. The NP president was reticent to add this connection, even though it was beneficial to them. In his opinion the NP was trying to get along with Graves in every way it could, but did not want to open up local territory to him. Agreements were made later for reciprocal switching of certain lumber mills, but disputes arose over the provision of spurs to Spokane industries already served by the NP.

123

Two or three passenger trains ran daily each way on the NP Moscow line in competition with the electrics. Transit time between Spokane and Moscow was an hour faster by the S&I. The NP tried a sleeping car for a while, without success, and then added café-observation service as an attraction. Fares were lower on the S&IE than NP, so the electric line carried more than its fair share; passengers from the NP Lewiston line changed trains at Moscow to take advantage of the lower charge.

Northern Pacific's fear of traffic abstraction was well founded. By 1910, the S&IE handled 31% more freight than the NP at Coeur d'Alene and carried the majority of passengers. The NP had made little effort to compete for passengers, at the most offering two trains per day. Graves went so far as to suggest to Elliot that the S&IE should take over all passenger service there. In the end, the NP continued to operate passenger trains to Coeur d'Alene, and on the P&L line, long after SC&P abdicated the passenger business.

After Hill acquired a controlling interest in the S&IE and divided his holdings between the NP and GN, Elliot told Graves that "the NP, as half owner of the property, must get every dollar that is fairly due to us from any and all property in which we have an interest." The GN had already cornered a substantial amount of the interchange traffic by establishing joint freight rates with the S&I on May 9, 1907. Pressed by Elliot, Hill confirmed that the NP and GN should participate equally in any business, freight, passenger or express interchanged by the S&IE. Immediate compliance with this directive can be seen from the relative number of freight cars subsequently interchanged by the S&IE with the parent companies:

	GN & NP Cars Interchanged	Ratio GN/NP Cars
1910	6320	68/32
1911	5712	51/49
1912	7117	50/50
1913	6987	48/52
1914	5977	51/49
1915	6049	47/53
1916	7999	50/50

Revenue generated by the two companies averaged $154 per car interchanged. On the passenger side, distribution was not so equitable. Through GN passengers averaged 1,567 per year during the same seven-year period, three times as many as the NP. Elliot grumbled that GN advertising matter was much more evident at S&IE stations than that of the NP and their agents pushed travel over the GN.

Competition between the NP and GN for interchange traffic resurfaced after the 1920 reorganization, since they no longer had financial ties to the railway. By 1927 the GN had 43% of the total business. Purchase of the electric lines by GN/SC&P resulted in head-to-head competition with the NP. Interchange with the NP continued, but to a lesser extent. For example, 1,599 NP cars (less than half the 1916 number) were exchanged in 1931: 83% at Spokane, 10% at Moscow, 5% at Rosalia and 2% at Palouse.

Interchange with the NP at Atlas, which entered the Atlas Lumber Company mill on track 1, was conducted on track 2. SC&P spur 3 extended from the electric main line to the mill (4).
(Northern Pacific Railway; Walt Ainsworth collection)

Chicago, Milwaukee, St. Paul & Pacific Railroad

The Chicago, Milwaukee & St. Paul Railroad completed its Pacific coast extension through eastern Washington in 1908. In later years the railroad name was changed to Chicago, Milwaukee, St. Paul & Pacific (CMStP&P) and also became known as the Milwaukee Road. The line paralleled the S&IE at Rosalia where an interchange track connected them; 250 cars were exchanged there in 1921. The Milwaukee Road built a depot at Rosalia, the third station for the town, but closed it 25 years later. Through tickets were made available from S&IE depots to the Milwaukee's main line stations. However, the introduction of train service at St. Maries hurt S&IE boat traffic to that point.

The S&IE and NP tracks paralleled each other through Rosalia and their depots lay almost in line as evident in this 1911 photograph, a pair of boxcars standing on the interchange track between the two railroads. In the foreground the interchange track between the S&IE and Milwaukee Road held three of the latter's cars. (Warren Wing Collection)

Four years after the coast extension, the Milwaukee opened a branch to Coeur d'Alene from Dishman. The branch crossed the electric branch to Liberty Lake, and beyond McGuires both lines were parallel. It competed with the S&IE for lumber business. Milwaukee's intentions were made clear by construction of a large freight depot at Coeur d'Alene.

In 1916, the Milwaukee acquired control of the Idaho & Washington Northern Railroad, whose line extended from McGuires to Newport and Metalline Falls. Interchange was conducted by the S&IE at McGuires. When first opened, I&WN had operated a passenger service from McGuires, connecting with the electric trains.

The Milwaukee became an aggressive competitor to the S&IE (and NP) for Potlatch lumber traffic, where the local mill was one of the largest in the northwest. Loads for both railroads were hauled

At Rosalia, on the Colfax branch, traffic was interchanged with the NP on the transfer track marked A until 1946. Track B connected with the Milwaukee Road that skirted Rosalia along the hillside. (USGS map)

At McGuires the switch for the Idaho & Washington Northern Railroad (later Milwaukee Road) transfer track was just beyond the highway crossing, freight cars awaiting movement. A shelter shed stood in the foreground and the white building on the south side of the main track was the substation and battery house. (Museum of North Idaho Trr-1-81)

over the Washington, Idaho & Montana Railway (WI&M) for the first part of their trip. Its western terminus at Palouse had connections to the S&IE and NP. At the eastern end, the WI&M interchanged with the Milwaukee Road at Bovill. From here, the Milwaukee offered its own route to eastern markets and by 1910 had won nearly the same amount of Potlatch Lumber Company business as the S&IE. By 1935, SC&P carried 55% of the traffic, which went to interline transfer (25% SIR, 20% GN and 10% OWR&N), while the Milwaukee Road got 25%. In August 1961, the Milwaukee Road bought the WI&M.

Oregon Railroad & Navigation Company

Northern Pacific management believed that the OR&N was initially behind the new electric line with the aim of cutting into NP business at Coeur d'Alene. This Union Pacific ancillary company was said to have delivered new rail to the Cd'A&S at rates considerably below tariff, offered incentives for lumber loads shipped via the OR&N, and touted locally for such business. NP President Mellen told James J. Hill that there was every reason to believe that the line would have never been built but for the encouragement extended by the OR&N. He reiterated this view to the NP chairman, admitting there was no possible way of checkmating the electric line; Mellen regarded the action as unfriendly and not at all in accordance with the general understanding of peace and goodwill with Mr. Harriman.

Even if this were an accurate reflection of OR&N motives, the Cd'A&S line could not have been wholeheartedly welcomed. After all, it was an OR&N competitor for traffic to and from the Coeur d'Alene mining district and the electric service gave a one hour shorter journey time from Spokane. Nevertheless, the company provided the Cd'A&S freight trains with an entry into Spokane. One of the first commodities interchanged there was sugar beet pulp from the OR&N's Waverly branch.

The OR&N gained the advantage in 1910 by opening a branch to Amwaco from the Spokane-Tekoa line to connect with its own lake steamer to Harrison. This adversely affected S&IE boat traffic, departure from Spokane having to be at least an hour earlier to make connection with the OR&N train at Harrison. A decade later, the Oregon Washington Railroad & Navigation (OWR&N) changed the route and abandoned the branch in 1933.

There was unhappiness at the S&I expansion through the Palouse, being a rival for routes owned by the OR&N:

Moscow-Pullman-Colfax
Colfax-Garfield-Seltice
Winona-Oakesdale-Seltice
Fairfield-Waverly (abandoned 1913)

The S&IE crossed the ORR&N/UP at grade near Thornton. The gates were normally closed across the S&IE track. (Michael J. Denuty)

Consequently, the S&I encountered some resistance during construction of its own line. The company had to go to court to cross OR&N tracks at Garfield. Another court visit resulted when side tracks in Moscow, surreptitiously laid at night, were ripped out by an OR&N crew.

Passenger service from Spokane to the Palouse towns over the OR&N was not competitive in journey time compared to the electric line. However, its Moscow-Pullman-Colfax service was a useful link and in 1930 eleven thousand passengers were carried by the twice-daily gas motor car service. Bus service by Union Pacific Stages gave the Inland lines severe competition during the 1930s.

While the two companies were in competition for agricultural traffic - over 80,000 tons of grain were carried annually from OWR&N stations between Colfax and LaCrosse in the mid-1920s - the S&IE handled loads originating at the Potlatch lumber mill and destined for the OWR&N. Interchange connection at Oakesdale was specifically laid for this traffic in 1923 to avoid movement through Spokane.

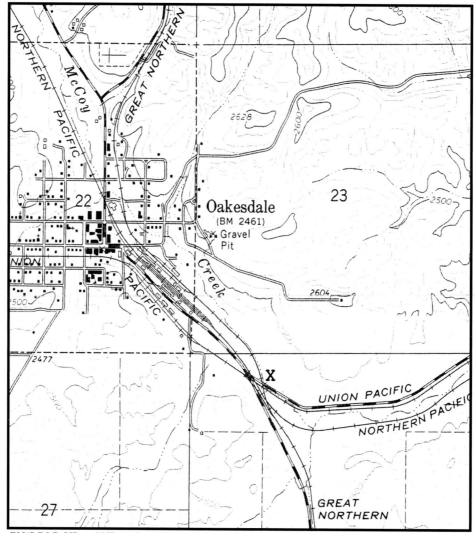

GN/SC&P, UP and NP tracks at Oakesdale. Traffic was interchanged with the UP at point X, the connection being installed in 1923 to facilitate lumber movement to the UP. (USGS map)

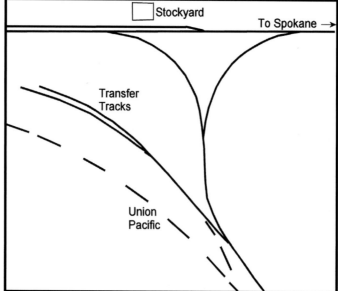

Chapter 5 contains an overall map of the Moscow terminus and a closer view of the Moscow wye is provided here. The tail gave access to two transfer tracks for interchange with the NP and UP.
(After a Great Northern Railway map)

A 1928 photograph of the UP interchange point, 3500 feet south of Oakesdale depot. The electric line (3) bisected the UP line (2) at the crossing of the NP line (1) at crossing (B).
(Northern Pacific Railway; Walt Ainsworth collection)

Track 8 extended from the tail of the Moscow wye. Track 4 connected track 8 to transfer tracks 6 and 7. Track 5 connected the transfer tracks to the UP and NP.
(Northern Pacific Railway; Walt Ainsworth collection)

A closer view of the Moscow transfer tracks 6 and 7, both of which were wired. On the left-hand side, the tracks of the NP (1) and OWR&N (2) ran into Moscow.
(Northern Pacific Railway; Walt Ainsworth collection)

Spokane International Railway

Daniel Corbin built the 140-mile Spokane International Railway (SIR) from Spokane to Eastport on the Canadian border. When close to completion in October 1906, the SIR laid a temporary connection to the electric line near McGuires so that its trains could enter Spokane. Corbin used this connection for several weeks. The newcomer also used the S&IE freight house in Spokane until its own was finished.

Spokane International became a competitor, building a 9.7-mile branch to Coeur d'Alene from its main line in 1911 to seek new business. Interchange facilities with the S&IE were established at Gibbs. Passenger service was introduced and although only one daily round trip was made, the S&IE did not need more competition at that time. The passenger train was eliminated about 1918, but freight continued.

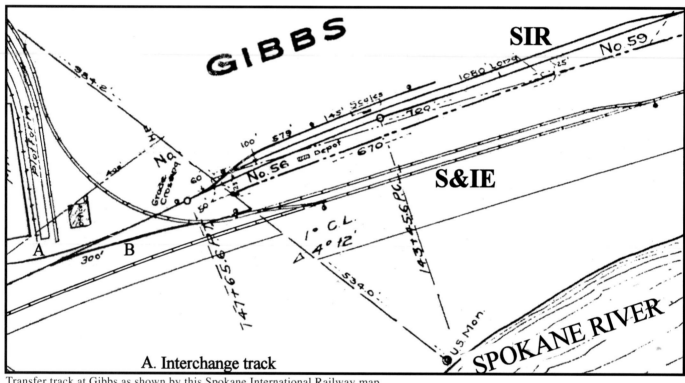

A. Interchange track

Transfer track at Gibbs as shown by this Spokane International Railway map.

Transfer track between the BN (ex-GN) and UP lines at Gibbs photographed in April 1972. (Michael J. Denuty Collection)

The SIR and Spokane & Inland signed a contract in April 1905 (before either road was operative) for the interchange of freight at agreed rates. Eastbound loads went via the Canadian Pacific and the Minneapolis, St. Paul & Sault Ste. Marie (SOO) railroads. Joint tariffs established between the S&I, WI&M and SIR to move Potlatch Lumber Company traffic in this way yielded about 30 car loads per day by 1910. Cars were collected from the WI&M at Palouse.

SC&P tracks 5, 7 and 8 extended from the wye at the north end of Palouse station to connect with WI&M tracks 3 and 4.
(Northern Pacific Railway; Walt Ainsworth collection)

Interchange with the NP at Palouse was over the connecting tracks 2 and 7 between the WI&M tracks 4 and 5 and the NP line 1.
(Northern Pacific Railway; Walt Ainsworth collection)

Such tariffs became a thorn in the side of the NP and GN parent companies, having been made with their major competitors. Management of both railways considered that lumber movement over the Spokane International was regrettable, but cancellation was impractical since the tariffs had ICC approval. They did stipulate, however, that short haul sacrifices be made by the S&IE to attend to the long haul business of the parents, too little attention having been paid to this factor. Success of this policy can be judged by Inland Empire Railroad data for the first nine months of 1921, with the GN, NP and SP&S jointly winning 71% of the 2,580 cars interchanged:

SP&S   29%
GN   21%
NP   21%
SIR   12%
CM&StP   10%
S&E   6%
OWR&N   <1%

The electric lines continued to interchange with the SIR with, for example, 700 cars in 1935, 90% of which were outbound.

Passenger travel to the east over the Spokane International was also promoted by the S&IE. The GN and NP instructed S&IE management to cancel this arrangement and the one with the Milwaukee too.

Union Pacific purchased the SIR in 1958. The track was later cut back from the lakeside to terminate at the Stimson Company mill. In December 2003, Union Pacific granted 1.4 miles of trackage rights to BNSF at Coeur d'Alene as part of BNSF's agreement to provide haulage services

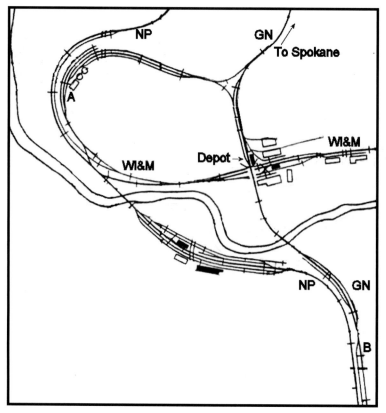

Track arrangement of the three railroads that entered Palouse. Interchange between the GN and the WI&M was at the sidings (A) shown upper left; interchange with the NP used the same tracks. From 1946 the GN and NP interchanged on purpose-built track at bottom right (B). (After a USGS map)

SC&P built a connection with the Spokane International Railway at milepost 6.88 near Millwood in 1934. Its primary purpose was to give the GN access to the local paper mill traffic. This photograph of the connection, looking east with the SIR track on the left-hand side, was taken in March 1973. (Michael J. Denuty)

for UP between there and Spokane. This allowed the UP to abandon most of its SIR branch to Coeur d'Alene.

Road Transport

After World War I, major improvements were made to highways that duplicated the rail routes. Automobile ownership rapidly increased. Regular bus service between Spokane and Coeur d'Alene, instituted in 1925, attracted many rail passengers. Buses between Spokane and Lewiston served most of the Inland towns. Road haulage firms sprang up, penetrating every area served by the S&IE. By the mid-1920s freight had all but disappeared from the Vera line due to road competition. Intermediate stations on the Coeur d'Alene line closed during the next decade for the same reason. Traffic generation diminished at Inland stations, notably between Spokane and Mount Hope where several had closed by 1941.

Sources

Northern Pacific Railway President's File Nos. 972, 1340, 1340-T, 1375.

Great Northern Railway President's Subject File No.8759 Spokane & Inland Empire Railroad General File.

Burg, Thomas E. White Pine Route: The History of the Washington, Idaho & Montana Railway Company, Museum of North Idaho, Coeur d'Alene ID, 2003.

Wood, John V. Railroads Through the Coeur d'Alenes, Caxton Printers, Caldwell ID, 1983.

Crowded trains were not unusual during the early years of operation as illustrated by the small Cd'A&S cars ready to depart from the Spokane terminal. (Museum of North Idaho Trr-1-34)

Chapter 9

TRAFFIC

PASSENGERS

Population of the towns served by the S&IE was not large. The 1910 census revealed close to 120,000 people (Table 9.1). Harrison and Wallace, serving the Coeur d'Alene mining district, added about 4,000 more. Forecasts promised rapid growth for the railroad's service area, stimulated by the new electric trains. It did not occur. By 1940, the population was less than 150,000.

Table 9.1. Population of Towns Served by the S&IE

	1910	1940
Spokane	104,402	122,001
Coeur d'Alene	7,291	10,049
Moscow	3,670	6,014
Colfax	2,783	2,853
Palouse	1,549	1,028
Oakesdale	882	690
Rosalia	767	596
Waverly	318	131

Encouraging passenger business, as measured by the average number of daily passengers in July, was experienced during the early years: 700 in 1904, 1,200 in 1905 and 2,000 in 1906. Crowded trains were not uncommon, particularly on weekends. Several thousand passengers were carried on the July 4, 1906 holiday, when 41 trains ran each way at 20-minute intervals.

The S&IE made every effort to stimulate passenger travel. Incentives included excursions, extra trains whenever necessary, and reduced fare arrangements. The company went to the extent of running a late evening train daily to Coeur d'Alene to carry theatergoers home from Spokane. Books of tickets for commuters and for 1,000 miles of trips were available at reduced rates. The railway company maintained 20 acres of waterfront land at Coeur d'Alene as a public park, adding a pavilion which brought many day-trippers to the town.

The Cd'A&S built Blackwell Park at Coeur d'Alene to help draw visitors to the town. (Ted Holloway collection)

135

The company promoted excursions to resorts and special events, exploiting any means to enhance revenue. Special trains for organized groups were arranged and their needs accommodated. One special ran directly from Moscow to Coeur d'Alene for a sports meeting. Illustrating the importance of such events to the bottom line was a large drop in revenue after termination of horse racing at the Alan racetrack in 1913. One notable event occurred in December 1936: a Great Northern twelve-car special train carried Weyerhaeuser officials to the company's mill at Coeur d'Alene. The train itself was an unusual visitor, consisting of eight first-class Pullman sleepers, two dining cars, a business car and a rear end club car, pulled from Spokane by an electric locomotive trailed by an oil-fired heater car, the latter normally assigned to the electrified section of the GN main line. Approaching the mill, the train stalled in snow. An NP locomotive, hastily purloined from a log train, rescued the special by pushing from the rear. In the meantime, steam had been piped from a nearby laundry to help keep the cars warm. The trip was completed successfully.

The S&IE encouraged special traffic to help swell the coffers. Great Northern operated such trains after acquiring the company. One special went to Coeur d'Alene in 1949, the last to carry passengers there, hauled by Alco model RS-1 No. 182. Great Northern coach No. 658 coupled to the locomotive was constructed from wood in 1913, refurbished with steel later, and had six sections for sleeping. (Museum of North Idaho Trr-3-12)

As part of the ongoing sales effort, an advertising agent was appointed to run a publicity department office in the terminal building. In order of expenditure the publicity media were (1) newspapers, (2) illustrated folders, timetables and maps and (3) billboards, passenger cars, and souvenirs. Advertisements were placed in local newspapers for towns along the lines. Rather than crowd the space with information, the company preferred brevity. For example, a catchy headline and brief facts about excursions were shown. In each of the suburban towns served by the railway, a small advertisement ran in the weekly newspaper: a local timetable display was varied by announcements of excursions or reduced long-distance fares.

Advertisements of train services.

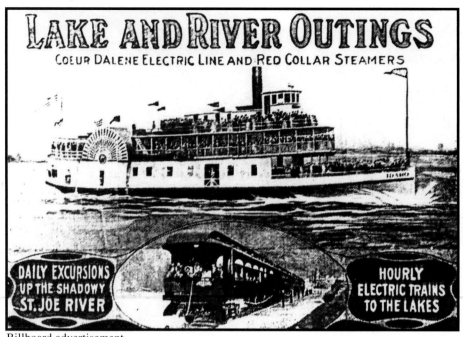

Billboard advertisement.

Folders and maps were of high quality because the company wanted to convey this impression of the rail system. The official timetable folder contained the electric train services, connecting steamers and steam railroads. Other folders dealt with vacation attractions in the area. Hotels and sporting goods stores were kept well supplied with literature. Station agents compiled mailing lists of clubs and groups.

Billboard advertising was found to be the most effective method, bringing quick and direct results. Thirty billboards throughout Spokane advertised excursions in the summer while eight in winter promoted regular services. Passenger cars displayed maps and timetables.

Residential and resort property companies were incorporated to stimulate travel over the railroad. Investors included the S&IE and directors thereof:
· Hayden Lake Improvement Company acquired land and built a hotel and recreational facilities.
· Liberty Lake Improvement Company aimed to develop residential property in the area.
· Railway Land & Improvement Company planned infrastructure for towns adjacent to the S&I right-of-way and sale thereof.
Further information on the three companies is given in Appendix D.

Despite all such efforts, the percentage of gross revenue from the railroad passenger business fell almost uniformly after Hill gained control. By 1916 only 50% came from this source and in ten years had halved again. Automobile ownership growth and bus competition were the major causes.

Table 9.2. Financial Performance by Railroad Division – 1914

DIVISION	Gross Revenue $	Net Revenue $*
Passenger		
Coeur d'Alene	182,449	33,823
Inland	217,047	897
Vera	40,284	21,110
Freight		
Coeur d'Alene	73,777	30,789
Inland	222,861	69,777
Vera	5,510	1,373

* Operating Expenses Deducted from Gross Revenue

Comparative performance by division was rarely revealed by the S&IE, but records for 1914 show passenger revenue exceeded operating expenses on three divisions, although none were particularly profitable (Table 9.2). The DC line produced the best net return. The Spokane & Eastern carried at least four times as many passengers as the Inland Empire Railroad:

	1923	**1924**	**1925**
S&E	576,690	477,482	454,416
IE	128,010	108,739	108,585

Both generated essentially the same gross revenue due to the difference in passenger journey length.

There was a precipitous decline in passengers between 1923 and 1928 due to the continued onslaught from road transport and onset of the Depression. Fewer than 50,000 passengers (137 per day) were carried most years after 1928, compared to 700,000 in 1923. By the late 1930s, the Coeur d'Alene line recorded about 30,000 passengers per year and the Inland some 4,000. Receipts from Coeur d'Alene line stations were only $5,535 in 1939, the last full year of operation, with ten stations taking less than $10 each for the year (Table 9.3).

Table 9.3. Passenger Results for the Coeur d'Alene Line in 1939.

SPOKANE, COEUR D'ALENE & PALOUSE RAILWAY CO.

Statement showing the number of passengers and revenue by stations on the line between Spokane and Coeur D'Alene for the period, January 1st, 1939 to December 31st, 1939.

Station	Number of Passengers	Revenue
Spokane	8,299	$ 2,147.52
Esperance	2	.18
Parkwater	183	18.49
Del Monte	22	4.60
Air Port	16	1.52
Orchard Ave.	339	39.32
Regan	343	33.98
Millwood	2,561	235.73
N. P. Ry. Subway	541	60.56
Sullivan	95	8.52
Wilbur Road	644	67.35
Pinecroft	819	91.41
Mt. View	169	18.95
Carders	176	22.31
Flora	369	61.12
Greenacres	587	67.35
Toledo	48	8.62
Liberty Lake Jct.	18	2.87
Liberty Lake	11	3.27
Seaton	60	12.47
Spokane Bridge	443	67.09
Curoe	3	.14
Signal Point	494	64.82
McGuires	424	72.59
Post Falls	3,153	384.38
Alan	186	60.00
Green Ferry Road	45	9.66
Ross	357	57.72
McCellan	103	13.93
Huetter	665	69.98
Atlas	79	18.02
Gibbs	785	114.30
Homes	26	3.90
Coeur D'Alene	7,285	1,698.64
Total	29,120	$ 5,535.31

Accounting Department
Passenger Receipts Division
May 1st, 1940

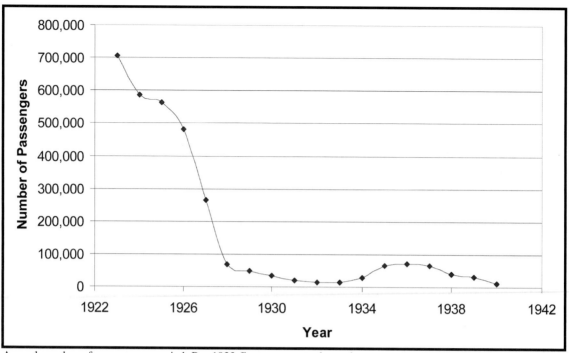

Annual number of passengers carried. Pre-1923 figures are not shown because streetcar passengers were included in available data.

With the decrease in passengers, mail became of increasing importance in sustaining revenue. Over half of the passenger business income came from this source during the 1930s (Table 9.4). Express traffic made a small contribution; the S&IE had negotiated a contract with Great Northern Express in 1907. Milk shipment was encouraged by the S&IE, but financial return was now poor.

Table 9.4. Sources of Passenger Business Gross Revenue

Source	1926	1931	1935	1939
Passengers	60%	26%	37%	31%
Mail	22%	62%	56%	60%
Express	12%	6%	4%	6%
Milk	6%	6%	3%	3%

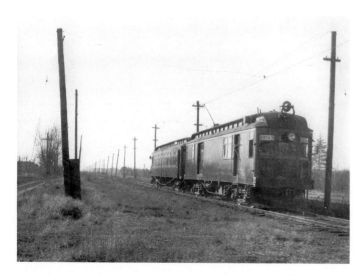

By the late 1930s, one trailer was usually adequate to carry the few passengers on the Coeur d'Alene line (Harold Hall, Warren Wing Collection)

Mail being unloaded at Spokane GN depot. Mail revenue became of increasing importance as passenger revenue fell.
(Clyde Parent, Richard Yaremko Collection)

FREIGHT

By the end of the first three years of Cd'A&S operation, freight contributed one-third of the company's gross revenue. This was a much greater proportion of gross revenue than most interurban railroads accomplished. The proportion continued to grow under the S&IE. By the time SC&P took over, 75% of the revenue came from freight.

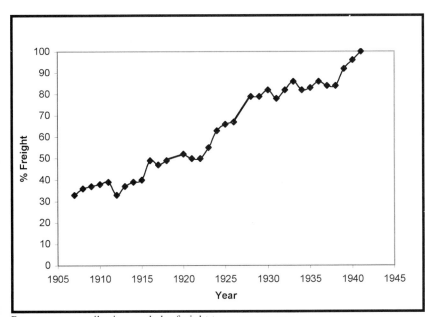

Percentage contribution made by freight to gross revenue.

Gross freight revenue generated by the Inland Division in 1914 was three times greater than the Coeur d'Alene Division (Table 9.2), the Inland carrying twice the average number of carloads daily. Traffic volume was consistently double that of the S&E between 1920 and 1925, although as noted in Chapter 2 the IE failed to cover operating costs.

A traveling freight and passenger

Washington State Sugar Company factory at Waverly owned by Daniel C. Corbin, builder of the Spokane Falls & Northern and Spokane International Railways. An OR&N branch provided rail service until the S&I built a spur to the factory. Reluctance of local farmers to grow beets restricted output and sugar production ceased after the 1910 season. The plant was sold in 1916 and equipment moved to Utah the following year. (Ted Holloway Collection)

agent did most of the freight soliciting for the S&IE. Local agents were expected to spend an hour or two daily with their customers and the traffic manager required daily reports of all freight handled at their stations. Inland depots were located close to those of competitors, so each agent was aware of all local freight movement. Seven station agents were employed between Spokane and Hayden Lake in 1912, but only two by 1934. Ten years later the Coeur d'Alene agent was the only one along the line, staying there until well after the BN merger. After cessation of passenger service on the Inland, agents remained at seven stations to support the freight business. By 1968, there were two agents, each responsible for dual agencies, and one at Moscow.

With respect to annual tonnage carried on the system, figures for 1908-1911 were in the range of 331,594 between 575,276 tons and averaged 438,190 tons. For the 1937 to 1941 period, annual loads were in the range of 261,037 to 280,368 tons except for 223,623 tons in 1938 when lumber production fell. Evidence presented to the ICC revealed that an average of 137,000 tons per year moved over the Spokane-Mount Hope

Loaded cars await dispatch from Washington Brick, Lime & Manufacturing Company plant at Freeman, over a 3,200-foot spur from the electric line. Daily output was 200 tons. (Ted Holloway Collection)

Table 9.5. Commodities Carried (by weight).

Products	1908	1911	1937	1938	1939	1940	1941
Forest	54%	51%	44%	38%	42%	55%	54%
Agricultural	20%	18%	33%	38%	35%	28%	29%
Mines*	5%	6%	8%	11%	11%	6%	5%
Miscellaneous**	21%	25%	15%	13%	12%	11%	12%

* sand, gravel and inward shipments of coal.
** machinery, agricultural equipment, oil and gas.

section in 1947-1950. Assuming that the Inland had continued to generate double the amount of traffic on the Coeur d'Alene line, the system total would have been close to 200,000 tons per annum.

Half of the tonnage consisted of forest products as shown in Table 9.5, except for years of reduced lumber production as in 1937-1939. This industry had been recognized as the potential major freight customer when the Cd'A&S was incorporated. Sawmills had hardly opened at Coeur d'Alene when train service began, but developed rapidly. Lumber became a major source traffic for the Inland, too.

Loaded flat cars at Coeur d'Alene. Logs and lumber were significant sources of revenue. (Museum of North Idaho Trr-1-11)

Of the lumber loads interchanged, 30 to 40% originated on-line, with the remainder coming from the WI&M and reciprocal switching. For example, in 1910 the Potlatch Lumber Company shipped 2,163 carloads via the WI&M for interchange with the S&IE:
- 47% for forwarding to the Spokane International (& SOO)
- 37% for forwarding to the Great Northern
- 16% to Potlatch-owned sales outlets near S&IE stations.

Potlatch Mill at Potlatch Idaho, served by the WI&M, was a major source of interchange traffic. Note that the two boxcars carried markings for the S&IE and Inland Empire railroads, respectively.
(Museum of North Idaho, Mil-7-35)

At the same time, the S&IE forwarded 1,263 cars that originated at Coeur d'Alene mills:
- 30% Spokane International/SOO
- 63% Great Northern
- 7% Chicago, Milwaukee & St. Paul

Eight flat cars loaded with forest products and two boxcars constituted the payload of this train hauled by two Class 700 AC locomotives, both marked Inland Empire.
(D. Cozine Collection)

Over three thousand cars also made local trips over S&IE rails in 1910: 2,426 loads of ties and wood for M.D. Wright at Monaghan (on the Hayden Lake branch) and 1,226 from his new Atlas Tie Company.

Lumber mills in the Coeur d'Alene region had a convoluted history. Changes in ownership/ identity and closures characterized the industry during the last century. Fires, bankruptcy and obsolescence were among the causes. Much of the story is told by Strong and Webb. Table 9.6

Access to the Stimson Lumber Company mill at Coeur d'Alene lumber was gained over the wye, the tail terminating in the mill, as demonstrated by this Burlington Northern class GP-7. (Ted Holloway Collection)

Table 9.6. Major Lumber Mills in the Coeur d'Alene Area

Mill	Notes
Rutledge Lumber Company	Built in 1916; became Potlatch Forests, Inc. in 1931; closed in 1987.
Blackwell Lumber Company	Incorporated in 1909; closed in 1937.
Coeur d'Alene Mill Company	Closed in 1929.
DeArmond Company	Built in 1960; became Idaho Forest Products in 1968 and Stimson Company in 2000.
Atlas Tie Company (Atlas)	Built in 1909; became Idaho Forest Products in 1968 and Stimson Company in 2000; closed in 2005.
Winton Lumber Company (Gibbs)	Became Northwest Lumber Company in 1946.
Ohio Match Company (Huetter)	Built in 1921; had several owners until purchased in 1993 by Crown Pacific; closed in 2001.
Louisiana Pacific (Post Falls)	Several owners before being purchased by L-P; closed in 1995.
Idaho Veneer Company (Post Falls)	Built in 1953.

summarizes ownership of the larger mills. Output of the few mills that survived in the area by 2001 made the branch the largest generator of lumber traffic for Burlington Northern Santa Fe in Idaho. By 2006 the primary sources of traffic were the Potlatch particle board and plywood plant, Idaho Veneer at Post Falls, and the Stimson stud mill at Coeur d'Alene.

Switching of the mills was governed by reciprocal agreements that allowed one railroad to switch for another. The S&IE did its own switching for most of its customers, gaining access over purpose-built spurs. Rutledge Lumber Co. (Potlatch Forest, Inc. from 1931 on), the principal shipper, was switched by the S&IE and also by the CM&St.P. Access to this mill was over an S&IE-owned spur that diverged from the Hayden Lake line approximately 0.5 miles east of the Coeur d'Alene depot. Northern Pacific switched the Coeur d'Alene and Blackwell mills for the S&IE. At the Atlas Tie mill, the S&IE and NP operated over their own tracks, connected by an interchange track. The S&IE and Milwaukee shared a joint track that served Winton Lumber Company at Gibbs. Smaller companies were treated the same way. For instance, the S&IE and SIR served the Lafferty Shingle Company, while the NP switched traffic bound for the S&IE at Coeur d'Alene Box Factory.

There was an unusual development in 1918, almost certainly to support the war effort. All four railroads agreed to unify the railway lines entering Coeur d'Alene. Unification required the S&IE to handle the local work, the other three railroads temporarily abandoning their service. Interchange was conducted at Spokane, except CM&St.P traffic and logs from the Spokane International that

Looking towards the BN wye from the mill in the previous figure, the Spokane International Railroad track crosses in the foreground. (Michael J. Denuty)

SC&P hauled lumber for the Blackwell Lumber Company; the cars were switched for them by the NP. At least two GN boxcars are evident in this splendid view of the mill. (Northern Pacific Railway; Walt Ainsworth Collection)

were transferred at McGuires. The S&IE borrowed a steam locomotive from the NP for $15 per day to work non-electrified lines. Duration of this agreement is unclear, but it was effective for at least eight months.

Agriculture accounted for one-third of the tonnage hauled in the 1930s, wheat growing being the major economy of the region south of Freeman. Most of the grain was billed to elevators at Seattle, Tacoma and Portland, but some went to the Spokane mills. Local and national companies improved grain-handling facilities. They arranged to operate railway-owned warehouses, sometimes enlarging them, and built elevators. Spurs were modified by the railroad to serve the new facilities.

Coeur d'Alene Mill Company (N) was located ¼ mile east of the passenger depot. Northern Pacific switched the mill for SC&P and CMSt. P&P. NP track 9 provided connection from the mill track (1) to the Hayden Lake line (4) that ran past the mill. Track 8 was a Milwaukee connection between its track 7 and the Hayden Lake line. (Walt Ainsworth, Northern Pacific Railway Collection)

Rutledge Lumber Co. mill, Coeur d'Alene, in 1927. (Northern Pacific Railway; Walt Ainsworth Collection)

Segments of the Inland lines that remained open after 1972 served the storage units. By the late 1970s, annual grain shipments were estimated by shippers as:

Location	Car Loads
Balder	200
Cashup - Manning	300
Crabtree and Sokulk	100
Seabury and Fairbanks	100
Spring Valley – Mt. Hope	200
Grinnell	100

Assuming a carload of 80 tons, this represented 80,000 tons per year. Around 20% was barley and the rest wheat. No inbound traffic was received, except for some 20 cars per year of agricultural chemicals delivered to the Mount Hope branch.

Large quantities of fruit and vegetables were carried until usurped by road transport. During the last four months of 1912, the S&IE dispatched 478 carloads, Greenacres shipping 45 cars, followed by Sharon, Moscow, Kiesling, Willow Springs, and Opportunity that loaded over 30 cars each. Fruit shippers also made use of express and less-than-carload facilities, the latter requiring the assignment of two or more cars in the refrigerator services that operated at that time.

A dozen stations were given stockyards when the lines were built and the S&IE made ten stock cars available. Records for 1909-1910 show an average of 1,500 tons of livestock (equivalent to 3,000 cows) moved per year. Several stockyards were abandoned by the time GN absorbed the rail system - loads were only one-fifth of the 1910 level.

Jefferson, a siding between Spring Valley and Mount Hope, was one of the stations that continued to get rail service for agricultural traffic during the 1970s. (Ted Holloway Collection)

Thornton, on the Colfax branch from Spring Valley, continued in operation during the 1970s. (Michael J. Denuty Collection)

Rail-served facilities at Steptoe on the Colfax branch were quite extensive by 1972. (Michael J. Denuty)

The S&IE provided spurs at numerous stations to promote business growth. This spur at Greenacres carried traffic for a local canning company. (Sheldon Perry Collection)

Location	Car Loads
Balder	200
Cashup - Manning	300
Crabtree and Sokulk	100
Seabury and Fairbanks	100
Spring Valley – Mt. Hope	200
Grinnell	100

Assuming a carload of 80 tons, this represented 80,000 tons per year. Around 20% was barley and the rest wheat. No inbound traffic was received, except for some 20 cars per year of agricultural chemicals delivered to the Mount Hope branch.

Large quantities of fruit and vegetables were carried until usurped by road transport. During the last four months of 1912, the S&IE dispatched 478 carloads, Greenacres shipping 45 cars, followed by Sharon, Moscow, Kiesling, Willow Springs, and Opportunity that loaded over 30 cars each. Fruit shippers also made use of express and less-than-carload facilities, the latter requiring the assignment of two or more cars in the refrigerator services that operated at that time.

A dozen stations were given stockyards when the lines were built and the S&IE made ten stock cars available. Records for 1909-1910 show an average of 1,500 tons of livestock (equivalent to 3,000 cows) moved per year. Several stockyards were abandoned by the time GN absorbed the rail system - loads were only one-fifth of the 1910 level.

Sources

Spokane & Eastern Ry. & Power Co. Annual Report to Washington State. 1920-1927.

Inland Empire Railroad. Annual Report to Washington State. 1920-1927.

Spokane, Coeur d'Alene & Palouse Railway. Annual Report to Washington State. 1927-1942.

Great Northern Railway President's Subject File No.8759 Spokane & Inland Empire Railroad.

Northern Pacific Railway President's File No.1604-2.

Street Railway Journal, October 12 1907, 30: 664. "Handling Freight on the Spokane & Inland System."

Flagg, Charles F. "The Possibilities of a Well-Conducted Department of Publicity," Electric Railway Journal, October 15, 1908, 32:1085.

Electric Railway Journal, October 8, 1910, 36: 633.

Railway Age Gazette, September 4, 1914: 423, "Hill System Electric Lines in the Northwest."

Strong, Clarence C. and Webb, Clyde S. White Pine: King of Many Waters, Mountain Press Publishing Co., 1970.

Great Northern Railway Historical Society, Reference Sheet No.243, June 1996, "Stories – Historical and Personal."

Accident scene at Gibbs on July 31, 1909, after the collision between eastbound and westbound trains. The leading car of the westbound No. 5 was telescoped between its partner trailer on the left-hand side of the photograph and the leading car of eastbound No. 8 on the right. (Sheldon Perry Collection)

Chapter 10

COLLISIONS

The first incident reported on the Cd'A&S was at Spokane Bridge, December 15, 1904. The 4:00 p.m. passenger train from Spokane ran into a motor baggage car, standing on the siding, through an open switch. Luckily, train speed was low. Flying glass cut both motormen, but no passengers were injured.

Accidents that warranted autonomous investigation are summarized below in chronological order. By far the most destructive occurred at Gibbs in 1909, where two passenger trains collided.

Freeman, Washington

A wreck occurred on the Spokane & Inland Railway at Freeman at 5:10 a.m. on September 15, 1907, in which the engineer O.W. Frost was crushed to death. Extras M2 and M5, both second-class trains, were going towards Spokane. Each crew knew the other was being operated.

Train M2 stopped at Freeman, ostensibly for switching and picking up cars. A man was left to protect the train and was about 600 feet behind when M5 came in sight. It was flagged, but not acknowledged by the crew. Brakes were not applied as the train passed the flagman and it continued to run at about 25 mph until train M2 was struck. When trainmen ran to electric locomotive M5, the engineer was found sitting in his cab seat crushed to death, his current turned fully on and air brakes not applied.

Washington State Transportation Division concluded that the motorman had become unconscious for some undetermined reason (no autopsy was mentioned). Company rules required that all trains of this class approach stations under control and responsibility for rear-end collisions was with the following train. Under the rules, train M2 need not have flagged, it being between switches on straight track and at a station. Collision could possibly have been avoided had two men been at the front of locomotive M5, or had the flagman put down torpedoes, thus alerting the head brakeman sitting in the locomotive's rear. The S&I general manager said that in future two men would be required for locomotives.

Gibbs, Idaho

No investigative report of this collision was issued by a state or government agency. Details given herein were therefore drawn from contemporary newspaper reports.

During July and August, 1909, the US government held a public lottery for the disposition of Indian Reservation land in three northwest states. Potential homesteaders had to register for the lottery in each state. Two of the registration sites were Coeur d'Alene and Spokane. Thousands of people came from all parts of the country despite long odds of winning. During the first two weeks of the 21-day registration period, the S&IE had found it almost impossible to carry the crowds between Spokane and Coeur d'Alene, despite extra service with trains departing every 20 minutes.

On July 31, 1909, two crowded trains collided at Gibbs station about 1½ miles from Coeur d'Alene. Special No. 5, westbound, and regular No. 20, eastbound, met head-on on a single line track. Seventeen people died and over one hundred were injured.

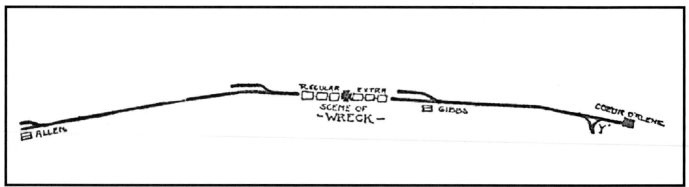

Sketch of Gibbs collision site.

Each train consisted of three cars. The eastbound train No. 20, of recent manufacture, was headed by motor, baggage and passenger car No. 8. The westbound special No. 5 was of lighter construction and consisted of motor baggage and passenger car No. 5, trailer No. 50 and a partner trailer.

A steam locomotive was sent from Coeur d'Alene to help with clearance at the site. (Museum of North Idaho Trr-2-3)

The motorman of the eastbound stopped his train when he saw special No. 5 approaching around a curve. The westbound collided at a speed of about 25 mph. Its leading motor car was telescoped, only twelve feet of the body remaining above the floor, the heavier motor car riding over the lighter vehicle. Contemporary newspapers presented graphic reports of the resulting carnage to passengers crammed in the small combination car. Workers from nearby Stack-Gibbs lumber mill rushed to help the injured. Medical staff were dispatched from Coeur d'Alene Hospital while physicians and nurses arrived from Spokane within an hour by special train. Incapacitated victims were moved to the local hospital while mobile casualties traveled to St. Luke's and Sacred Heart hospitals in Spokane for treatment.

Jay Graves, president of the S&IE, authorized an official statement the following day. In part, he said, "The company will make a full, thorough and complete investigation, fixing the blame where it belongs without

Closer view of the remains of car No. 5 from the opposite side of the tracks. (Museum of North Idaho Trr-2-5)

fear or favor and will make the result of the investigation public. The accident is of such an appalling nature that the public is entitled to be fully informed concerning its cause. As to the injured persons and the relatives of those who lost their lives in the wreck, the company wants them to understand that it will act fairly and justly with them and that it is unnecessary to hire a lawyer to enforce their claims….We want to be fair and deal justly with everyone and we hope all will come to us in the same spirit."

General Manager Clyde M. Graves announced on August 3 that "We have made a sufficiently full investigation to determine that the company is legally liable for any legitimate damages sustained by reason of the wreck and this legal liability it does not intend to question….The company has decided to ask (for) a public investigation."

Evidence pertinent to the collision was given at two separate hearings. One was a coroner's inquest held in Coeur d'Alene on August 6, 1909. A nine-member committee of attorneys and businessmen, appointed by the Chambers of Commerce of Spokane and Coeur d'Alene, and officers of the railway company conducted the second investigation, on August 17-18.

Principal facts disclosed during the hearings were as follows. The road operated under standard code rules. Track and equipment were in good order. Trainmen were competent and of many years experience, on both steam and electric railways. During the rush they were obliged to work overtime, but this in no way affected their efficiency. Men and cars of the westbound train were late in reaching Coeur d'Alene from the west. Orders for their westbound trip were issued before they arrived and the assistant trainmaster received and receipted for these orders contrary to the rule. The conductor and motorman did not sign the register. The order specified that No. 5 should meet eastbound special No. 4 at Alan (6.5 miles from the terminus). No. 5 was bound to keep out of the way of eastbound No. 20 under the rule that made extra trains always inferior to regular trains with respect to movement.

The assistant trainmaster delivered the order to the conductor, at the same time telling him that eastbound No. 20 was late (25 minutes). He instructed the conductor to pull his train down to the wye (¼ mile from the depot), such movement being permissible within station limits, where No. 20 would clear the way for No. 5. Temporary operating arrangements, to expedite train reversal, required eastbound trains to reverse on the wye and back into the terminus. The conductor gave verbal instructions to the motorman and handed him a copy of the order. He did not, however, require the motorman to read the order aloud in the conductor's presence as required. He also failed to exhibit the order to the brakemen; both were unaware of it.

Having instructed the motorman, the conductor went into the car and began taking tickets as the train departed. The motorman kept right on past the wye, regardless of instructions, while the conductor did not notice that the train failed to stop there. If he had paid attention to the operation of the train instead of collecting tickets, the collision could have been avoided. Approaching the point of collision, the motorman should have seen the eastbound No. 20, 800 feet away.

Conflicting evidence was presented with respect to the subsequent deceleration of No. 5. An experiment conducted at the collision site with a train similar to No. 5 demonstrated that at the estimated speed, the train could have stopped within 200 feet. Indeed, No. 20 had done this immediately prior to the collision. Failure by the motorman to keep a good lookout was thus cited as an element in the cause of the wreck. The only excuse offered by the motorman was that he understood that the order referred to No. 20, instead of special No. 4, for the meeting at Alan. He was badly injured, breaking both legs. The motorman of No. 20 had jumped out after stopping his train, so avoided serious injury.

The six-man coroner's jury found that "the collision was caused by the running of special No. 5 out of the Coeur d'Alene yards without orders on the time of regular train No. 20, from Spokane; by the failure of the conductor and motorman of special No. 5 to register out as required by the rules; by the failure of the company to stop the practice of allowing the conductor to register for the motorman and in not requiring the brakeman to be informed of the contents of the train's orders."

The nine-man committee found that the motorman and conductor caused the wreck by violating the rules. While the assistant trainmaster violated a rule by signing in for the conductor's train order, no blame was attached to him. The company was exonerated – unlike the findings of the coroner's jury.

By June 1912, the S&IE had awarded $345,488 in compensation. Settlement of certain claims through litigation was not finalized until 1916. Damaged cars were repaired except for motor combination car No. 5, the remains of which were used to construct a motor baggage car.

McGuires, Idaho

On July 1, 1915, an S&IE electric passenger train, running as extra 43, collided with an Idaho & Washington Northern Railroad freight train at the intersection of the two railroads at McGuires, Idaho. This resulted in injury to 27 passengers and 7 employees.

Both lines were single track, crossing at grade at an angle of about 45 degrees. Normally a gate was locked across the I&WN track. Trains on that road were required to stop and swing the gate across the S&IE track, before using the crossing. S&IE trains were not required to stop if the gate was set against the opposing line and the way seen to be clear. At night the position of the gate was indicated by a lamp mounted on a mast on top of the gate; a green light showed to trains having the right-of-way, and a red light to trains required to stop.

The I&WN freight extra, consisting of a steam locomotive and 32 cars, arrived at McGuires at 11:16 p.m. The train stopped before the engine reached the crossing. A brakeman went ahead, unlocked the gate and changed its position to stop trains on the S&IE track. He observed that the lamp was lit, as did the engine crew. The train then started and while passing over the crossing at about 4 mph it was struck between the eighteenth and nineteenth cars by S&IE westbound passenger extra 43, consisting of motor-passenger car No. 43 and one trailer, running at about 25 mph. The force was such that two freight cars, loaded with cement, came to rest at right angles with the electric track. Both passenger cars derailed and were badly damaged.

Extra 43 approached the crossing at about 40 miles per hour. The motorman said he looked for the signal light on the crossing gate, but did not see it. A yardmaster was in the motorman's compartment with him. Within 400 or 500 feet of the crossing the motor-passenger car headlight revealed a train on the I&WN track. He immediately applied the emergency brake but was unable to stop in time to prevent the collision.

The Interstate Commerce Commission concluded that the cause of the accident was failure of the motorman to properly control the speed of his train approaching the crossing and to know the position of the gate governing the use of the crossing. Under company rules he should have approached the crossing at such a speed that he could have stopped his train clear of the crossing had the signals been set against him or had the crossing been obstructed. In the event of a gate signal light not being visible, as claimed by motorman, the rules stated that this should be regarded as a stop signal. In addition, he violated company instructions that unauthorized persons were prohibited from riding in the motorman's compartment. The ICC found that the method employed by the S&IE and the I&WN railroads to control the use of the gate crossing at McGuires by trains was inadequate and did not afford proper protection. The S&IE subsequently installed an interlocking tower and signals.

Sources

Railroad Commission of Washington. Second and Third Annual Reports, p.67, Investigation Report, September 18, 1907.

Interstate Commerce Commission Report, August 15 1915, Investigation of a Collision which Occurred at the Intersection of the Tracks of the Idaho & Washington Northern Railroad and the Spokane & Inland Empire Railroad at McGuires on July 1 1915.

Inland Empire Quarterly, Inland Empire Railway Historical Society, 4, No.4, p.4.

Spokane Spokesman Review.

Coeur d'Alene Press.

Trolley wire was installed over two tracks at the GN Spokane depot on Havermale Island to allow electric passenger trains to enter the station. An eastbound train passes the Express Company office at the station in 1938. (Harold Hill, Warren Wing Collection)

Chapter 11

SYSTEM WIDE TOUR

This chapter presents a photographic tour over the interurban system. Infrastructure and examples of the industries served by the company are illustrated (in milepost order). Various eras are encompassed. The tour begins on the Coeur d'Alene line from the Great Northern depot, followed by views of the Vera line and continues south from Inland Junction.

To set the scene, descriptions of two journeys made on the interurban system by Clyde Parent are presented below. Clyde was the leading authority on the interurban and traveled over it many times. Permission was kindly granted by the Inland Empire Railway Historical Society to reproduce the text, quoting directly from their publications.

SC&P TO OAKESDALE

After the demise of the local city electric lines, I was working as night dispatcher for the Spokane United Railways [SU], which by 1940 was nothing but a bus line. The interurban lines run by the Great Northern Railway to Coeur d'Alene, Moscow and Colfax were still using electric locomotives for freight service in the fall of 1940.

So I thought it would be nice to take a trip on the line south of Spokane while it was still electric. Through the SU Railways, I got a pass. I planned to take a freight train leaving the Spokane Yards about noon to Oakesdale, where it was scheduled to meet the northbound freight from Moscow about 3:00 pm, so I could be back in town by six or seven in the evening.

The conductor on the southbound freight leaving Spokane that day was Tom Smith, whom I had known in times past as conductor on passenger trains. Young Dow, whose father was also a motorman on the electric lines, was at the master controller of the #704 and #706 on the point.

Taking a lunch, a flashlight and my camera which I think was a 2¼ x 3½ Voightlander "Bessa" loaded with black and white film [several photographs included in this chapter were taken on the trip], I swung aboard the caboose and climbed into the cupola to wait until we rolled out of the yard.

The DC switching motor finally backed into the rear of our caboose and coupled on. After the crew tested the air and exchanged insults with our crew (motorman, conductor and two brakemen), they shoved our train, about eighteen assorted cars and the two AC locomotives, out through the yards, over the wooden bridges, past the gas works and under east Sprague Avenue, to the breaker between the AC trolley wires. Then the two folded pantographs on top of the locos suddenly sprang to life, jumped up and started gliding under the catenary wire, feeding 6600 volts, 25 cycles alternating current to the two "700" type units, which suddenly pulled all the slack out of the train, and as the rear motor dropped off, started up the grade south of Third Avenue as easily as if they had nothing but the caboose tied on.

By now I was standing on the rear platform of the caboose with my camera and recorded scenes: the gravel pit at Pantops, just east of the Spokane city limits, then as we rolled up the grade, through Moran, Parkview, Keisling, Valleyford and Freeman, finally coming to an easy stop just north of the huge wooden Rock Creek trestle.

All trains were required to stop before venturing out on the spectacular Rock Creek bridge, and as you can see from the photo, it was high, long and curved and according to crews, shaky, dilapidated, treacherous and about to fall in. However, trains used it about twelve years more until 1952, when it was the main reason for the abandonment of all track between Mt. Hope and Spokane. Even after that, it stood for years withstanding the efforts to bring it down with bulldozers, winches and even dynamite.

We sneaked over the top of this bridge slowly, waved to the bridge tender and headed through the forest towards Mt. Hope.

Here the train was broken in two and the twin "700" class locos were used for switching cars in and out of the sidings. At that time there were no grain elevators at Mt. Hope, only storage sheds. After motorman Dow and conductor Smith had put the train back together with the help of the brakemen, we once more proceeded south towards Waverly, where more switching was done, but this time from the head end, which left the caboose about a quarter mile up the curved grade northwest of the town.

Next stop was Spring Valley where two "600" with #606 on the point headed the Colfax branch freight. Here freight cars were exchanged, the 606 wyed and started back for Colfax with a train and we once more headed south on the Moscow branch.

At Oakesdale, we arrived before the northbound from Moscow, so we went in the "hole" to eat lunch and wait for the other train. When this train did arrive, its double set of motors was headed by #701 and was pulling so much tonnage that I was informed that the crew would have to "double the hill" between Spring Valley and Silver Hill. This, of course, meant taking one part of the train to Silver Hill first, cutting it off, then going back to Spring Valley with the motors and caboose, bringing the rest of the train up the hill, then putting it together again for the downhill trip to Spokane. I had planned to be back in Spokane sometime during the evening, but this maneuver meant the train would not arrive until midnight or even later.

When we left Spring Valley northbound with only about 24 loads, I decided I would not return with the crew to double the hill. When we finally ground to a stop at Silver Hill, which was just this side of Keisling, I told the conductor goodbye, dropped off and walked the ties six miles in the dark (luckily I had my flashlight) from there to 29th and Myrtle in Spokane, the end of the bus line, where I collapsed gratefully into a bus seat.

VERA LINE

Nothing to me was more pleasant than to spend a Sunday afternoon riding this line. Arriving at the terminal building at Main and Lincoln about 11:30 a.m., I would first see what type of equipment they had ready for the Sunday rush to and from Liberty Lake and to Coeur d'Alene Lake, which of course ran on the faster line with multiple-unit trains. I did not always have enough money for this trip.

So I bought a round trip ticket to Liberty Lake and walked over to where car #210 was waiting to be loaded, with destination sign "VERA" in the upper right front window and "LIBERTY LAKE" below. I gave the motorman (one-man car) my ticket and then sat on the first transverse seat where I could see everything up front.

Then I watched as he rang up the fares collected on the "OHMER" fare register, which was operated from the motorman's position and showed the amount collected on a large readout in the front of the main passenger compartment where all could see it. The #210 was the largest of the Vera cars and the only one built by the

Niles Car Company. So we glided out of the terminal on time, and rolled up to Post Street where a few more passengers boarded and were duly "rang up" on the Ohmer Register.

Then east to Howard and Washington Street where a large metal sign hung from the span wires proclaiming "INTERURBAN TRAINS STOP HERE" and more people boarded our car. From there we sneaked out of town on Main to Trent and east Madelia. Then east on Sprague, still on half points (half speed) to where, east of the city limits, the line curved south from Sprague to a private right-of-way. There was a passing track there, but no train was there and we did not stop. Then for the first time on the private right-of-way the motorman wound up the controller ten points and we sailed through the countryside at speed, with the chime whistle blowing for the crossings.

Here I noticed the air whistle on the #210 was not on the roof, but underneath the cab floor and when it was blown set up vibrations in the cab. Why this was done, nobody seemed to know – of course, the valve which the motorman used to sound the whistle was on the floor of the one-man cars which may have had a bearing on it.

Crossing the "Appleway" at Park Road after making the Edgecliff stop required much whistle-blowing, then down under the UP tracks and north and east around the Jack Tire Company's factory. Dishman showed up next and looking east along the tracks and trolley wire I could see a two car train waiting for us to take the passing track (eastbound trains must take the siding for another train of the same class).

After passing this train and stopping at the depot, we were off again on ten points, parallel and just north of the Appleway. Then we began to pass and overtake autos on the highway to my enjoyment. The speed limit was 30 miles per hour in those days and even though some were going faster than that, we sailed right by them on the private right-of-way just north of Sprague Avenue, much to my exhilaration. Stopping at Opportunity to let a few passengers off, we were soon gliding along again, and at True's Oil spur we veered northeast and away from the highway. Through Vera and at Flora Junction the motorman steps down to register our train in a little booth by the tracks.

Then east through Greenacres, an agency station on the Coeur d'Alene-Hayden Lake line, which was double tracked. A stop at Liberty Lake Junction to align the rails and then we are south towards Liberty Lake. But first another stop, at the Milwaukee tracks, a long look up and down the steam rails and then with a long blast of the whistle we are sailing down the single track branch line.

Sitting by an open window, the smell of new mown hay and the wild flowers mingling with the ozone from the car motors, no pollution, but just floating along on the rails, passing the cars on the highway, what could be better? Soon a long blast on the chime whistle as we pass waiting autos on the side roads, then slow down for the spring switch into the loop. The motorman sets his K28 controller on three points and we are soon stopping with a whoosh in front of the agency station of Liberty Lake. Here everybody gets off with their picnic basket, towels and swimming suits and fan out over the big park, while some head for the bath houses.

So I hung around the little depot where the telegraph key clicks continuously and the agent appears to be too busy to talk to me until #210 pulls out with a few passengers for Spokane. The main part of this little wooden station is occupied by the agent and all his apparatus while on each side and parallel to the tracks are open air waiting places with benches and a roof for rainy weather.

Clyde Parent occasionally published short commentaries regarding his interurban trips.

The trailers where the ladies rode with their escorts, if any, were quiet smooth running coaches, but I always preferred to ride in the baggage passenger motor car, when I could not ride in the cab. In this coach you could hear the sound of the gears growling low, then higher and higher as the train gathered speed. Then the musical sound of the air pump, as it started slowly, then faster and faster. The chime whistles were built that a motorman could blow them into overtones for a shriller, louder warning. It got so we could identify the motorman by the way he did, or did not, use the overtones at crossings and stations. At each agency station the motorman was required to blow one long and four shorts, then as the order board was or was not changed, two shorts in acknowledgment. Later, some motormen added another whistle of a different tone to the existing one, for a more pleasing sound.

Sources

Clyde Parent, "SC&P to Oakesdale", Inland Empire Railway Historical Society, Rail Quarterly, 5, Summer 1978, p.1.

Clyde Parent, "Vera Line", Inland Empire Railway Historical Society, Newsletter, March 1988, 22, No.3, p.1.

Electric trains entered the GN Spokane depot at the east end, over the main line 232-foot steel truss Havermale bridge. (Harold Hill, Warren Wing Collection)

After passing under Division Street bridge, eastbound car No. 60 branches off right from the GN line to take the 1927-laid connection to the SC&P tracks. Standing in the coach yard behind were three Pullman cars, with "Harpswell" built in 1913 to plan 2410, in the center. (Harold Hill, Warren Wing Collection)

Further east along the connecting line from the depot. The GN depot tower, GN yards and the John Deere & Low Company building were evident in the background. The SC&P freight yard was behind the photographer. (Harold Hill, Warren Wing Collection)

Looking north over the SC&P Spokane freight yard in June 1927, the freight house is at the center of the left edge of the photograph. Letter D denotes GN tracks and the white lines mark the old Lake Shore & Eastern Railway right-of-way.
(Northern Pacific Railway; Walt Ainsworth Collection)

Looking west towards the Spokane freight house circa 1907. The main tracks that led to the original passenger terminal are in the center and an electric locomotive was at work in the freight yard. (Sheldon Parry Collection)

The same location as the previous illustration almost seventy years later, in June 1973. By 1975 the Spokane to Coeur d'Alene daily freight train operated from the ex-NP Erie Street freight yard and a decade later from Yardley terminal. (Michael J. Denuty)

The main tracks 3 and 4 crossed the GN/NP transfer track (1) near Trent Avenue (F), protected by a watchman housed in the SC&P shanty (B). Water tank C and bridge D belonged to the GN. (Northern Pacific Railway; Walt Ainsworth Collection)

Inland Junction in October 1970 with BN switcher No. 475 on the Coeur d'Alene leg of the wye. (Michael J. Denuty)

This photograph was taken from the East Spokane interlocking tower. The tower's interlocking system included semaphore signals on the SC&P double tracks 5 and 6 which crossed Napa Street bridge E, and the OWR&N single track main line at crossing C. Track 7, connecting SC&P to the OWR&N, dated back to 1903. Switch B provided a lead track 3 to the Spokane Union depot, crossing SC&P tracks at G. (Northern Pacific Railway; Walt Ainsworth Collection)

For several miles from the Spokane International shops to beyond Millwood the SC&P and SIR lines paralleled each other. Spokane International track, with heavier rail, is on the left in this view looking east near Byrd Street in March 1973. (Michael J. Denuty)

This old battery house was located adjacent to the Coeur d'Alene line at Esperance (renamed from East Spokane around 1917). No record of this building was found in the valuation records. The battery probably became redundant after the City Substation opened in 1911. (Michael J. Denuty)

Passengers boarding at the Millwood depot. The hip roof was unusual for the Coeur d'Alene line. (Harold Hill, Warren Wing Collection)

Coeur d'Alene double tracks 4 and 5 extended under concrete bridges X and Y that carried the NP main line. Beyond the bridges, shelter shed C was at the NP Subway station. Track 3 belonged to the Spokane International Railway.
(Northern Pacific Railway; Walt Ainsworth Collection)

Greenacres depot photographed from the cab of No. 20 traveling west in 1937. Evidence of the second track remained. (Harold Hill, Warren Wing Collection)

Crowds filled the rudimentary depot at Liberty Lake Junction as they transferred from a main line eastbound train to the Liberty Lake branch train. Both trains consisted of the smallest motorcar and trailer types. New second track to Spokane Bridge can be seen behind the trains. (Museum of North Idaho Trr-1-99)

Liberty Lake depot, the branch terminus, was similar to the one built at Hayden Lake. (Ted Holloway Collection)

Right-of-way extended through farming country near Spokane Bridge. The Cd'A&S depot there shipped an average of 100,000 pounds per month of milk and cream during 1906. (Harold Hill, Warren Wing Collection)

Motor baggage car No. 152 moving away from Spokane Bridge shelter shed, alongside several Cd'A&S boxcars. (Museum of North Idaho, Trr-1-91)

Post Falls frame depot built in 1905 and sold thirty years later. (Museum of North Idaho Trr-1-58)

Looking east from motor baggage and express car No. 152 at the Post Falls depot in 1904. Northern Pacific's Fort Sherman branch line was on the left, the depot visible in the distance. (C.A. Libby, E. Hemingway Collection)

On the outskirts of Post Falls, this is a spur (4) from the Fort Sherman branch (1) which crossed SC&P (2) and CMSt.P&P (3) tracks to reach Rubedew Lumber Company. The group of structures in the foreground was Post Falls Box and Manufacturing Company. (Northern Pacific Railway; Walt Ainsworth Collection)

Blackwell Lumber Company's Coeur d'Alene mill lay on the west side of the Spokane River. Both NP and CMSt.P&P switched the mill so each built a bridge at Gibbs to carry their mill spurs over the river. The SC&P track (4) went under the NP bridge at A. The CMSt.P&P bridge along track (2) was covered. (Northern Pacific Railway; Walt Ainsworth Collection)

Ground-level view of the SC&P line (2) passing under the NP bridge (A) to Blackwell Lumber Company. The electric line was now paralleled by the Spokane International Railway branch to Coeur d'Alene (1) which had curved in from the north (left). The Gibbs mill can be seen in the distance. (Northern Pacific Railway; Walt Ainsworth Collection)

April 1973 view of the line passing the lumber mill at Gibbs with the SIR interchange track ahead. (Michael J. Denuty)

Looking north from near the Coeur d'Alene substation towards the yard tracks in August 1972. Sixty years earlier, a two-stall engine house stood near where a ramp was now located. (Michael J. Denuty)

Aerial view of Coeur d'Alene circa 1930 looking east, showing the SC&P passenger depot, car barn, freight house and docks in the foreground with the Milwaukee Road freight house and tracks behind. (Ted Holloway Collection)

The two-story depot was replaced in 1965 by this office at 601 Northwest Boulevard. The building was empty when photographed in March 2002. (C.S. Carter)

Motorman's view as he approached Coeur d'Alene passenger depot around 1910. The depot was on the right, track to Hayden Lake lay ahead and the car barns were on the left. (C.A. Libby, Ted Holloway Collection)

The same location as in the previous illustration, photographed in 1972. The single track served the Potlatch Forest mill. (Michael J. Denuty)

In 1927, the Hayden Lake line (4) crossed NP tracks 1, 2 and 3 that extended south along Third Street to the Coeur d'Alene Mill Company. The NP passenger depot on Third Street was identified as D. (Northern Pacific Railway; Walt Ainsworth Collection)

The same crossing of NP tracks 1, 2 and 3 as previous, viewed east along the Hayden Lake line (4). (Walt Ainsworth, Northern Pacific Railway Collection)

Hayden Lake line along Front Avenue at 6th Street, Coeur d'Alene. (Northern Pacific Railway; Walt Ainsworth Collection)

Looking east along Mullan Avenue from 8th Street. (Northern Pacific Railway; Walt Ainsworth Collection)

At the corner of Mullan Avenue and 11th Street, the Hayden Lake line (2) turned north and track 1 to Rutledge Lumber Company mill continued east along Mullan Avenue. This junction was ¾ mile from the depot. Track 3 was a little-used spur. Telephone booth C was used for movements to and from the mill. (Northern Pacific Railway; Walt Ainsworth Collection)

Entry to Rutledge Lumber Company mill. (Northern Pacific Railway; Walt Ainsworth Collection)

Two-car train traversing the loop at Hayden Lake. (Sheldon Perry Collection)

Photographs of the Vera line in early days are quite rare. This one was taken looking west at University Road and what appears to be a warehouse that was under construction. (Ted Holloway Collection)

One of Hillyard's class SD-9 units at work alongside Sprague Avenue on the Vera line, by that time an industrial spur from Flora Junction. (Harold Hill, Warren Wing Collection,)

On the outskirts of Spokane housing developments were exposed to the S&I line. (Ted Holloway collection)

Overhead wires on the right-hand side delineate a spur, hidden by weeds, which led from Moran siding. (Ted Holloway Collection)

Parkview was 9.35 miles from Spokane. A shelter shed was located here until 1939. (Ted Holloway Collection)

Willow Springs was one of the largest (15 by 18 feet) shelter sheds on the Inland lines. It was erected in 1908, removed in 1939 and the station abandoned in 1942. (Sheldon Perry Collection)

Only the foundation of Kiesling depot remained in front of the substation, when this circa 1940 photograph was taken. (Ted Holloway Collection)

Valley Ford depot was the first example of this distinctive design that could be seen by a southbound passenger. It was removed in 1939. (D. Cozine collection)

Mount Hope depot, similar to Valley Ford, photographed as a train departed for Spokane. (Warren Wing Collection)

Clyde Parent, quoted in this chapter, busy at West Fairfield. (Ted Holloway Collection)

Panoramic view of Waverly with the electric line curving through the town. (Ted Holloway Collection)

Waverly's train order signals are conspicuous in this photograph of a small roadway vehicle ready to leave on the main track. Great Northern enlarged the system's work equipment fleet in 1927, but No. 99252 on the adjacent track was an ex-S&IE outfit car renumbered into the GN series. (Clyde Parent, Ted Holloway Collection)

The two-story Spring Valley depot was located at the Spokane end of the wye. The building was destroyed by fire in 1936 and replaced by a tool house from Kiesling converted to a shelter shed. (National Archives)

Landscape at Konah, mile post 42. (Ted Holloway Collection)

The Milwaukee Road main line crossed over the Moscow branch at Seabury. The branch was cut half a mile beyond here in 1972. (Ted Holloway Collection)

The NP and OWR&N already had depots at Oakesdale near 100 feet in length, so the S&I built one of comparable size, extra space being assigned to the freight room and office. The depot is shown in 1969, two years before retirement.
(Robert W. Johnston, Warren Wing Collection)

Oakesdale in March 1973 with the S&I depot on the left and the NP depot on the right, both owned by Burlington Northern by that time.
(Michael J. Denuty)

The two freight trains standing at Oakesdale were almost certainly the pair that Clyde Parent traveled on as described in the text. (Clyde Parent, Ted Holloway Collection)

Oakesdale substation was one of ten similar buildings built for the AC lines. (Ted Holloway Collection)

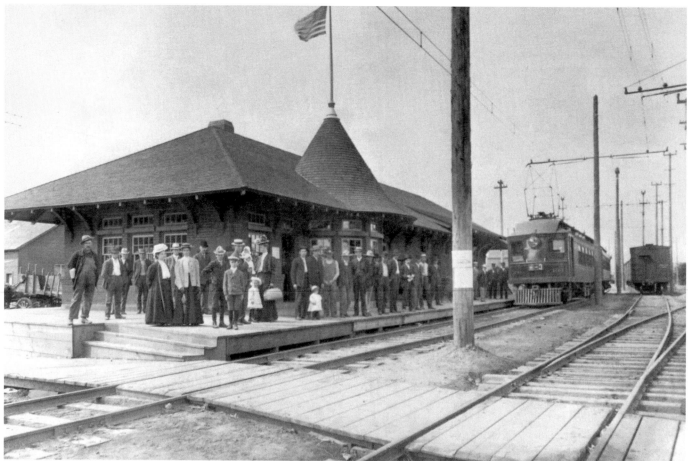

Newly built Garfield 90-foot depot was a mirror image of Oakesdale. The arriving train was headed by S&I motor baggage and passenger car No.100. (Sheldon Perry Collection)

Sixty years later Garfield depot was little changed apart from the absence of the wooden platform.
(Robert W. Johnston, Warren Wing Collection)

The first depot at Palouse was this temporary structure. When replaced, the redundant material was sent to Moscow to build a depot. Boxcars caught by the photographer were S&IE 40-foot No. 1992 and 36 foot, 10 inch No.1633, supplied by different manufacturers. (Warren Wing Collection)

A 112-foot brick veneer depot, the largest of the distinctive style, was erected at Palouse in 1908. (Sheldon Perry Collection)

Looking south in 1970 from a road bridge over the cut made by the S&I at Palouse. The depot had lost its conical roof over the office by that time. (Ted Holloway Collection)

Looking down and east from the Palouse depot over WI&M facilities and the concrete retaining wall. (Sheldon Perry Collection)

The camera foreshortened this view of Ringo in the 1970s. (Ted Holloway Collection)

The 90-foot depot built at Moscow in 1912 had a frame structure with drop siding walls, a 13-foot operator's bay and a hip roof. New management had started to reduce expenditure and the exterior was no doubt cheaper than brick veneer.
(Robert A. Johnston, Warren Wing Collection)

A 1970s view of the Moscow depot and surrounding area. (Sheldon Perry Collection)

The electric line crossed the Northern Pacific P&L line over this bridge one mile north of Rosalia depot. The bridge was of wood construction in this 1927 view, but a steel bridge was provided later. (Northern Pacific Railway; Walt Ainsworth Collection)

Rosalia, one of the brick-style depots, had two GN work equipment cars present when the depot was photographed in 1969. As at Palouse, the depot had lost its conical office roof. (Robert W. Johnston, Warren Wing Collection)

Milwaukee Road's main line crossed over the Colfax branch at the south end of Rosalia. (Michael J. Denuty)

Steptoe in the early days. The depot is the one-story building in the center of the photograph. (Sheldon Perry Collection)

Entering Colfax, the line crossed the UP tracks. Prior to 1928 the crossing was controlled by an S&I-built interlocking tower. (Sheldon Perry Collection)

Sentinel rock on the approach to Colfax. (Sheldon Perry Collection)

Bridge 76.5 over the Palouse River was just beyond the Colfax UP crossing. (Sheldon Perry Collection)

View of Colfax depot, built in 1912, from the street side. (National Archives)

After the 1910 flooding at Colfax, a new site relative to the river was chosen for the depot when it was built. (National Archives)

Joint use of track between Spokane Bridge and Gibbs by the Milwaukee Road and Great Northern from 1945 resulted in the S&IE-built bridge at Spokane Bridge becoming redundant. This April 1973 photograph shows the Milwaukee Road bridge and the remaining piers of the S&IE bridge in the foreground. (Michael J. Denuty)

Chapter 12

ABANDONMENT

Little of the interurban system remains today. One readily identifiable remnant remains at Coeur d'Alene, extending from the substation to the wye. Dismemberment occurred over a period of almost sixty years. Significant events were the closures of Liberty Lake and Hayden Lake stations in 1928 and 1931, respectively; abandonment of the track north from Mt. Hope in 1952; devastation of the Inland lines by Burlington Northern in 1972; and removal of much of the Coeur d'Alene line in the 1980s.

Electric operation ceased in 1941. Clyde Parent reported that the last electrified service ran on September 30, 1941.

Coeur d'Alene Line

Ostensibly, the first abandonment was circa 1905 when the connection between the main track and the Spokane Traction streetcar line along Boone Avenue was removed. The main track was then realigned to yield right-of-way for the Spokane International Railway.

The south track of the double track between Liberty Lake Junction and Spokane Bridge was removed in 1920. The entire double track from Spokane was in poor shape by that time, needing new ballast and 10,000 ties. Instructions were issued in October 1927 to remove 12.6 miles of the second track from Liberty Lake Junction to Recreation Park in Spokane, and six months later for the remainder. Work was completed in 1928.

According to Interstate Commerce Commission (ICC) records, the last passenger train departed from the Spokane Terminal depot on May 20, 1927. The Great Northern passenger depot was used instead. Ownership of 1.16 miles of double track extending from the Terminal depot site was transferred to Spokane United Railways in March 1931.

The ICC authorized abandonment of the 2.2 miles from Liberty Lake Junction to Liberty Lake on May 21, 1928, the branch having been left open for freight after withdrawal of passenger service. No freight was shipped from there during the preceding six months; logging near the branch was completed, and less than two tons of freight had arrived.

On May 18, 1931, the ICC authorized abandonment of 1.65 miles of track, including the loop at Hayden Lake. This segment extended to Honeysuckle Farms. After discontinuance of passenger service, freight revenue had averaged only $345 per annum. Authority to abandon the remaining 5.63 miles of the branch from Coeur d'Alene to Honeysuckle Farms was granted on April 8, 1940. Deferred track maintenance had resulted in SC&P facing expenditure of $27,200 for renewals. Carloads handled were less than 20 per year, mostly fruit and vegetables, with none in 1939. Although declining freight traffic was due partly to diminishing farm production, the principal reason was movement by road transport agencies. Rail service was cancelled on May 8, 1940, and track was removed the same year.

The Chicago, Milwaukee, St. Paul & Pacific branch to Coeur d'Alene paralleled the electric line from Spokane Bridge. In 1945, the Milwaukee Road and GN jointly decided to operate over one track, each company contributing segments joined by crossover switches. As a result, two segments of the GN line were abandoned: the first 4.4 miles extending east from Spokane Bridge at milepost 18.89, including the Spokane River bridge and almost to Post Falls at milepost 23.32, and, secondly, approximately 2.3 miles from milepost 27.26 to milepost 29.54 at Atlas. Joint operation became effective on October 21, 1945, having been decided by the ICC three months earlier. Redundant track was removed the following year. The Milwaukee Road dispatcher controlled movement over the joint line. Following the demise of the Milwaukee Road in 1980, Burlington Northern bought its segments of the line.

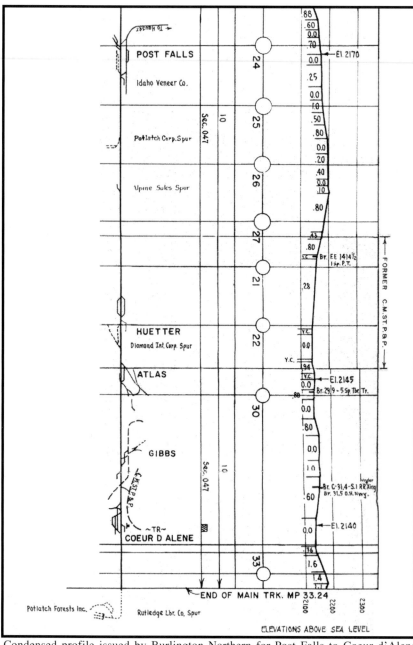

Condensed profile issued by Burlington Northern for Post Falls to Coeur d'Alene dating from January 1984. Mile posts (circles) are GN except for the Milwaukee Road segment. (Burlington Northern)

The ex-NP branch from Hauser Junction to Coeur d'Alene paralleled the GN/Milwaukee Road joint line between Post Falls and Huetter. In 1973 Burlington Northern put in connecting tracks between the lines at these two stations, the plan being to abandon the corresponding ex-NP segment.

The ex-GN line that extended east from Coeur d'Alene to the Potlatch Forests mill was abandoned circa 1988 after the mill closed, allowing track removal from the city streets. Between Post Falls and Coeur d'Alene substations, the right-of-way remained open, although normally unused beyond the Coeur d'Alene wye.

At Spokane the main line had been cut between bridges 1.3 and 1.5 by mid-1973. The ex-SC&P freight yard at the west end of bridge 1.3 could still be accessed over the transfer track. Bridge 1.5 was removed in April 1974, but bridge 1.3 remained until August 1987, explosives being required for destruction.

In December 1983, BN filed notice of abandonment of 14.4 miles extending from Greenacres to Post Falls and implemented six months later. Traffic from Spokane had already been rerouted over the ex-NP branch from Hauser Junction and the connection installed at Post

Complete abandonment of the line out of Spokane did not occur until 1987, but the main line was cut at the east end of bridge 1.3 by June 1973, as shown here. (Michael J. Denuty)

There were a number of spurs along the Coeur d'Alene line between Parkwater and NP Subway stations. In 1986 Union Pacific granted BN running rights over its parallel Spokane International Railroad track, on the left-hand side here. Thus, BN maintained access to the spurs after abandoning the line. (Michael J. Denuty)

Falls in 1973. Abandonment of the Carders-Greenacres section took place in December 1985. This was followed by abandonment of Spokane-Carders in April 1987, track removal east from Orchard Road being underway by May 1987. Union Pacific granted BN trackage rights over six miles of Spokane International main line from the SI yard to beyond Millwood. This allowed BN to maintain service to several isolated spurs along the abandoned line.

Vera Line

Operation within Spokane was on streetcar tracks to the city limits at Havana Street. They were retained by the S&E after Spokane United Railways took over the streetcar system in 1923. At the same time, the streetcar tracks along Riverside Avenue in Spokane, between Madelia Street and Smith Street, were taken out. Spokane United Railways had granted permission for S&E cars to operate over and along its Sprague Avenue streetcar tracks east from Madelia Street and rejoin the connection to the Opportunity line near Regal Street. After withdrawal of Opportunity/Vera passenger service, parts of the associated streetcar track were given to Spokane United Railways and the rest removed.

In 1928 the Opportunity line proper was terminated at the Spokane end, 2.08 miles of track from Havana Street to Edgecliff being removed. Thereafter, the line became an industrial spur from Flora, on the Coeur d'Alene main line. It remained intact for almost thirty years before abandonment in three stages:

· The 1.25 miles Vera-Flora segment closed in 1956 and track removed the following year. Connection was made to the Union Pacific at milepost 6.89 near Dishman to give access to the residual track.
· Closure of the 4.04 miles from Dishman to Vera was approved by the ICC in July 1963 and track removed later that year.
· With ICC approval, the remaining track between Dishman and Spear saw its last service on August 31, 1979. Removal of the tracks occurred soon afterwards.

End of the line at Mt. Hope. The line terminated 0.07 miles north of the station depot, following the rerouting of traffic over the Union Pacific. (Ted Holloway Collection)

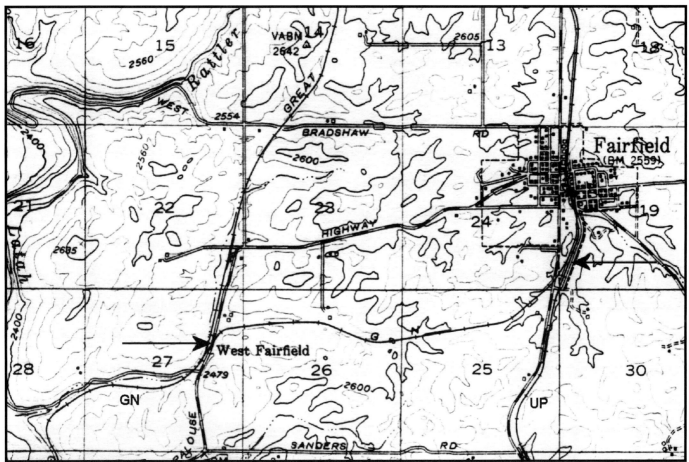

The Connection from West Fairfield to the Union Pacific at Fairfield, opened in 1952, is shown between the arrows. Part of the old OWR&N right-of-way between Fairfield and Waverly was utilized in construction. (USGS)

Inland Lines

In 1948 Great Northern Vice-president G.F. Ashby contacted President Gavin to propose abandonment of the track between East Spokane and West Fairfield, thereby eliminating the expensive maintenance of several old timber bridges due for renewal at a cost of $520,000 (specifically the Parkview, Sharron, Little Rock Creek and Rock Creek bridges). Funds for renewal already had approval by the GN directors.

The plan was modified later to shorten the segment to Mt. Hope since this retained

Connection to the UP line is shown leaving the Inland at West Fairfield and crossing the highway. (Michael J. Denuty)

205

Great Northern Alco 1,500 hp model RS-2 No. 208 heads past the OR&N Mica depot after Inland trains were rerouted over the Union Pacific from Spokane to Fairield. (Ted Holloway Collection)

worthwhile traffic and increased the estimated net saving. Union Pacific and the GN signed an agreement dated September 26, 1950, that granted the GN trackage rights between Spokane and Fairfield over its Manito line for an annual fee of $25,000 plus an amount dependent on traffic volume.

Great Northern built a 2.6-mile connecting line from a junction at milepost 31.11 south of West Fairfield to the UP tracks at Fairfield. Two bridges were necessary and the maximum grade in both directions was 1.7%. Service over this route began on September 17, 1952, with ICC blessing. The 22.87 miles of track from 0.9 mile north of Mt. Hope to Spokane (2.16 miles south of Inland Junction) was abandoned the same day and subsequently removed.

The tunnel on the Colfax branch was declared structurally unsafe in 1967. As a result, the line from Manning to Colfax was closed in that year, 5.62 miles of track being lifted in 1968-9. Colfax traffic was handled by the UP under ICC service order No. 992, dated 26 May, 1967.

Burlington Northern reorganized the ex-GN Inland and ex-NP Spokane-Moscow lines in 1972, having acquired them in the 1970 amalgamation. The ex-NP line was retained, but the ex-GN West Fairfield connection to the UP and portions of the Moscow line were abandoned. Abandonment of the following sections became effective May 29, 1972:
   · West Fairfield to UP Fairfield, 2.52 miles; track removed between June and December, 1973.
   · Seabury to Oakesdale, 5.11 miles; track removed between August and December, 1973.
   · Crabtree to Garfield, 3.79 miles; track removed by 1973.
   · Garfield to Grinnell, 5.54 miles; track removed between April and August, 1973.
   · Viola to Estes, 4.32 miles; track removed by 1973.

Remaining segments of the Inland effectively became branches of the ex-NP line. A new NP-GN connection at Rosalia gave access to both Spring Valley and Manning. Others were reached through existing connections at Palouse and Moscow and a new connection laid by BN at Oakesdale; Garfield got a new connection to serve industries at the ex-GN station.

All these branches were eventually abandoned, contractors removing the tracks in almost every instance:

- Spring Valley - Mt. Hope, 15 miles, 1983.
- Rosalia-Spring Valley, 5.8 miles, 1986.
- Rosalia-Balder, 4.8 miles, 1985.
- Balder-Manning, 20.6 miles, October 10, 1980; track removed between March and December 1981.
- Spring Valley -Fairbanks, 5.68 miles, 1983.
- Fairbanks-Seabury, 2.07 miles, November 10, 1980; track removed around 1981.
- Oakesdale-Crabtree, 6.97 miles, June 1, 1978; track removed by May 1979.
- Palouse-Grinnell, 4.85 miles, 1983.
- Palouse-Viola, 6 miles, service discontinued in December 1984.
- Estes-Moscow, 3.72 miles, 1984; track removed in 1984.

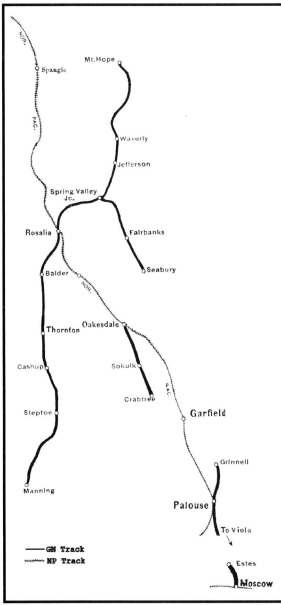

Evidence presented to the ICC by Burlington Northern outlined the reasons for abandonment. Traffic from the Crabtree branch had dropped to eight carloads in 1975 with the growth of truck haulage to the Snake River for barge transportation. Grinnell faced similar competition, losing money by 1982. Despite loading over 200 grain cars per year in 1980 and 1981, the Mt. Hope branch had an annual net loss close to $15,000. Car weight restriction on that branch prevented jumbo, covered hopper car utilization. The same restriction applied to Fairbanks, which had experienced fluctuations in annual car loadings. Nevertheless, it was marginally profitable, handling up to 90 cars for the sole shipper and so remained open a few more years.

Amalgamation of GN and NP lines in 1972 by Burlington Northern. The remnants of the GN became spurs for the P&L line. (author)

Fairbanks became the terminus for a line from Spring Valley when Seabury closed in 1980. (Ted Holloway Collection)

207

Looking south from Oakesdale in June 1972. Boxcars stand on the siding, and an industry spur leads to the old warehouse. The tall structure beyond the depot and substation belonged to the Inland Empire Pea Growers Association. A connection between the ex-NP and ex-GN lines was installed here by BN to provide access to the Oakesdale to Crabtree spur. (Michael J. Denuty)

The Crabtree elevator was served by the spur from Oakesdale. (Ted Holloway Collection)

Spring Valley was one of the last surviving stations on the old Inland line. (D. Cozine Collection)

The last station on the Colfax branch from Spring Valley was Manning after closure of the tunnel. (D. Cozine Collection)

Track between Viola and Estes was removed in 1972, Estes becoming the end of a spur from Moscow. It stayed open for a decade to handle grain traffic. (Ted Holloway Collection)

Sources

Interstate Commerce Commission, Finance Docket No. 6808, Abandonment of Branch Line by Spokane, Coeur d'Alene & Palouse Railway Company, Decided May 28, 1928.

Interstate Commerce Commission, Finance Docket No. 6774, Abandonment of Lines by Spokane, Coeur d'Alene & Palouse Railway Company, Decided May 10, 1928.

Interstate Commerce Commission, Finance Docket No. 7612, Abandonment of Lines and Trackage Rights by Spokane, Coeur d'Alene & Palouse Railway Company, Decided July 23, 1929.

Interstate Commerce Commission, Finance Docket No. 8713, Spokane, Coeur d'Alene & Palouse Railway Company Abandonment, Decided May 18, 1931.

Interstate Commerce Commission, Finance Docket No. 12770, Spokane, Coeur d'Alene & Palouse Railway Company Abandonment, Decided April 8, 1940.

Interstate Commerce Commission, Finance Docket No. 14854, Chicago, Milwaukee, St. Paul & Pacific Railroad Company Trustees et al. Abandonment etc., Decided July 3, 1945 (unpublished).

Interstate Commerce Commission, Finance Docket No. 16876, Great Northern Railway Company Trackage Rights, etc., Decided December 26, 1951.

Interstate Commerce Commission, Finance Docket AB-6, Sub Nos. 39, 134 and 146, 1975-1983, Application of Burlington Northern Inc. to Abandon Line of Railroad..., state of Washington, (unpublished).

Great Northern Railway President's Subject File No. 14474. Connection with UP and GN Between Fairfield and Waverly.

APPENDIX A

An inventory of Spokane and Inland Empire Railroad Company operating property made in 1919 contained a description of buildings. These are reproduced in Tables A.1. and A.2. for the Coeur d'Alene and Inland Divisions, respectively.

Source

Great Northern Railway President's Subject File No.9128. Spokane & Inland Empire Railroad History of Properties – Operating Property. 1919.

1919 Inventory of Spokane and Inland Empire Railroad Company Buildings

Town	Building	Size
Coeur d'Alene Division		
Spokane*	Terminal	-
	Freight House Brick	14x300
	Frame Ice House	14x14
	Frame Office E of Sheridan Street	20x30
	Scales	11x16
	Frame Section Bunkhouse	10x32.3
	Annex	5.4x9.4
	Frame House	8.5x9.4
	Fr. Supt. Office, Hamilton & Olive	30x50
	Annex	18x18
	Fr. General Store	40x150
	Corr. Iron Store Oil House	17x25
	Fr. Shed	21.4x42.6
	Brick Traction Car Barns	118.6x200
	Brick Car Barns, Cincinatti & Superior	52'x200'
	Brick Machine Shop	40.5x200
	Frame Office	9x18
	Frame Oil House	8x17
	Frame Sand Dryer	10x12
	brick Blacksmith Shop	36.5x83
	3 Fire hydrant Shelters	8x8
	Hand Car House	8x10
	Pattern Shop Frame	20x24
	Gravel Bin	27x27
	Carpenter Shop & Garage	40x58
	City Substation Brick	93.4x112
	Frequency Substation Brick	102x162 (L-shaped)
	26 Frame Houses (on 10 streets)	Various
	Frame Shed	12x24.5
Pinecroft	Frame Transformer	7x14
Parkwater	Frame Shelter	8x12.3
Esperance	Frame Shelter	5.6x6.4
Del Monte	Frame Shelter	6x7
Orchard Ave.	Frame Shelter	8x12
Millwood	Frame Shelter	12x32
NP Subway	Freight Platform	10x12
Carders	Frame Transformer	7x14
	Telephone Booth	4x4
	Frame Shelter	6x10
Greenacres	Frame Section House	20x24
	Frame Signal Tower	12x14
	Substation Brick	45x50
	Frame Depot	16x53
	Frame Tool House	7.2x10
Toledo	Frame Shelter	10x24
Liberty Lake	Covered Platform	20x120

	Frame Privy	5.4x18
Seaton	Frame Shelter	6x7
Spokane Bridge	Frame Shack	9x12.4
	Frame Pump House	8x12
	Water Tank	11x12
	Section House	22x24
	Freight Depot	20x46
	Toilet	8.4x9.3
McGuires	Frame Shelter	8x12
	Frame Freight Shed	8'x12
	Concrete Substation	32x45
	Brick Battery Room	32x89.5
Post Falls	Depot	20x45
	Privy	5x8
	Tool & Hand Car House	-
Alan	Telephone Booth	4x4x11.6
Ross	Frame Shelter	10.3x12.4
	Brick Battery Station	32x79.4
	Annex	8x9
	Telephone Booth	4x4x11.6
Huetter	Frame Pass. Depot	9.2x143
	Frame Freight Depot	8x14.3
Atlas	Frame Shelter	6x9
Gibbs	Frame Shelter	10x12.4
	Telephone Booth	4x4x11'8"
Coeur d'Alene	Frame Depot	30.5x93.5
	Frame Freight Depot	20x176
	Frame Ice House	18x44
	Frame Tool House	12x16
	Frame Lightning Arrestor	20x27
	Brick Substation	32x148.8
	Frame Pavillion	55x110
	Frame Band Stand	15' diam.
	Log Dock	18'x810'
	Passenger Dock	55'x600' condemned
	Frame Old Engine House	34x75.3
	Frame Scale House	14x16.4
	Car Barn	41.5x150.5
	Machine Shops	46.3x124.3
	Annex	21x47.5
	Blacksmith Shop	21x47.5
	Building on Log Dock	27x32
	Building on Log Dock	12x24
	Office on Pass. Dock	16x64
	Office on Pass. Dock	10x12
	Shop	18.5x29.4
	Shack	12x24
	Shack	18x22
	Shack	10.4x12.4
	Coal Bin	30x80.2
Penn. Ave.	Frame Shelter	10x12
Johnsons	Frame Section House	20.4x23x12
	Frame Tool House	10.3x13.3x12
Dalton	Frame Depot	12x30.3
Honeysuckle Farm	Frame Shelter	8.3x12.3
	Frame Freight House	10x20
	Frame Telephone Booth	4x4x11.8
Farr	Frame Shelter	10x12
Dishman	Frame Depot	14'x40
	Frame Loading Platform	10x15
Spear	Frame loading Platform	8.4x12
Edgecliff	Frame Shelter	6.7x12.3
Opportunity	Frame Depot	8x20
Manzanola	Frame Shelter	6.2x9.3

Vera	Frame Shelter	6.2x9.3
Inland Division		
Pantops	Frame Shelter Shed	6.2x6.8
Glenrose	Frame Shelter Shed	6.2x6.8
Pinegrove	Frame Shelter Shed	6.2x6.8
Morgan	Frame Shelter Shed	6.2x7.2
Piedmont	Frame Shelter Shed	6x8
Parkview	Frame Shelter Shed	6x6
Hillby	Frame Shelter Shed	6x8
Willow Spring	Depot	16.2x18
Kiesling	Depot	15xx46
	2 Frame Toilets	5.8x6.2
	Brick Substation	33.8x42
	Frame Coal House	8x10
	Frame Bunk House	10.5x24.5
	Frame Toilet	4x4
	Frame Shed	9.7x12
	Frame Tool House	8.3x10.3
Sharon	Frame Shelter Shed	6x7
	Frame Freight House	10x12
Belair	Frame Shelter	6x7
Excelsior	frame Shelter	6.2x7.2
Valley Ford	Frame Water Tank	9x16
	Frame House	10x13.5
	Frame Depot	22.8x57.8
	2 Frame Toilets	5x6 each
	Frame Bunkhouses	16.4x24.4
	Frame Tool House	8x10
Larkin	Frame Shelter	6x9
Rubeck	-	7x18
Freeman	Frame Depot	16.5x54
	Frame Transformer H	8x8
Ochlars	Frame Shelter	6x6
Mt. Hope	Brick Depot	22.22x52
	2 Frame Toilets	5x6 each
	Frame Bunkhouses	9.4x22.8
	Frame Tool house	8x10
Treat	Frame Shelter	6x6
Rattler's Run	Frame Shelter	6x6
Lenox	Frame Shelter	6x6
West Fairfield	Frame Shelter	9x13
Saline	Loading Platform	12x66
	Frame Shelter	6x6
Bound Brook	Frame Shelter	6x6
Waverly	Frame stock Yards	32.4x33
	Brick Depot	25x63
	Track Scales	-
	2 Frame Toilets	5x6
	Frame Bunk House	10x22
	Frame Shelter	6.2x7.2
Jefferson	Frame Shelter	6.2x7.2
Spring Valley	Brick Depot	40x80
	Frame Storehouse	25x60
	Frame Bunk House	21x38
	Frame Transformer H	4x5
	Frame Switch Tower	10x15
	Frame Asst' Rd Mstr Shack	20x24
	Frame Tool & Car House	14x20
	Frame Lineman's Shack	13x23
	Frame Stock Pens	31.5x40
	3 Toilets	5x5
	Water Tank	10x12
	Frame Shack	10x12
	Frame Tent House	12x14

Rollins	Frame Pump House	10.5x14
	Frame Shelter	6x7
Rosalia	Brick Depot	22.6x90.3
	Stock Pens & Scale	32x84
	Frame Warehouse	50x100x12
	Frame Bunk House	12.3x20.3
	2 Frame Toilets	5x6
Broadview Farm	Loading Platform	10x30
	Frame Shelter	6x7
Barley	Frame Shelter	6x7
Balder	Frame Shelter	6x7
Harris	-	-
Stoneham	Frame Shelter	8x8
Thornton	Frame Depot	38.8x20.5
	Frame Bunk House	11.3x35
	Frame Tool House	10.5x12.2
	Stock Pens	50x57
Barnes	Frame Shelter	6.3x7.3
Cashup	Frame Shelter	6x7
	Frame Shed	18x18
	Frame Shed	12x24
Lynn	Frame Shelter	6x7
Bankson	Frame Shelter	6x7
Steptoe	Frame Depot	17.2x40.4
	Stock Pens	48x108
	Section House	22x24
	Transformer House	3.3x3.3
	Bunk House	10x24
	Tool House	8x10
	2 Toilets	5.3x6.2
	Tel. House	3x3
	Car House	10x12
Blackwell	Frame Shelter	6.2x7.2
Rye	Frame Shelter	6.2x7.2
Manning	Frame Shelter	6.2x7.2
Harpole	Frame Shelter	6x9
Lincoln	-	-
Fairbanks	Frame Depot	10x20
	Stock Yards	16x33
	2 Toilets	4x5
Seabury	Framd Shelter	6x7
Geary	Frame Warehouse	50x10x12
	Frame Shelter	6x7
Dan	Frame Shelter	8X8
Oaksdale	Brick Depot	22.4xx90.3
	Stock Yards & Scales	50x50
	Warehouse	50x150x12
	Bunk House	16.4x24.4
	Tool & Hand Car House	10x10
	Ice House	9.8x11.2
	Coal Shed	18x20
	2 Toilets	5.8x5.8
Robinson	Frame Shelter	4.5x7
Sokulk	Frame Shelter	6x7
Elmer	Frame Shelter	6x9
Davidson	Frame Shelter	5x7.5
Crabtree	Frame Shelter	6x7
	Milk Loading Platform	6x12
Garfield	Brick Depot	22.6x90.6
	Frame Bunk House Carbody	10.7x39
	Ice House	20x30
M.P. 68	Stock Yard & Scales	50x92
Ladlow	Frame Shelter	6.2x7.3
Grinnell	Frame Shelter	6x7

Palouse	Brick Depot	24.5x110
	Toilet	4.8x11.2
	Bunkhouse Fr. Carbody	10x39
	Frame Tool & Hand Car	8x10
	Freight Elevator	7x12
	Stock Yards	23x112
	Sand Box	14x32
Ringo	Std. Stock Chute	-
Cove	Milk Platform	5.2x24
	Frame Shelter	6x7
Viola	Frame Shelter	6x7
	Frame Freight Shed	8x10
Poe	Frame Shelter	6x7
Avery	Frame Shelter	6x7
Estes	Frame Shelter	6x7
Moscow	Frame Bunk House	11.2x36
	Frame Tool House	9x16.5
	Frame Depot	28x90
	Frame Stockpens & Scales	50x70
	Frame Old Depot	20x38
	Pump House	18.8x36.8
	Coal Shed	8x10

* Buildings owned by both Divisions.

Source: Great Northern Railway President's Subject File No.9128,
Spokane & Inland Empire Railroad History of Properties – Operating Property. 1919.

APPENDIX B

Table B.1. shows the location and type of bridge on the railroad system.

Table B.1. Bridge Summary

Mile Post	Bridge Number	Location	Type
SPOKANE - HAYDEN LAKE			
0.90	0.9	Olive Street	Overhead timber bridge on new connection to GN depot, 1927.
1.30	1.3	Spokane River	Three 125 foot Howe trusses; 2 tracks;replaced by one TPG span and one 120 foot pony truss, 1944 and one 175 foot thru truss, 1946; with four-span timber approach east end; one track.
1.36	1.4	Dakota Street	Three-span pile trestle.
1.58	1.5	Spokane River	One 100 foot and two 150 foot Howe truss spans; replaced by steel structures by 1964.
1.59	1.6		CMStP&P overcrossing.
2.00	2.0	Helena Street	Eight-span pile trestle; removed 1929.
2.08	2.1	Medalia Street	Vera line undercrossing; pile trestle; removed 1929.
2.30	2.3	Napa Street	Undercrossing.
7.85	7.7	Trent Road	Overcrossing.
7.88	7.8		Northern Pacific Railway overcrossing; steel bridge replaced by concrete bridge 1916.
7.89	7.9		Northern Pacific Railway overcrossing; steel bridge replaced by concrete bridge 1916.
10.68	10.7		Three-span timber bridge.
11.89	11.9		Three-span timber bridge.
18.68	18.7		Single-span timber bridge; filled 1939.
19.26	19-A	Old Line	Abandoned 1915.
19.35	19.3	Spokane River	Five-span plate girder bridge built 1910.
19.68		Old line	Bridge.
20.90	20.9		40 foot bridge; filled 1939.
21.33			45 foot bridge.
29.91	29.9		One-span timber bridge.
30.05			CMStP&P overcrossing until 1945.
30.74			Northern Pacific overcrossing.

30.88	30.7		Subway; three-span timber bridge.
31.45			Spokane International Railway undercrossing.
32.66			Bridge.

INLAND JUNCTION - SPRING VALLEY

1.81			Northern Pacific Railway overcrossing.
2.27	2.3	Fourth Avenue	Five-span frame trestle; 78 feet.
2.41	2.4		Five-span frame trestle; 72 feet.
3.03	3.0	Altamont Street	Seven-span frame trestle.
3.75	3.8		Trestle: 38 foot steel span and trestle approaches, 1942.
4.55	4.5		Highway undercrossing.
5.23			Six-bent trestle; filled 1930.
	5.4		Filled 1915.
9.25	9.2		Country road overhead bridge.
9.55	9.5		?
9.89	9.9		Five-bent pile trestle.
11.54	11-A		Six-bent trestle; 78 feet.
13.46	13-A	Stephens Creek	48-bent frame trestle.
15.89	15.7		Overhead road crossing bridge.
16.48	16.5	California Creek & Road	17-span pile trestle, 228 feet; 80 foot steel span and trestle approaches, 242 feet; 1942.
	19A		Filled 1915.
21.08	21.1		Filled 1916.
23.17	23.2	Rock Creek	Trestle and deck truss, 1,057.5 feet; rebuilt 1917.
24.63	24.6		Two-bent pile trestle.
25.20	25.2		Four-bent pile trestle, 64 feet.
25.59	25.6		Four-bent pile trestle.
25.81	25.8		Two-bent pile trestle; filled 1930.
26.31	26.3		Two-bent pile trestle; filled 1930.
	26.9		Filled 1915.
28.23	28.3	Rattlers Run	Pile and frame trestle.
28.64	28.6		Undercrossing, six-bent pile trestle.
29.44	29.4		Six-bent pile trestle.
29.63	29.6		Six-bent pile trestle.
31.64	31.6		Two-bent pile trestle.
31.93	31.9		Two-bent pile trestle; filled 1930.
32.15	32.1		Undercrossing, three-bent pile trestle.
33.47	33.5		Undercrossing, three-bent pile trestle.
33.77	33.8		Six-bent pile trestle; filled 1929.
34.19	34.2	Latah Creek	42-bent pile trestle; three steel deck spans and trestle approaches, 1929.
35.09	35.1		Creek.
35.38			Creek.
38.57	38.6		Single-span pile trestle.
39.46			16 foot trestle.
39.54	39.6		Single-bent pile trestle.

SPRING VALLEY - MOSCOW

43.04			Filled 1916.
43.38	43.8		Seven-span pile trestle.
43.84	43.8		Three-span pile trestle.
44.07	44.1		Three-span pile trestle.
44.62	44.6		Single-span pile trestle.
45.04	45.1		Single-span pile trestle; filled 1921.
47.24	47-A		Road, 400 feet.
47.31			CMStP&P overcrossing.
47.78	47-B	Seabury	Road, 160 feet.
49.00	49.0		Three-span trestle.
52.95			Bridge.
54.14	54.1		Four-span pile trestle.
54.50	54.5		Three-span pile trestle.
56.07	56.1	Longwill	Three-span pile trestle.
56.78	56.8		Single-span pile trestle; filled 1930.
60.43	59-A		Pile bridge.
60.53	59-B		Pile bridge.

61.46	61.5		Seven-span pile trestle; 36 foot steelspan and six-span pile trestle, 1942.
62.37	62.4		Three-span pile trestle.
62.92	62.9		Three-span pile trestle.
63.09	63.2		Five-span pile trestle.
63.19	63.3		Seven-span pile trestle; filled 1930.
63.61	63.6	Hampshire	Five-span pile trestle.
64.21	64.2		Seven-span timber trestle.
64.31	64.3		14-span timber trestle.
64.58	64.6	Garfield	Silver Creek and OWR&N; pile and frame trestle; replaced by 38 foot steel span and 21-span timber trestle.
64.68	64.7		Seven-span timber trestle.
65.18	65.2		Four-span pile trestle.
65.53	65.5		Four-span pile trestle.
65.91	65.9		Single-span pile trestle; filled 1930.
66.85	66.9		Seven-span pile trestle.
65.18	65.2		Four-span pile trestle.
65.53	65.5		Four-span pile trestle.
65.91	65.9		Single-span pile trestle; filled 1930.
66.85	66.9		Seven-span pile trestle.
69.65	69.7		Three-span pile trestle.
	69.9		County road pile trestle; 38 foot steel span and 5 trestle spans, 1930.
70.63			County road bridge.
70.83			Bridge.
71.29	71-A		Bridge.
75.96	76.0	Palouse	WI&M Railroad and Palouse River, 100 foot Howe truss, 39 foot I-beam, 38 foot I-beam, 52-span timber trestle; three SH DPR spans and 35 foot thru beam span, 1951.
77.16	77.2		County road nine-span pile trestle.
82.90	82.9		Filled 1915.
83.00	83-A		
85.46	85.4		Five-span pile trestle.
87.61	87.6		Five-span pile trestle.
88.19	88.2		28-span timber trestle.

SPRING VALLEY - COLFAX

40.33	40.3		Pile bridge.
41.24	41.2		10-span frame trestle.
43.04			Filled 1916.
45.87	45.9	Rosalia	12-span pile trestle.
45.91			Possibly filled.
46.88	46.9		Four-bent pile trestle.
47.06			Milwaukee Road overcrossing.
48.12	48.2		Nine-span pile trestle.
48.39	48.4		Three-span pile trestle.
49.87	49.9		Single-span pile trestle.
52.42			State road No.3.
55.17	55.2	Thornton	Four-span pile trestle.
59.36	59.3		Four-span pile trestle. Filled 1929.
61.36	61.4		Private road, five-span pile trestle.
61.64	61.6		Private road, five-span pile trestle.
65.02	65.0		Single-span pile trestle; filled 1930.
65.84	65.8		Three-span pile trestle.
66.41	66.4		Three-span pile trestle.
66.87	66.9		Four-span pile trestle.
67.45	67.5		Four-span pile trestle.
68.08	68.1		Timber trestle.
68.61	68.6		Five-span timber trestle.
68.81	68.8		Eight-span timber trestle.
68.97	69.0		Nine-span timber trestle.
69.52	69.5	Rye	11-span pile & frame trestle.
69.87	69.9		Five-span timber trestle.
70.65	70.6		Single-span pile trestle; filled 1930.
71.21	71.2	Manning	Six-span timber trestle.
71.59	71.6		Palouse River, 150 foot Howe truss and trestle approaches; truss housed, 1928.

72.34	72.3	Palouse River, 150 foot Howe truss and trestle approaches.
72.38		Tunnel 655 feet (milepost 72.38 to 72.51)
72.56	72.6	Palouse River, 150 foot and 100 foot Howe truss spans.
74.05	74.1	Five-span pile trestle.
75.91	75.8	Palouse River, 150 foot Howe truss and 27-span timber trestle.
76.37	76.3	Palouse River, 100 foot Howe truss span and 46-span timber trestle; Howe truss housed in 1928; most of trestle filled, 1938.
76.55	76B	Palouse River.

APPENDIX C

A summary of side tracks and connections taken from information supplied by James C. Mattson is presented herein. Additional data regarding the length of tracks have been added from official maps and plats. Table C.1. describes the Coeur d'Alene and Vera lines. Table C.2. describes the Inland lines.

The following abbreviations are used:

EE – Entry from East; WE – Entry from west.
NS – North side of main track; SS – South side of main track.

NE – Entry from North; SE – Entry from South.
ES – East side of main track; WS – West side of main track.

Table C.1. Side Tracks and Connections for Coeur d'Alene and Vera Lines.

Mile Post	Track
	SPOKANE - HAYDEN LAKE
0.00	Spokane Terminal.
1.10	GN/NP transfer track crossing until 1911.
1.20	Connection to GN depot, 1927.
1.23	GN/NP transfer track crossing from 1911.
1.49	Vera line junction NS (between shops and bridge 1.5).
1.66	CMSt&P crossing.
1.63	Inland Junction: wye switches 1.63 west, 1.75 east, 1.78 south..
2.08	Mill spurs WE-SS.
2.30	UP junction.
2.32	CMSt&P crossing.
2.33	UP crossing
3.05	Concrete Block spur WE-SS.
3.05	Recreation Park: several tracks and streetcar connections.
4.37	Pike Lumber Spur EE-SS, 1950.
4.48	Landis Oil Spur EE-SS, 1927; Esperance spur, 1939.
4.61	Parkwater Lumber Spur EE-SS 1946; extended from Esperance spur 1939.
4.75	Byrne-Ferris Spur EE-SS, 1952.
5.04	Lennox Furnace Spur WE-SS, 1950; relocated in 1956 to 5.17.
5.35	Columbia Electric Spur WE-SS, 1952.
5.63	Brown Trailer Spur EE-SS, 1952.
5.75	Spokane Natural Gas Spur EE-SS, 1957.
5.81	Building Supplies Spur EE-SS, 1966.
6.33	Orchard Avenue Siding 6.33 to 6.87 SS 1933; shortened in 1940 to 6.68.
6.88	Spokane International Railway connection WE-NS, 1934.
7.82	Spur EE-SS.
8.45	Sullivan Siding 8.45 to 8.76 NS.
9.54	Washington Real Estate Spur WE-SS, 1909.
12.43	Inland Empire Paper connection, 1930-1945.
12.82	Flora Junction renamed Vera Junction circa 1935: wye track, 1910; abandoned, May 1947.

13.34	Greenacres Spur EE-SS, 792 feet.
13.51	Cannery Spur 415 foot EE-NS; removed in 1940 and replaced in 1945 by Rogers Brothers Seeds spur.
15.56	Liberty Lake Junction wye 15.56 & 15.94 SS.
18.84	Spokane Bridge siding 18.84 to 19.16 NS; end of double track 19.13; line change 19.07 to 20.15, 1909.
19.07	Line change 19.07 to 20.15 in 1909.
19.13	End of double track.
22.37	I&WN connection WE-NS.
22.45	McGuires Spur EE-SS.
22.54	I&WN Crossing.
23.58	Stevens & Peterson Spur WE-NS 1928; removed 1931.
23.77	NP spur crossing.
23.89	Post Falls Siding 23.89 to 24.00 SS.
24.08	Idaho Veneer Spur, 1964.
25.65	Alpine Sales Spur, 1976.
25.82	Alan Siding 25.82 to 25.99 SS; removed in 1942.
26.43	Ross Spur WE-SS; removed in 1942.
28.38	McClellan Spur EE-NS; removed in 1940.
29.23	Ohio Match Spur: 902 foot EE-SS.
29.62	Spur WE-NS.
30.05	Wrights Mill Spur: 2327 foot EE-NS, 1909.
30.12	CMStP&P transfer track WE-SS, 1922.
30.73	Winton Lumber Company Spur WE-SS, 1919; removed 1953.
31.02	Spur EE-NS.
31.15	Gibbs Interchange track EE-NS.
31.26	Winton Lumber Company Spur WE-SS, 954 feet.
31.79	Coeur d'Alene wye 31.79 and 31.95.
31.95	Coeur d'Alene yard 31.95 to 32.57.
32.54	CMSt&P crossing.
32.69	NP crossing.
32.82	Spur EE-NS.
33.18	Kennedy's Spur.
33.22	Rutledge Mill Spur, 1916.
33.27	Spur NE-WS.
33.71	Newtons Spur NE.
33.90	Kennedy Spur NE.
34.24	Woodlawn Spur SE-ES.
37.28	Dalton Siding 37.28 to 37.45 ES.
38.80	Corbin Spur SE-WS, 1907.
38.99	Atlas Tie/Ramage Spur: 2075 feet WE-SS.
39.97	Spur SE-SW.
40.03	Hayden Lake loop track switch.

LIBERTY LAKE JUNCTION - LIBERTY LAKE

15.72	West wye switch.
15.79	South wye switch.
16.00	CMSt&P crossing.
17.10	Siding 17.10 to 17.25 ES.
17.49	Spur SE-ES.
17.50	Liberty Lake loop track switch.

VERA LINE

4.57	Granite Point Siding SS; removed 1928.
6.12	Edgecliff (Station 8), end of track, 1932.
6.18	UP undercrossing.
6.20	Morrison Seed Spur WE-SS, 1930 - 1950.
6.27	Washington Brick Spur WE-SS, 1942.
6.31	Jack Tire Rubber Spur, 392 feet.
6.32	Ace Sand and Gravel Spur EE-NS, 1947.
6.43	Plywood Distributors Spur EE-NS, 1968.
6.49	Spear Spur, 567 foot converted to 722 foot siding in 1952.
6.97	UP connection, 1957.
7.10	Appleway Fuel Company Spur: 588 feet, EE-SS, 1947.
7.13	Dishman Siding 7.13 to 7.22.

7.97	Spokane Fruit Growers Spur (Spokane Fertilizer Company from 1950): 352 feet, WE-NS, 1914.
9.33	Opportunity Spur: 1,341 feet, EE-NS.
9.35	Independent Fruit Spur WE-NS.
11.00	Trues Oil Spur: 313 feet, WE-SS, 1923.
11.14	Gillespie Spur: 414 feet, WE-SS, 1947.
11.16	Clay Spur WE-SS; moved 1947 to 11.14.
11.19	End of track, 1957.
11.23	Vera Lumber and Fuel Spur: 296 feet, 11.29; removed in 1948.
12.45	Flora Siding 12.45 to 12.56.
12.60	Junction with main line.

Table C.2. Side Tracks and Connections for Inland Lines

Mile Post	Track
SPOKANE (INLAND JUNCTION) - SPRING VALLEY	
1.78	South wye switch.
1.88	Siding 1.88 to 2.18 WS.
2.46	Spokane Asphalt spur SE-WS, 1910.
3.76	Altamont spur NE-ES.
4.84	Gravel pit spur, 1907.
5.23	Gravel pit spur SE-WS.
5.89	Glenrose/Rosedale Greenhouse spur: 300 feet, SE-WS, 1945.
6.27	Pinegrove spur: 999 feet, NE-WS, 1910.
7.68	Moran siding 7.68 to 7.89 ES with Spokane Fruit Growers Company spur: 552 feet; siding shortened, 19
8.05	Jacobson's spur SE-WS, 1945.
9.25	Parkview siding 9.25 to 9.47 WS.
10.37	Latta spur: removed 1908 and relaid at Willow Springs.
10.55	Willow Springs spur: 409 feet, NE-SW; removed in 1942.
10.80	Siding 10.80 to 11.09 WS.
12.55	Kiesling spur: 760 feet, SE-ES; retired, 1941.
13.35	Sharon spur SE-WS, 361 feet; retired in 1947.
14.98	Excelsior siding 14.98 to 15.25.
16.05	Gravel Pit No.2; sand spur.
16.20	Jones spur: SE-ES, 404 feet; removed in 1940.
16.76	Valleyford siding 16.76 to 16.98 ES.
17.25	Valleyford Brick spur.
19.24	Freeman siding 19.24 to 19.45 ES with spur.
20.42	Inland Brick spur: SE-WS, 3196 feet.
21.93	Ochlare spur.
25.22	Mount Hope siding 25.22 to 25.54 E; shortened in 1958; with industry spur, 1,103 feet.
25.81	Treat spur: 386 feet, NE-ES; removed in 1938.
27.47	Meeker spur; removed by 1919.
27.56	Loke spur NE-WS; removed, 1942.
28.09	Rattler's Run spur NE-WS; removed, 1941.
29.01	Lenox spur 308' SE-ES; removed, 1941.
30.22	West Fairfield siding 30.22 to 30.59 ES; shortened, 1942.
31.11	Connection to UP, 1952.
31.96	Saline spur SE-WS; removed, 1942.
33.91	Waverly house track 33.91 to 34.04 ES; extended 217 feet in 1959.
33.91	Waverly siding 33.97 to 34.04 WS; shortened in 1959.
35.02	Clifton spur: 315 feet, NE-WS; removed, 1953.
35.50	Dale spur: 383 feet, NE-WS; removed, 1950.
36.61	Jefferson spur: 397 feet, SE-WS; extended north to 36.49 for siding, 1942.
38.14	Durkee siding 38.05 to 38.23 WS; removed, 1941.
40.00	Spring Valley wye, north switch.
SPRING VALLEY - MOSCOW	
40.21	Spring Valley wye, east switch.
45.14	Fairbanks siding: northbound 45.14 to 45.43 ES.
45.17	Fairbanks siding: southbound 45.17 to 45.36 WS; removed by 1940.
47.48	Seabury spur: 717 feet, NE-WS and extended 112 feet; extended to 47.65 for siding, 1942.
49.76	Geary siding 49.76 to 50.05 ES with spur: 301 feet, SE-ES; modified andshortened to 49.87, 1942; remo

52.73	Grange Supply spur NE-SW, 1934; removed, 1949.
53.06-53.97	Oakesdale siding 53.10 to 53.34 (53.50 until 1931); ES and industry track; house track.
53.80	UP crossing.
53.83	NP crossing.
53.97	UP interchange track, 1923; moved to 53.88, 1944.
54.36	E.B. Parkman spur SE-ES; removed circa 1925.
56.03	Robinson spur SE-WS, 397 feet; extended in 1955.
57.31	Sokulk siding 57.31 to 57.69 ES and industry track, 516 feet; siding connected thru industry track, 1941.
60.78	Crabtree siding 60.78 to 61.09 ES; removed, 1942.
60.86	Crabtree spur: 600 feet, NE-WS connected in 1942 at 61.01 for siding.
64.71	Garfield siding 64.71 to 64.96 ES.
64.72	Garfield spur 1276 feet NE-WS.
65.34	UP spur crossing.
65.35	NP crossing.
68.68	Ladow spur NE-WS.
68.84	Ladow siding 68.84 to 69.05 WS and industry spur, 345 feet; center removed and ends reconnected thru
70.90	Grinell spur NE-ES, 553 feet, 1907; connected at south end for siding, 1942.
70.92	Grinell siding 70.92 to 71.24 WS; removed, 1942.
73.40	Horn spur: 959 feet; removed, 1916.
75.72	Palouse wye 75.72 to 75.81.
76.09	Palouse siding 76.09 to 76.29 ES.
76.23	Spur WS
76.29	NP interchange track NE-WS.
78.70	Ringo spur: 536 feet, NE-WS.
82.38	Viola siding 82.38 to 82.60 ES; removed, 1943.
82.42	Viola spur NE-WS, approxiamately 600 feet connected to main track at 82.60 for siding, 1942.
82.51	Spur SE-ES laid by GN; connected for siding 82.51 to 82.71, 1952.
84.53	Poe spur; removed, 1939.
87.09	Estes spur: 695 feet, NE-WS; shortened to 595 feet in 1930; connected to main track at 87.28 for siding,
89.94	Tertelling spur SE-WS, 1952.
90.25	Moscow siding 90.25 to 90.39 WS.
90.57	Wye, east switch 90.57, west switch 90.70 to UP and NP interchange.

SPRING VALLEY - COLFAX

40.21	South wye switch.
42.63	Rollins spur: 710 feet, SE-ES.
45.09	NP crossing at grade.
45.52	Wasington Refining spur, 1929-1940.
45.60	Rosalia siding 45.60 to 45.79 WS.
45.66	Uni-Chem spur SE-ES, 1965.
45.71	INP interchange connection NE-ES,
46.11	CMSt.P&P interchange connection SE-WS.
46.85	Broadview Farms spur SE-WS; removed, 1927.
48.26	Early spur: 512 feet, NE-WS; removed, 1951.
50.53	Balder spur: 969 feet, NE-WS, 1909; connected to main line at 50.68 for siding, 1941.
51.11	Harris siding 51.00 to 51.26 ES; removed, 1941.
52.39	Stoneham Stone and Mueli spur: 361 feet, 52.39 SE-ES; removed, 1959.
54.78	UP crossing.
55.22	Thornton Potlatch spur NE-ES, 553 feet; siding 55.30 to 55.38 WS.
55.30	Thornton siding 55.30 to 55.58 ES.
59.65	Cashup spur: 1,189 feet, NE-WS; shortened, 1956.
64.44	Steptoe siding 64.44 to 64.81 ES with industry spur NE-ES, 898 feet;changed to industry siding by 1953
66.59	Blackwell siding 66.59 to 66.79 WS with industry spur, 532 feet; removed, 1961.
69.66	Rye spur SE-WS, 787 feet; removed, 1947.
71.12	Manning spur: 467 feet, NE-WS.
72.25	Work spur NE-WS; removed, 1928.
75.14	Colfax wye 75.14 to 75.32 ES.
76.21	Spur NE-ES.
76.46	Two UP crossings at grade.
	End of track.

NE - North entry to spur; SE - South entry to spur
ES - East side of main track; WS - West side of main track

APPENDIX D

Hayden Lake Improvement Company

Hayden Lake lies eight miles north of Coeur d'Alene and forty miles northeast from Spokane. A potentially attractive resort area, it lacked development and accessibility until the turn of the twentieth century. In 1902, local landowner C.B. King announced the opening of a new "summer hotel" on the west shore of the lake; thirteen rooms included accommodation in the owner's house. Camping sites, ten cottages and a rudimentary activity center known as the "wigwam"were soon established. Transportation needs were met four years later when electric train service started to the lake.

As noted in Chapter 9, the S&IE actively promoted business that would stimulate passenger traffic over its lines. To this end, Hayden Lake Improvement Company filed articles of incorporation on December 12, 1906. Incorporators were the railroad's second vice president, A. L. White; its traffic manager, W.G. Paine; and local landowners, H.B. King and W.G. Malloy. Objectives were to lease, buy and sell real estate and personal property; purchase or construct hotels, billiard rooms, club houses, or other buildings for amusement purposes; acquire, lay out, plat town or city lots; improve and operate ball grounds and racetracks. Aubrey White was appointed president and Paine as vice president. One thousand shares, $100 each, were issued. By 1909 the railroad held 96% of the stock, acquisition being structured so as to keep it clear of mortgage liens that secured the railroad's bonds and so retain the option to sell the property.

The new company immediately purchased a 140-acre tract owned by C.B. King and H.B. King. Accommodation, waterfront land and a one-half mile racecourse were included in the sale. Price was reported as $70,000. A few weeks later, the company announced construction of a first-class, Swiss-style chalet hotel. Kirtland K. Cutter, a leading architect in Spokane, designed the two-story hotel. Construction was well underway by April 1907. A spur was installed from the electric line for materials delivery. Thirty-five 11 by 16 foot guest rooms were provided, with or without baths, and equipped with long-distance telephone. Steam heating and electrical lighting were installed. The hotel front had a full-length, 16-foot-wide veranda facing the lake with the main entrance at the rear. Covered walkways led from the central 40-foot-square lobby to the two-story dining hall/ kitchen (53 by 73-foot frame) and the "wigwam" (33 by 64 feet). Interior décor emulated Native American design, two fireplaces in the lobby being representative of teepees. Specialists were brought in to plan the grounds and landscaping.

The hotel opened on July 20, 1907 under the name "Bozanta Tavern." Rates were $3 a day with all meals furnished, or $20 per week. Less expensive, electrically-lit, two- or three-room "cozy log cabins" were available north of the hotel. Cooking was not allowed in the cabins and there was no plumbing in most of them for some years; a staff member came around every morning to empty chamber pots. By 1909 the company had found that many tourists preferred to camp out, so a site was developed for this purpose. In view of this preference, it was rather surprising that a plan to increase the number of rooms in the hotel was announced in 1911. New S&IE management did not implement the plan.

Tennis, croquet and golf facilities were established and rapidly became the main attraction for patrons. The instructor from Spokane Country Club laid out the nine-hole golf course. It was extended to 18 holes in 1912. Swimming, boating and fishing were promoted at the lake: free bathhouses, diving boards and rowboat hire were available. During summer months, Saturday night dances were held exclusively for guests.

A most distinguished guest traveled over the electric line and dined at the resort on September 28, 1909. President William Howard Taft arrived by special train at the NP Spokane depot and spent the morning touring the city. After lunch, he departed for Hayden Lake at 2:44 p.m. from the S&IE Terminal depot. At Spokane Bridge an Idaho reception committee boarded; the president waved to several hundred people as he passed through Post Falls and delivered a 15-minute speech to the crowd assembled in front of the Coeur d'Alene hotel, cut short by departure of the train. Taft declined an offer of a round of golf at Hayden Lake. Dinner at the Bozanta Tavern was made up largely of wild game dishes, cub bear steak being the climax. Returning, the special train left Hayden Lake at 8:00 p.m. The president was transferred near the OR&N crossing, on the east side of Spokane, to his special train waiting on the NP track to carry him to north Yakima.

Naturally, travel by train to the resort was encouraged. Sunday and weekend rates to Hayden Lake were available and special 25-ride family tickets were issued at commuter rates. The GN and NP railways issued tickets for long-distance travel with stopover privileges at Spokane and Hayden Lake. Several trains ran to and from Spokane daily, the "Campers Limited" leaving Spokane Terminal shortly after 4:00 p.m. and enabling businessmen to take dinner with their families. A 7:30 a.m. departure from the lake gave arrival in Spokane convenient for the business day. The depot was designed to give an appearance consistent with that of the hotel.

By the end of WWI, many patrons reached the hotel and golf course by automobile. Annual gross revenue in 1918 was $3,827 (including $2,634 rent) against operating expenses of $10,449. By that time, the S&IE had made loans to Hayden Lake Improvement Company that totaled $117,174. With its stock holding, loan notes and interest thereon, the S&IE's financial involvement in the company came to $228,332. Value of the property was estimated as $32,425.

After Spokane & Eastern Railway & Power Company acquired the property in 1920 as part of the receivers sale of the S&IE, management concluded that there was less incentive to operate this "unprofitable enterprise" than formerly and leased the hotel to "an individual who could easily make it profitable." Coeur d'Alene Golf Club leased and operated the resort's golf course. In April 1928, the Spokane, Coeur d'Alene & Palouse Railway, having acquired the facility as part of the purchase of the electric railroad, agreed to accept an offer for the hotel and resort property from the golf club. Sale price was $30,000, repayment spread over a few years. The club, which became a successful operation, bought the depot and a cottage in 1931 for $500.

Liberty Lake Improvement Company

Liberty Lake Improvement Company sought to develop the resort for the planned branch line. Directors were Spokane businessmen, at least one of them an associate of Jay Graves. The area was promoted under the name "Wicomico" to support land sales there and improvements were made to a local hotel. The S&IE annual report for 1909 informed stockholders that the railway had built up a first-class summer resort at Liberty Lake. Electric Railway Journal gave further details, noting that Liberty Lake afforded the finest bathing beaches in the county and Inland management had laid out a 35-acre park, built a $10,000 pavilion (50 by 100 feet), a 500-foot floating pier, bath houses and various devices for bathers. In 1921 the Spokane & Eastern Railway & Power Company completed sale of the property for $40,926.

Railway Land and Improvement Company

This company was formed on October 2, 1905 to buy, develop and sell land adjacent to the Spokane & Inland right-of-way. Incorporators included Jay Graves; W.G. Paine; railroad contractor D. D. Twohy; and real estate developers Fred B. Grinnell and Arthur Jones. By mid-1906 the company owned several thousand acres. Sales of town lots and acre tracts began on July 1, 1906 at Valleyford (10 miles southeast of Spokane) where the company owned 1,480 acres. Special trains for prospective buyers were organized over the newly-opened line during the next several weeks. Buyers were fewer than anticipated. In August 1909 the entire holdings of the company, about 1,800 acres, were sold at auction. Minimum bid prices were set at a half or less of the appraised value of the land to motivate bidders.

Sources

Great Northern Railway, President's Subject File No.9128, *S&IE History of Properties – Non-Operating Property*, 1919.

Northern Pacific President's File No.1340-T.

Spokane and Inland Empire Railroad. *Golf at Hayden Lake*, no date.

Electric Railway Journal, February 27 1909, 33: 364. "Parks Served by the Inland Empire System of Spokane".

Spokane Spokesman Review.

INDEX

Page numbers shown **Bold** indicate an illustration.